JOBS, ROLES AND PEOPLE

JOBS, ROLES AND PEOPLE
The New World of Job Evaluation

Derek Pritchard
and
Helen Murlis

NICHOLAS BREALEY
PUBLISHING
LONDON

First published by
Nicholas Brealey Publishing Limited in 1992
156 Cloudesley Road
London N1 0EA

© Derek Pritchard and Helen Murlis 1992

ISBN 1 85788 007 2

British Library Cataloguing in Publication Data
A catalogue record for this book is available from the British Library.

Phototypeset by The Midlands Book Typesetting Company, Loughborough.
Printed and bound by The Bath Press, Avon

Acknowledgements

The authors would like to thank and acknowledge Celia Barker of Hay Management Consultants for the chapter on Equal Value, Linda Boots for her care and effort in preparing the manuscript, and the many Hay clients and colleagues on whose experiences we have drawn in preparing this book.

We would also like to thank those management consultancies whose methods are quoted, for their permission to do so.

Finally we would like to express our thanks to both our families for their patience and help while this book was being written.

Derek Pritchard
Helen Murlis

Contents

1 Introduction: Job Evaluation in the Nineties

Job evaluation is the process of assessing the relative size or importance of jobs within an organisation.

Its primary purpose – though by no means its only use – is to provide a rational basis for the design of pay structures.

The majority of sizeable organisations in the UK, and many smaller ones too, use some kind of job evaluation as a component of their pay determination processes. Many of these are extending its use to job levels not previously covered. There is also continuing growth in the application of common job evaluation systems across job groups which were previously dealt with separately, as part of the growing trend towards harmonisation of employment conditions.

A significant proportion of organisations which have not previously used job evaluation are introducing it, or at least actively considering the possibility. Some who abandoned outdated approaches are returning to using newer forms, to assist with the effective management of pay relativities.

It is clear to practitioners in the field that activity and interest in job evaluation is at a high level, and that it continues to provide one of the foundations of pay management in most organisations. But it is also abundantly clear that job evaluation is meeting increasing challenges to many of the practices and assumptions traditionally associated with it, and to its relevance and validity in today's organisations and the environment in which they operate.

While there has always been some debate on these issues, its intensity increased dramatically in the latter part of the 1980's and the start of the 90's in the wake of the radical changes which were taking place in most organisations in that period and are still continuing apace. The increasingly competitive economic environment has caused major structural change in most businesses, bringing with it changes in the nature of jobs and how they relate to each other. Profound changes are occurring in attitudes to work, jobs and employment, with greater emphasis on flexibility and empowerment, and less on hierarchical control. The proportion of 'knowledge workers' continues to grow, and the effective development of highly skilled people is recognised by many organisations as one of the keys to competitive advantage. Pay markets themselves have become fragmented because they are now more finely tuned and specific to different specialisms, functions, regions, industries and so on.

There has been a period of intense re-assessment and development of job evaluation in response to these changes focused in particular on the processes by which it is applied, and the way its results are used. The development of computer assisted processes during this period is just one example of this.

Unfortunately, most existing texts on job evaluation pre-date this period of debate and development, and present a view of job evaluation practice during the 70's and early 80's: a period during which orthodoxies developed in the 1960's remained relatively unchanged. This historical view regrettably gives fuel to many of the criticisms of job evaluation practice. For example, in the current standard text books on personnel management and salary administration there are many long chapters on the constitution and membership of 'the steering committee' and 'the evaluation panel' containing the implicit assumption that these have to exist. These do little to reassure the manager or human resource specialist who is reviewing current practice and is concerned about bureaucracy! In practice, many users of job evaluation today do not have a steering committee or an evaluation panel : these are just one way of handling the process, appropriate in some circumstances, totally inappropriate in others.

Our objective in this book is to challenge some outdated thinking and present an up to date view of job evaluation in practice today, consider its continuing relevance and validity, and describe how it is developing and changing to meet the demands placed upon it.

One of the problems facing the actual or potential user is that all too frequently job evaluation is presented as a 'package' or 'scheme' – or as a series of competing packages or schemes. People often talk for example about 'installing' a job evaluation scheme. Claims and counter claims are made about the advantages and disadvantages of one 'scheme' over another.

With this system driven view of job evaluation, it is profoundly difficult to assess the validity of some of the challenges which are raised – or to see how to change things to respond to the challenges – without the risk of baby joining the bathwater.

To overcome this, we will describe job evaluation as a *process*, which like other processes contains a number of separate but connected steps, from consideration of why you are doing it in the first place right through to determining how you are going to use the results. It is intended that this process view will provide both a conceptual and a practical framework to help in the understanding and design of appropriate approaches to meet the wide variety of circumstances and requirements which may occur.

It is not our intention to act as apologists for, or defenders of, job evaluation, nor to attack it. All too often the debate is simplistic and polarised, with job evaluation being alternately presented as a 'Good Thing', or as a 'Bad Thing', to be replaced by the more fashionable 'Good Thing'. In fact it is not a 'Thing' at all, but a diverse range of approaches which can be used to achieve the important but fairly limited objective of assessing the relative size or importance of jobs in an organisation.

Job evaluation is not a panacea : it does not of itself produce pay structures or make pay decisions, though it is sometimes wrongly credited with this power. It is a useful and important tool, but just one of a number of tools which need to be used in conjunction with each other to address pay and broader human resource issues. This has always been the case – the organisational and environmental changes of the last few years have not created this situation. They have simply made it more apparent and reinforced the necessity to design processes and combinations of processes accordingly.

The book is organised into three main parts.

In Part I (Chapters 2–4) we explore the current challenges to job evaluation and the ways in which practice is responding to these.

In Part II (Chapters 5–10) we cover in more detail the main steps in the job evaluation process and describe the range of practices available for each step, while in Part III (Chapters 11–14) we focus on the way job evaluation results are used.

We recognise that not all readers will work their way systematically through from start to finish, but may want to focus on specific chapters of particular interest to them. For this reason we have tried to make each chapter reasonably self-sufficient, even though this may at times cause some overlap in the issues covered.

PART I: CHALLENGES

2 The Challenges to Job Evaluation

Introduction

In order to review and analyse the ways in which job evaluation practice is changing and developing in the current environment, it is helpful to begin with a consideration of some of the major challenges which are being presented to it, and which are driving many of the changes which are taking place.

The three major areas of challenge which require consideration are:

Relevance in a fragmenting pay market, which is dealt with in this chapter.

Job evaluation is primarily concerned with internal relativities between jobs. Pay markets are increasingly fragmenting, demanding different pay rates for jobs of similar size depending on market scarcity. How can these conflicting requirements be reconciled, and is there a case for purely market based pay?

Relevance to the way today's organisations are being managed (Chapter 3).

Organisations are changing rapidly and fundamentally. There is widespread de-layering and breaking down of traditional 'pyramid' hierarchies. Team and project relationships are taking over and even large, complex organisations are becoming more fluid, and less structurally defined. Within these organisations, there is a need to move away from restrictively defined 'jobs' to more broadly defined 'roles', with an emphasis on flexibility, and making maximum use of people and their abilities. Traditional job evaluation practice is often seen as reinforcing the old hierarchical model. How is modern practice responding to these challenges, and how does it relate to pay determination based on skills or competencies?

The need for greater efficiency and less bureaucracy (Chapter 4).

Traditional job evaluation is often seen as a centralised bureaucratic process, demanding on time and resources. Organisations in all sectors are seeking approaches which are significantly more efficient, less bureaucratic, and can be devolved or decentralised without loss of consistency. How is job evaluation practice responding to these demands?

Relevance in a fragmenting pay market

The nature of pay markets
Pay markets are no longer homogeneous, even if they ever were (a claim made for the 1970's).

At industry level, there are now significant differences in pay practices between various sectors. A company for example with businesses in more than one sector – say chemicals and pharmaceuticals, a fairly common combination – is therefore operating in two quite distinct pay markets. In addition, different functions, specialisms or occupational categories may be paid quite differently, with jobs of the same 'size' as measured using job evaluation attracting different market rates. Most organisations are familiar with the higher market rates which I.T. specialists or medical doctors for example have attracted over the years. But such market pressures, driven as they are by supply and demand, are typically very specific and relatively short term. Thus a period of heavy capital investment in process industries can cause a shortage of control and instrumentation engineers and result in raising market pay for these jobs.

Pay in the UK can also have a strong geographical component, notably at more junior levels where local recruitment is the norm. The debate of a few years ago on the 'north–south divide' is an oversimplification, and market pay can be affected by small changes in geography. Thus market rates for office staff in a city centre may be quite different from those on an industrial estate ten miles away, and can be affected by factors like availability of public transport facilities.

To complicate matters further, these factors of industry, function and geography have different degrees of importance at different job levels. Generally speaking, at lower job size levels, geographical

factors will dominate. For middle range management and professionals, function gains in importance, while at more senior level,
industry sector is the major factor. Finally, at the highest management levels, company performance and international markets are the
main driving force. These relationships are shown diagrammatically
in Figure 2.1.

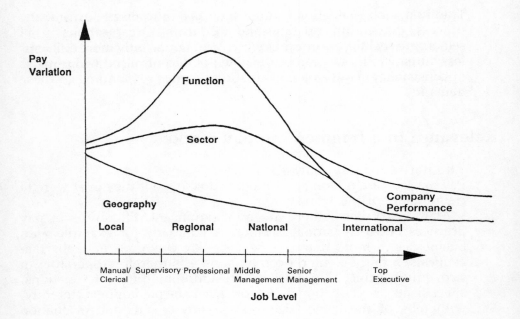

Figure 2.1   Factors causing pay differences.

In these circumstances, what is the relevance of job evaluation,
with its emphasis on internal relativities, and its apparent neglect
of external market forces? Why not simply pay the market rate for
each job?

This is a challenge not to the method of job evaluation which
may be used, or to any aspect of the process by which it is applied,
but to the basic purpose of job evaluation and its relevance in a
fragmenting pay market. To explore this challenge, it is helpful
to examine how typical job evaluation based pay structures are
designed.

Job evaluation based pay structures
These are normally based upon the premise that pay at the individual
level depends upon:

- The job, and its size relative to others.
- The business or organisation in which the job exists, its strategic requirements, economics and ability to pay.
- The market.
- The individual – for example his/her performance, length of service, etc.

These requirements are frequently combined in a pay structure with the general form illustrated in Figures 2.2 and 2.3. In the case of Figure 2.2, pay is directly related to job size on an individual job basis, whereas in Figure 2.3 (see p. 8), the job size spectrum is sectioned off into grades.

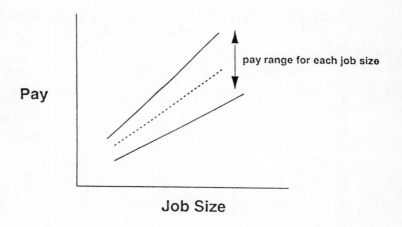

Figure 2.2   Typical job evaluation pay structure. (a)
Pay directly related to job size.

The balance between the organisation's requirements and economics on the one hand, and the market on the other provides the basis for decisions on how high to pitch the whole structure, and how much to move it each year. Individual characteristics (e.g. performance or length of service) are accommodated by progression through the pay band or range for each job or grade which the structure generates. Of course in some organisations these factors are not taken into account, and so the structure is much simpler as in Figures 2.4 and 2.5.

While details may vary enormously, this is the basis of a high proportion of pay structures using job evaluation. It is also a basis

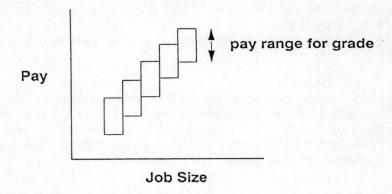

Figure 2.3   Typical evaluation based pay structure. (b)
Pay related to grade.

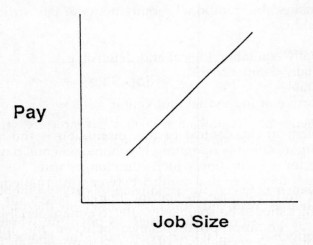

Figure 2.4   Pay structure without performance/service ranges. (a)
Pay directly related to job size.

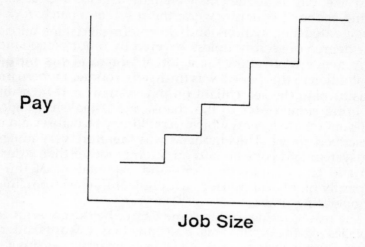

Figure 2.5   Pay structure without performance/service ranges. (b)
Pay related to grade.

which satisfies the traditional requirements of pay structures, that
they should be:

- Internally equitable, logical and defensible
- Externally competitive
- Affordable
- Supportive of individual motivation

A problem in the context of this discussion is the assumption
that the organisation is operating in a homogeneous pay market or
market sector – a situation which is no longer true.

There is thus a potential conflict between internal equity on the
one hand and response to specific market forces on the other.
Such conflict should be soluble by effective managerial judgement,
to arrive at an appropriate balance between the internal and
external forces. Nevertheless it does cause many organisations some
difficulty, and has led to the challenge under discussion here.

Pay structures in the 1970's
To understand the current position, there is a need to examine the
way pay structures were typically operated in the 1970's.

Prior to the widespread introduction of job evaluation in the 1960's and 70's, pay arrangements were fairly chaotic and lacking in logic – being as they frequently were, the result of a patchwork of history, fragmented negotiations and short-term decisions all clothed in a fair degree of secrecy unless covered by union negotiations.

A major motivation for a lot of organisations introducing job evaluation in this period was (in an environment where unionisation was turning the searchlight on pay systems and their differentials) to bring some order to the chaos, and establish a logical basis of internal relativities on which to build pay structures along the lines described above. The emphasis was therefore very much on order, on system and control, and on internal rather than external issues. To add to this, pay decisions and negotiations at the time were typically highly centralised, with little influence from line managers or operating units.

The result, influenced to some degree by the government incomes policies of the time, was a strong bias towards internal equity and internal control and away from market sensitivity. The pay structure, rather than providing a framework, was treated as a rigid constraint. If specific market forces arose which the structure could not accommodate, they were either ignored, or at best dealt with subject to feelings of guilt.

In addition, in an environment where fixed increments were the only form of progression permitted under incomes policy, the relationship between pay progression and individual performance was in general very weak. There could be little differentiation *in practice* between movement for high and low performers, even though *in principle* the structure previously allowed for this.

Thus in practice, pay in many organisations in the 70's was almost exclusively driven by job evaluation, with market considerations largely restricted to a blanket once-a-year decision on inflating the whole structure (often within strict guidelines). Performance rewards largely disappeared or went underground to re-surface (see below) as a form of 'grade drift'.

This was never the intention of job evaluation, but nevertheless it was the way it was used and perceived for many years. Not surprisingly in this environment, employees and managers soon realised that the only way to increase pay significantly and respond to market pressure was to have the job re-evaluated or re-graded. This put severe strain on many evaluation systems, increased the need for control mechanisms, and added further to the perception of job evaluation as an instrument of rigid control and bureaucracy, preventing what were seen by people outside the process as 'sensible' pay decisions.

How often does one still hear comments like:
'I'll never be able to recruit a programmer at that job size (or grade)'.

'The job evaluation scheme won't allow us to pay the right salaries to engineers/accountants/... etc.'.
'The job evaluation scheme won't let us pay our people properly'.

Comments like this illustrate the common perception that 'the job evaluation scheme' pays people – not that it is just one component of the pay determination process.

Of course managers and employees don't always give in so easily. Living and operating in the real world, with practical problems of recruitment, retention and motivation to solve, they have to find ways round the constraints of an over-rigid pay structure, and often display considerable ingenuity in doing so – ingenuity and effort which could better be directed towards solving business problems. One of the most time-honoured approaches is simply to keep rewriting the job description and resubmitting it, until the evaluators give in and re-grade the job.

This of course is the first step on the slippery slope for any job evaluation scheme, and if the practice becomes widespread, the whole integrity of the evaluation process can rapidly decline.

In our experience, failure of a job evaluation process can very often be traced directly back to over-rigidity in pay structure design – particularly over-narrow bands, insensitivity to performance issues, and inflexibility in responding to market pressures.

Market based pay structures

Given this situation, some commentators and not a few chief executives looking for instant flexibility suggest that internal relativities should be ignored, and that pay decisions should be based simply on market considerations.

Unfortunately, this alternative is not without some fundamental difficulties.

In the first place, pay markets are imperfect. Only a small percentage of people are actually entering or leaving 'the market' at any point in time, and most people will spend a relatively long time in a particular organisation in between interchanges with 'the market'. It thus lacks the continuous flux which is needed for conventional supply and demand relationships to operate fully. This can make it difficult to define what 'market' pay actually is for a particular job, since there may be significant differences between recruitment levels and steady-state levels within organisations.

It is also extremely difficult to measure market pay rates with precision on a job-by-job basis. Ironically, probably the best way of doing this is to use job evaluation as the basis for using market data, so as to ensure that valid like-for-like comparisons can be made.

The relative stability of employment patterns also means that for most people in most organisations, internal relativities *do* matter. Often they matter more than the external market, notably in times of stability or recession. The requirement for 'fairness' in pay arrangements is still strong, and likely to remain so for some time to come, and is usually taken to imply that pay should bear a reasonable relationship to the relative contributions from jobs and people within the organisation. Pure market pay cuts right across this concept.

From a business point of view, there are also difficulties. For most organisations, pay is one of the most important items of cost, and in many of these it is the largest single cost item. Increasingly, businesses are recognising the need to manage pay strategically. Pay markets are, by their nature, outside the control of the organisation, and subject to relatively short-term fluctuations. Most business managers would not be happy to have one of their major cost items handled on a basis which is outside their control and relatively short term.

Pay structures in the 1990's

It is apparent that in the current environment neither pay structures which are rigidly driven by job evaluation nor those which are purely market based will satisfy most organisations' requirements. Each is an oversimplification and neglects the basic reality that both internal relativities and external market forces need to be reflected. At times, these requirements will be in conflict, and judgements will need to be made about how to achieve the right balance in the particular circumstances. No simple formulaic structure can substitute for this need or replace managerial judgement. This is a reflection of the fact that pay can no longer simply be administered, with control handed over to structures and systems. It requires managing, using structures and systems to provide a framework for the managerial judgements required.

Thus in the 1990's, pay structures need to be seen as providing such a strategic framework, within which judgements can be made and decisions taken. It is no longer tenable for them to be seen as rigid constraints, seen to be preventing necessary decisions. Otherwise – 'The job evaluation system won't let us pay our people properly'.

The value of job evaluation in this environment is that it can provide the strategic framework, independent of market fluctuations and pressures, so that when decisions are taken on responding to these, there is a firm baseline to start from. Decisions can then be taken rationally, and managed over time.

This does, of course, represent a substantial evolution which has taken place since the 1970's, in the strategic role and purpose of job evaluation.

As illustrated in Figure 2.6, it has changed from being largely an instrument for the control of uniformity to a tool to help manage diversity, with the recognition that it is only one of several tools which are required and which need to be used together.

The ways in which job evaluation is applied, the methods and processes used, and, most importantly, the way its results are used, need to reflect this evolution.

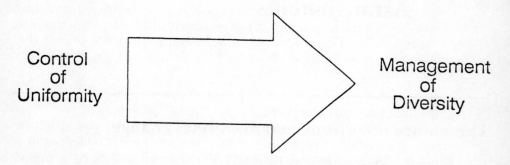

Figure 2.6   Evolution of purpose of job evaluation.

3 Application of Job Evaluation in Today's Organisational Arrangements

The nature of current organisational change

The late 1980's were and the early 90's are proving to be a period of unprecedented organisational change across virtually all sectors of the economy.

Whereas previous periods of change have altered the size and shape of many organisations, they tended to leave the basic organisational principles and architecture unchanged. In contrast, we are currently experiencing a much more radical period of change, in which the fundamental nature of many organisations is changing, with major implications for how jobs and roles are defined and treated. Among the main features of these changes are:

De-layering of organisations to yield much flatter structures.

Traditional, heavily layered structures emphasised hierarchical control. Whole layers of hierarchy existed mainly to supervise and control other layers, rather than add value in their own right. The IT revolution has rendered many middle management jobs superfluous.

In the new flatter structures with wider spans of control, supervision is less intrusive, and each layer has to be justified in terms of the unique added value which it generates.

Increasing recognition of project and team work

The traditional pyramid emphasised vertical reporting relationships, and in many cases resulted in a series of functional 'drain-pipes', with formal integration between them only at very senior levels. In reality, many working relationships are horizontal or diagonal across the structure – which the hierarchical view did not recognise, and indeed frequently inhibited. The need for project and teamwork – both formal and informal – is an increasing feature in today's organisations. 'Matrix' organisations are a characteristic of many knowledge based businesses.

Organisational flexibility

A feature of teams and projects is that they require constant grouping and regrouping, as different skills and perspectives are brought to bear on specific issues, which demands considerable flexibility in the organisation. Traditional hierarchical structures imply a permanence and stability of organisation which is incompatible with the need for flexibility.

Multiple reporting relationships

The hierarchical model emphasised a singular boss–subordinate relationship. In today's environment an individual may have 'reporting' relationships with an administrative boss responsible for work allocation and resourcing, with one or more technical leaders for guidance on the content of work, and with one or more project leaders.

Job flexibility

Flatter, more flexible organisations with less hierarchical control require jobs themselves to be more flexible and responsive to varying demands, not constrained by the hierarchy and structure.

Jobs designed to expand, not constrain

It is becoming recognised that the narrowly defined jobs in tradi-tional hierarchies frequently failed to make best use of the abilities of the jobholders, since the scope of jobs was structurally constrained. Increasingly jobs are being designed to allow them to expand to the level of ability of the jobholder, rather than the other way round.

'People make jobs'

To some degree this has always been so, and the separation of jobs and people has always been something of an oversimplification. However, in structurally defined jobs, it has been a workable and convenient separation. In the more fluid organisations which are emerging, the separation is increasingly difficult, and the more broadly defined roles which are being created require consideration of both traditional 'job' and 'person' aspects.

Organisations built along the lines described above have existed for some time, but until recently have mainly been found in areas where the business is naturally project-driven or where there is an acceptance of rapid rate of change as a way of life – for example in high technology companies, consultancies, software houses and so on.

The major change which has occurred in the last few years is the application of the same kind of organisational principles to much larger organisations previously associated with traditional structured hierarchies and strong functional separation. For example, many financial institutions are building customer service teams, bringing together skills which were previously organised in separate functions. In many manufacturing environments, plants are now operated by integrated teams bringing together craft and operating skills, and there is steady progress being made on multi-skilling and overlap of activities between previously highly separate jobs.

In this environment, the challenge to job evaluation is at two levels.

- Can it cope with the kind of jobs which exist in these new structures and organisations?
- More fundamentally, is it still appropriate to consider the evaluation of jobs in this environment?

Job evaluation – coping with new organisations

For job evaluation to cope in this environment, three main issues require consideration.

- Job definition.
- The basic method of job evaluation used.
- Assumptions which have developed around the method.

Job definition

Failure of job evaluation to cope in these new organisations can frequently be traced directly back to the way jobs or roles are defined in the first place, and how this definition is communicated to the evaluators.

Traditionally, the vehicle for job definition and analysis has been the job description. Often, these have been long and detailed, and have emphasised the features that are relevant to the kind of hierarchical organisation in which the job existed, i.e.

- Specific tasks and duties.
- Position in the hierarchy.
- Procedural controls/limits to authority.
- Reporting relationships.

Not surprisingly, many users of job evaluation find difficulty in expressing today's more flexible roles in these detailed, restrictive terms. However, it is wrong – and dangerous – to assume that it is impossible to define these roles with the necessary degree of precision. It is simply that different approaches are needed. Flexibility in job design should not be an excuse for woolliness. However flexible a job is, it should be possible to define that degree of flexibility and the nature of the role with clarity.

Any role within an organisation, however flexible, can be considered in terms of the simple input/processing/output model shown in Figure 3.1.

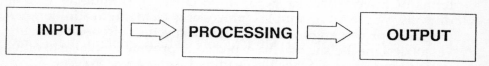

Figure 3.1   Model of a role applicable to any organisational arrangement.

For a role to justify its existence, it must be possible to define in some way what is expected from it, the output. Similarly, the kind of input that is needed to power this output – in terms of skills, knowledge, capability, etc. – should be definable, as is the processing of the input which is required to yield the results, in other words the kind of difficulties, problems and challenges which need to be overcome en route.

This type of approach to jobs is not new, and has been applied to some kinds of jobs for a long time. It simply needs extending to a wider range of jobs. Consider for example a project engineer in a manufacturing company.

It has long been realised that to try to write a detailed description of tasks and activities would for such a job be a long and fruitless occupation. Apart from the number of individual tasks involved, they are different at the various stages of the project. Also, each project is different in its requirements, and at any time the engineer might have several projects underway, each at a different stage.

What it is possible to define is:

- The 'output' expected, in terms of the complexity, scale and importance of projects which the engineer would typically be expected to undertake, and the technical and financial freedoms which he/she would need in order to deliver.
- The 'input' required in terms of the level of experience, skills and knowledge which would be needed to undertake this kind of project.
- The 'processing' required in terms, for example, of the amount of original design work which would typically be required for projects of this type, or the complexity of relationships with sub-contractors involved in the project.

What would therefore emerge from this process is a broad but precise role statement for the project engineer, not a detailed task analysis.

In most companies with such jobs, it would probably also be clear that project engineers exist at different levels. The more senior ones, able to provide greater input based on higher levels of capability, will typically be asked to take on more important outputs, in terms of project size, range or importance, or outputs of greater difficulty with a more complex 'processing' element. In addition, if a particular project engineer is expert in a specific field – say pressure vessel design – he/she may be expected to provide guidance to other projects in this area as well as leading his/her own projects.

This can generate a series of role statements for the various levels of engineer, identifying the features which differentiate between the levels in terms of input, output and processing – which of course is perfectly satisfactory information on which to base the evaluation of each defined role.

What is happening in the newer organisations that we have described, is that more and more jobs need treating in ways akin to this, and not necessarily described in terms of structures, tasks and hierarchies if these are no longer relevant or appropriate. More detailed discussion of job definition and analysis is given in Chapter 8.

Features of the evaluation method itself

Even if jobs or roles can be defined satisfactorily in the new organisations, the second potential difficulty might arise with the evaluation methodology itself.

If the method includes criteria or factors which materially affect the assessment of job size, and which directly and explicitly relate to organisational features or concepts which are changing, then these factors or criteria require re-examination. These criteria may include factors within points factor rating schemes, or questions in computer aided job evaluation questionnaires. For example:

- Factors explicitly relating to hierarchical position will lock in the importance of hierarchy.
- Factors explicitly relating to number of people supervised, which will reinforce the traditional view that the only way to bigger jobs is by climbing the structural hierarchy.

This is not to say that such factors may no longer have any importance.

However flexible and flat the organisation is, it is still an important feature *for some jobs* that they supervise large teams, that they have the skills to do so, and carry the responsibility for their work – for example, a production unit manager, working alongside our project engineer. On a factor explicitly relating to numbers supervised, the production manager would (rightly) score heavily, while the project engineer would probably rate zero.

But the project engineer may require as much, if not more, skill in influencing and directing other people's activities, and in organising complex work relationships. He/she may also carry as much responsibility for the work of others, even though those people do not 'report' in the conventional hierarchical sense.

To achieve a sensible balance between these jobs, we need either:

- More factors, carefully weighted so that the particular characteristics of each job can be accounted for and balanced in a way that reflects the new organisation and its values;

  or

- Factors which are less narrowly defined, and which make no explicit organisational assumptions. For example factors covering interpersonal skills, and organising skills could be applied to both our example jobs, and allow them to be compared in a way which is independent of any hierarchical assumption.

In general, the latter is to be preferred as the basic measuring instrument. Approaches with large numbers of specific factors may require constant re-tuning of factors and weights to make them respond to changing organisational models and values. Factors which are expressed more conceptually and which make no explicit organisation assumptions are more likely to stand the test of time. Who knows, for example, what kind of organisation changes we will see in the second half of the 1990's?

Evaluation assumptions – myths and legends

Even when the factors or criteria themselves make no organisational assumptions, a common problem is that people using them and interpreting them often do. Examples illustrating this point are given below:

- It is common practice for evaluators to use 'rules of thumb' about the gap in job size or rating between boss and subordinate, reflecting the normal kind of relationship in the traditional pyramid. When whole layers are stripped from the pyramid, these rules of thumb will no longer apply, and if enforced will produce results which do not reflect the new organisation. Similarly, as outlined earlier, it may be increasingly difficult to define a single 'boss', and the nature of 'bossness' is very variable. Any blanket rule of thumb will almost certainly be too simplistic in this kind of environment.
- It is also common practice to overlay evaluation factors or criteria which do not in themselves contain explicit organisational assumptions with interpretations which implicitly make such assumptions. For example:

    Factors to do with organising skills or interpersonal skills are interpreted as 'numbers supervised', or even so far as 'up to ten people supervised gives level x, up to 20, level y', and so on.

    When using factors to do with output or impact on results, it is common practice to use resources controlled as a proxy for impact – presumably on the assumption that the impact from a job is in some way proportional to resources controlled. While this just might have been acceptable in a pyramid hierarchy, it certainly is not in today's organisations.

Given the prevalence of assumptions like these, it is not hard to see why there is often a view expressed that job evaluation 'does not work' in more flexible, less resource orientated environments.

Most evaluation methods gather around them a whole series of these assumptions – the myths and legends of job evaluation. Like other myths and legends, they often can be traced back to something real in history. If evaluators spend many years considering jobs in traditional hierarchies it is understandable, and supportable, that they will build up a series of practical rules of thumb, and bits of guidance to help them achieve consistency. These rules of thumb will probably work quite well as long as the model of organisation is not changed. If, as is currently happening, the model changes substantially, then the rules of thumb must also change, or the job evaluation approach will not produce sensible results and will be considered 'not to work'.

Some of these rules of thumb may be written down: more are

likely to remain in the heads of evaluators – passed on like real myths and legends round the evaluation campfires.

The practical challenge for job evaluation practitioners is to tease out what assumptions and interpretations are actually being used, to test out their validity against the new organisational arrangements, and discard or modify those which are inappropriate.

The relevance of job evaluation in new organisations

The previous section outlined the ways in which job evaluation can be applied in new organisations, and is based upon observation of how, in practice, it is successfully being used in a wide range of organisations which have undergone radical change.

However some commentators go beyond challenging its practicality and question its validity and relevance as an approach in this environment, even suggesting in some cases that its presence can inhibit organisational change along the lines described. Many of these challenges, when examined carefully, are actually about *how* job evaluation is conducted, and are based upon traditional assumptions of how it works. These issues have been dealt with in the previous section.

Thus, for example, it is sometimes claimed that job evaluation inhibits the development of flexible organisations because of its reliance on restrictive, detailed job descriptions with an emphasis on tasks, activities and hierarchy. This is based upon the incorrect assumption that job descriptions have to have these undesirable characteristics – though an understandable one if based upon observation of typical job descriptions on 1975 assumptions.

As outlined earlier in this chapter, it is perfectly possible to develop clear definitions of broadly based flexible roles, which can be evaluated accordingly.

A related claim is that the factors typically used in job evaluation reinforce the old order. Again, as outlined previously, factors and the interpretations around those factors can be cleansed of outdated organisation assumptions to ensure that they are relevant.

One is therefore drawn to the conclusion that many such challenges are made from a perception of how job evaluation practice was, and not how it is today.

Perhaps more substantial is the proposition that in today's environment we should not be considering the concept of *jobs* at all as the basis of pay arrangements, simply paying *people* according to the skills and/or competencies which they demonstrate. Based upon this argument, we see the emergence of a variety of 'skills based pay' or 'competency based pay' schemes.

The appeal of such approaches is that they attempt to recognise the importance of people much more than traditional pay structures based on job evaluation were seen to do, and have the attraction of encouraging the acquisition of new skills which are required to make multiskilling and job flexibility work in practice.

There are three main problems with basing pay *purely* on consideration of skills and competencies.

First, business success is ultimately about outputs. Skills and competencies are about inputs, so pay arrangements based *purely* on these factors present a potentially dangerous conflict. How people are paid is one of the most important ways in which an employer communicates with employees, and the values which the pay system embodies will be perceived to be the values which the company holds. There is thus a very real risk that pure skill/competency based pay would encourage an input culture, at variance with the real business requirements.

The second business based argument is one of cost. Paying for the acquisition of greater skills or competencies is only justifiable in business terms if it yields a net benefit, either in greater or more effective outputs from the same resource, or the same outputs from a smaller resource. This puts a great onus on business managers to ensure that the skills which are paid for are the ones needed, and that an appropriate balance of levels and types of skill is maintained, in line with the outputs required. Simply paying for skills which are not used or needed is a cost with no return.

It also puts a great onus on the organisation's ability to measure skill and competency levels, if these are the only bases on which pay decisions are to be made and progression controlled. One must question the current ability of most organisations and indeed most managers to undertake this measurement with precision and confidence across the broad spectrum of roles. The potential result is cost escalation through 'competency drift' in place of 'grade drift'. Even with the apparently over-rigid processes used to control conventional grading, grade drift is still a problem; 'competency drift' could be much more severe. These problems are beginning to emerge with some of the skills based pay systems implemented in the mid/late 1980's – now seen by some organisations as 'transitional' policies used to improve the skill base.

The third problem is one of comparability between different occupational groups or functions.

Much of the work which has been done on skill/competency based pay has been on relatively homogeneous groups or job families, where the nature of work is broadly similar, but may exist at different levels. Examples include:

- Skill based pay schemes for production operators, to support and encourage flexibility, teamwork and breaking down of restrictive working practices.
- Similar schemes in craft areas to support multiskilling initiatives.

- Career structures for groups of scientists, engineers or other professionals.

Where the population is broader and not homogeneous, it is usually necessary to break it down into families so that the skill/competency definitions and levels which form the basis of the structure can be made sufficiently precise and relevant. Thus while for each family it is possible to define progression based on skills/competency in an internally coherent way, it is difficult to make:

- Comparisons between families (for example how would level 3 in an operator family compare with level 3 (or 2 or 4) in a craft family).
- Comparisons between a single family treated in this way and the rest of the organisation which may be using more traditional approaches.
- Comparisons with the market.

These comments apply to the idea of pay arrangements *purely* driven by skill/competency consideration.

In reality many 'skill based/competency based' pay schemes contain a combination of a framework of broad bands or role levels, with progression through and between them geared to skill/competency assessment. The bands provide a basic form to the structure, enabling communication of the various broad levels of role, and also providing a series of safety barriers against wholesale escalation.

Job evaluation approaches (or 'role sizing' as it is sometimes called in this context) can be used to underpin the basic framework and ensure comparability between families, or with the rest of the organisation.

This points to the fruitless nature of much of the highly polarised debate on job evaluation versus skills and competency which has been conducted over the last few years. We described in an earlier section the inadequacy of pay structures based purely on job evaluation, since they neglect vital aspects of the people doing the jobs. In this section we have outlined the inadequacy of pure skill or competency based approaches since they focus only on people and lose sight of the requirements of the business in terms of outputs and achievement, and do not enable the management of relativities across a broad spectrum of roles. The argument about which is 'better' is missing the point, and symptomatic of an unfortunate tendency to seek panaceas.

There is now a growing realisation that it is not a question of choosing between job evaluation, skills and competencies as the basis of pay arrangements, but of seeking ways in which these complementary methods can be combined to yield a more balanced approach to pay.

Jobs, roles and people – achieving the balance

To explore how these approaches can be used in a complementary way, it is necessary to define some of the terms we will use. At least part of the misunderstanding between advocates of different approaches arises because of differences in the way words are used.

For this discussion, we will refer to 'roles' rather than jobs, as signifying an entity within an organisation which takes account of the organisation's requirement (the traditional 'job' view), and the person doing it. We will also use the long established Hay/McBer definition of a competency:

> 'an underlying characteristic of an individual which can be shown to have a causal link with high performance in a defined role'.

An important feature of this definition is that it stresses the fundamental links between competencies, role and performance. For the purposes of this discussion, we will also distinguish between 'skills' and 'competencies', as follows:

- Learnable skills, knowledge and expertise, which we will call 'skills'.
- Behavioural characteristics which can be demonstrated to differentiate high performers in a given role (e.g. concern for order, achievement drive, etc.). These we will call 'competencies'.

In order to define a role in terms which take account both of the organisation's requirement for some kind of output or achievement, and the characteristics of the person which will enable the achievement, we need to define the 'blueprint' for a role in terms of:

- Achievements and outputs required by the organisation.
- Skills, knowledge and expertise required in the role.
- The competencies which characterise the role.

This is illustrated in Figure 3.2 (a).

As shown in Figure 3.2 (b), this model can be broken apart into two more familiar components. The first is the combination of output and skills which is the basis of classical job evaluation – the input and output factors referred to earlier. The second is

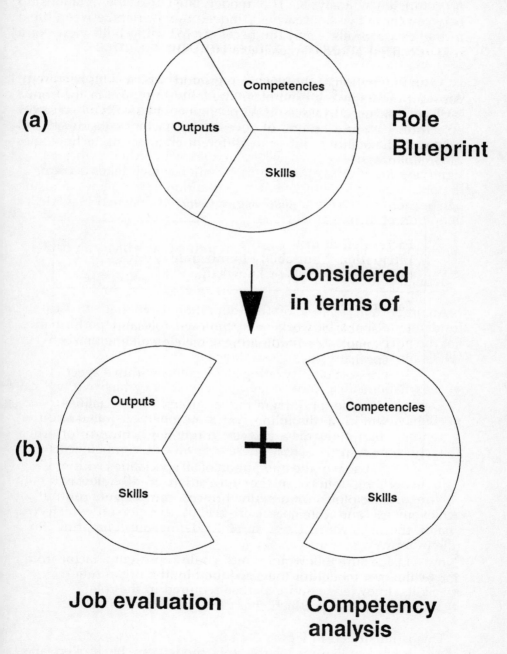

Figure 3.2   Jobs roles and people.

the combination of skills and competencies, which is the basis of competency analysis. The model illustrates the relationship between these two approaches – indeed the overlap between them in the area of skills – and the necessity for using both views of a role in concert in order to characterise it fully.

As an illustration of the 'common ground' which skills represent, consider the following examples. The first is a typical factor from a 'skills matrix' used to assess levels of engineer in a skills based career structure. It would be one of several skill factors considered and relates to the ability to integrate different engineering technologies or disciplines.

Skills matrix factor

Factor definition
Integration 'Your ability to integrate directly technologies, skills or knowledge'.

Factor levels

1. Capable of working within own speciality.
2. Capable of co-ordinating some elements within a speciality.
3. Capable of integrating all elements within a speciality.
4. Capable of integrating a group of specialities within a discipline, or a number of relevant disciplines on a project, component, process or system.
5. Capable of the integration of all specialities within a discipline, or the integration of all relevant disciplines on a major project, component, process or system.

Now consider the following, which could represent a factor from a job evaluation model for the same job family.

Job evaluation model factor

Factor definition
Integration 'The requirement to integrate directly technologies, skills or knowledge'.

Factor levels
1. Required to work within own speciality.
2. Required to co-ordinate some elements within a speciality.
3. Required to integrate all elements within a speciality.
4. Required to integrate a group of specialities within a discipline, or a number of relevant disciplines on a project, component, process or system.
5. Required to integrate all specialities within a discipline, or integrate all relevant disciplines on a major project, component, process or system.

This illustrates the essentially complementary nature of the two approaches, with skills being the common ground, achievements being particular to job evaluation and competencies being particular to competency analysis. It also illustrates the sterile nature of debating whether job evaluation or competency is 'better', since each on its own gives an incomplete view of a role, but used together can give a powerful perspective of a role, in whatever kind of organisational environment it exists.

This three-part model of a role illustrated in Figure 3.2 is particularly powerful because it provides the means of linking and integrating a wide range of human resource management processes, many of which have previously been handled separately – indeed in many organisations they have been the responsibility of quite different departments.

Some of these are illustrated in Figure 3.3, which shows how the role blueprint expressed in this way can be used to provide a common basis for

- Job evaluation, hence pay structure.
- Selection.
- Training.
- Development.

It also provides the essential basis for performance management processes as illustrated in Figure 3.4. The classical approach to performance management is based upon the agreement of targets

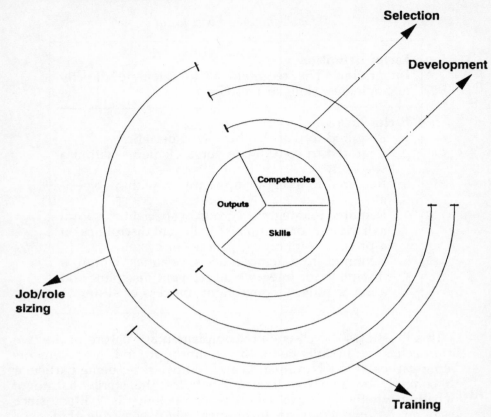

Figure 3.3   The role blueprint in relation to common HR processes.

and objectives, followed by the assessment of achievement against these. In terms of our model, it only addresses the 'output' segment of the role blueprint. Modern thinking and practice in this area now recognises that for most jobs, simply using achievement against target is an incomplete view. Indeed for some jobs, it may be profoundly difficult to identify sensible targets, yet there are clearly different levels of performance between individuals (e.g. research scientists, airline cabin crew, etc.).

The best current approaches to performance management are based on determining, for each job type, an appropriate balance of performance criteria based on achievements against objectives, demonstration of the required skills, and of the differentiating competencies. Performance management processes along these lines can therefore also feed off the same role blueprint, and enable the achieved reality to be compared with the requirement as set in the blueprint.

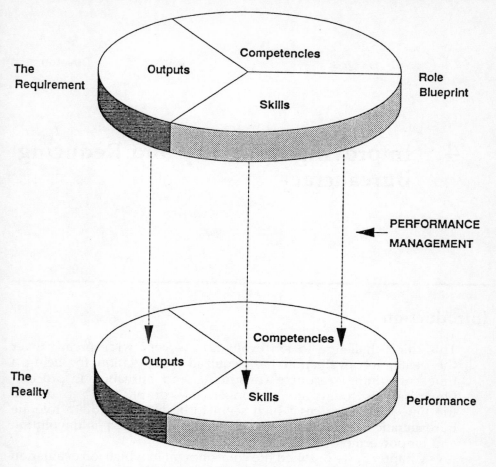

Figure 3.4   Performance management.

Wider adoption of this integrated approach to defining roles will undoubtedly produce over the coming years a much more constructive combination of processes (rather than competition between them), and more integrated approaches to this complex – but critical – issue.

4 Improving Efficiency and Reducing Bureaucracy

Introduction

This third challenge to job evaluation is very widespread. Over the years, job evaluation has acquired a reputation for being a time consuming, resource consuming and bureaucratic process. Organisations today are no longer able or prepared to devote the time and resources which seem to be required, or to tolerate bureaucratic approaches when the order of the day is devolution and empowerment.

In Chapter 2, we outlined the environment in which job evaluation was introduced by many organisations in the 60's, 70's and even into the early 80's. As described there, job evaluation was used as an instrument of control to bring order to pay structures, and was frequently applied in a highly centralised way, in line with the prevailing organisational culture of the day. Thus it is not surprising that processes were used which reflected the need for system, order and control, which nowadays would be regarded as bureaucracy. It is easy in hindsight to be critical of these processes, but it is important to recognise that while they may be inappropriate for today's needs, they satisfied the requirements and culture of the time.

Problems with traditional approaches

The major areas in which traditional approaches are criticised for taking time and resources are as follows:

Job description preparation – and reading

Long, detailed job descriptions were often a feature of traditional job evaluation processes.

Frequently, the motivation behind the growth in length and detail was a positive one – the wish to make sure full justice was done to the job, and that no detail which could affect evaluation was missed. This was, of course, reinforced by the high focus on job evaluation as the primary determinant of pay, so that jobholders and their managers felt obliged to put every last detail in – and rewrite the description periodically with even more detail – in an attempt to increase the score.

Preparing such descriptions absorbed much time on the part of the jobholder and manager, and in many organisations trained analysts were also used, to interview jobholders/managers and prepare descriptions for approval. In some cases, sizeable teams of full-time job analysts were maintained for this purpose alone.

Apart from the time and resource absorbed by this approach, the resulting long descriptions were frequently of little use for other purposes, apart from feeding the job evaluation process. Thus, for example, because the essential features often became lost in a mass of detail, they were not particularly useful for providing the basis for performance management or for recruitment. In some cases, entirely different descriptions had to be prepared for these purposes, adding to the time consumption.

In addition, detailed concentration on tasks and duties in the description often produced a document which was restrictive and encouraged the attitude 'I won't do it unless it is in my job description', leading to many of the criticisms of inflexibility noted in the last section.

Job evaluation committee or panel

The conventional use of a job evaluation committee has many strengths – drawing on a wide range of expertise, enabling debate about jobs from different perspectives, enabling a consensus view to be reached, building ownership of results, etc.

Unfortunately, however, it can be slow, and if applied to large numbers of jobs, can consume excessive resources.

Some features of past practice (which still persist in some places today) have exacerbated the problem. Again, like the pressures for longer job descriptions, these were often the result of the best motives, to make sure that jobs were given fair treatment, but often had the effect of slowing the process to unacceptable levels, or bogging it down in a mass of procedural detail. For example:

● Large committees: In order to ensure fair representation,

particularly where a number of different groupings are involved, large committees have often resulted, sometimes in excess of 12 or 15 people. At this size, committees can become virtually unmanageable, consensus can be difficult to achieve, and the rate of progress can be very slow.

- Presentations by jobholders/managers/representatives: In addition to long job descriptions, some organisations' committee processes involve lengthy inputs from the jobholder, manager and/or representative. One of the authors once saw a jobholder arrive for such an input complete with overhead projector and a large folder of slides. Again, while the aim is praiseworthy, the result is to slow the process down even more.
- 'Observing' the work: In some cases, particularly in schemes for manual workers, the process includes the whole committee visiting the workplace and observing the work done. Again, praiseworthy for attention to detail, but enormously time consuming, and also increasing the focus on specific tasks and duties.

It is not surprising that in some cases committees sometimes only dealt with a handful of jobs in a full day's deliberations.

Review processes

In order to spread the load, larger organisations frequently set up a number of committees to deal with different parts of the business. This was also done in many cases in order to decentralise the evaluation process to different business units. In order to maintain consistency across the various committees, review processes are necessary, and in some cases these can be an elaborate and time-consuming second tier in the process, sometimes 'second guessing' the results of the separate committees.

Current practice

In today's environment, such practices are no longer acceptable, and much more efficient processes are demanded – and used.

In exploring the ways that modern practice has responded to these kinds of criticisms, it is important to recognise that they are issues about the evaluation process, not about the underlying method or measuring stick used. Recognising this is important for users of job evaluation who are experiencing some of the problems itemised above since it will help determine the most appropriate course of action. The tendency to see job evaluation as a 'package' may result in a decision to change the whole package, with all the costs and resource implications of that decision, when in fact the basic methodology and the results which it has produced may be perfectly satisfactory. In such cases, relatively straightforward developments of the process may be possible, and yield major gains in efficiency.

Thus even a conventional committee based approach in today's environment can be made much more efficient by the use of shorter, sharper job descriptions, smaller panels, and a range of computer based tools to help the administration of the process.

But beyond these straightforward refinements, a wide range of application processes is now available, each with different characteristics, enabling the most appropriate process to be selected to suit a particular set of requirements. It is important to stress that there is no single 'best' process to suit all circumstances – careful selection and design is necessary to get the right balance of characteristics to meet the needs of the organisation.

These processes are described in more detail in subsequent chapters. In the following section we review some of the options available to address the issue of process efficiency, and outline the main criteria for process selection.

Process design criteria

The major considerations in designing the right process are illustrated in Figure 4.1.

In the inner circle are shown the primary 'hard' considerations on which the choice should be based, while in the outer ring are a range of environmental issues which may also have an important bearing on determining the best process.

Purpose
Possibly the most important issue affecting process choice is the basic purpose of the whole exercise – why job evaluation is being undertaken at all. In most cases, the answer will be to provide some kind of input to pay arrangements, but the nature of this input, the way the results are to be used, and the additional objectives to be met will largely determine the choice. A few examples will illustrate:

• If the requirement is purely to arrive at a simple grading for a large number of jobs as quickly and efficiently as possible, then it is likely that a computer assisted questionnaire based approach, or a classification method underpinned by job evaluation, would be the primary choice, since efficiency is the dominant consideration.

• If, on the other hand, additional outputs are required in terms

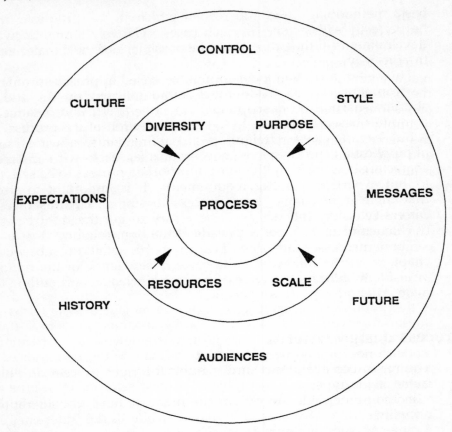

Figure 4.1   Factors affecting process choice.

of organisational analysis or clarification, then the debate in a conventional committee may be the best choice, even though it is less rapid.

- Similarly, job evaluation is frequently used as the vehicle for building common pay arrangements across different groups of employees. A participative panel with representatives from all these groups can often provide the essential joint involvement to support this.
- Where the requirement is to link pay closely to career or professional development – as for instance for a group of engineers or scientists – then a specific job family computer model may be the best choice, using factors linked explicitly to career development issues, and underpinned by conventional evaluation.

Scale

The second major influence on process choice is the scale of the exercise, in terms of the numbers of jobs to be covered. Thus, if the requirement is simply to evaluate a few dozen senior management jobs, then a straightforward panel process is probably the best choice, since the investment required to develop models and sophisticated frameworks would not be justified. Conversely, to apply the same process to several thousand jobs elsewhere in the same organisation would probably not be the best choice, and one would be looking to computer assistance or simplified frameworks.

Diversity

The diversity of the job population to be covered has two main components:

Diversity of job type

If the population is large but highly homogeneous in terms of the kind of work undertaken (e.g. several thousand clerical staff) then a relatively simple classification framework or job family model, underpinned by job evaluation, may be the best choice. A requirement to evaluate a similar number of jobs in a much wider range of job types would probably be best satisfied by a broadly based computer aided questionnaire method, to accommodate the diversity.

Organisational diversity

One of the major trends in recent years has been the decentralisation of many HR processes, including job evaluation. Processes for successful decentralisation need to accommodate the need for maintaining consistency between units, and computer aided approaches are particularly valuable in this context.

Resources

The ultimate determinant of the process is the amount of time and resource which can be devoted to it, and the way this resource is distributed. Thus straightforward panel processes may not require tremendous investment of time and resource to get them started, but do present a continuing resource requirement throughout initial implementation and beyond into the maintenance phase.

Computer aided methods on the other hand may require greater initial resource investment to develop the necessary questionnaires and models, but the resource requirement for evaluating the bulk of jobs and for the maintenance stage drops very significantly. This is illustrated graphically in Figure 4.2.

While these considerations will largely determine the choice of process, the 'softer' environmental and cultural issues noted in Figure 4.1 also need to be taken into account.

If, for example, the whole style, culture and history of the organisation have been characterised by highly participative processes, then a clearly management driven job evaluation process may not be culturally acceptable – and vice versa. It should however be noted that job evaluation is frequently used as a component of cultural change, and so one might design into the process a carefully measured degree of culture mismatch in order to support the change process.

As a practical example of this, a large manufacturing company had among its broader human resource management objectives a sharpening of managerial accountability, and a greater focus on output and results achievement. Its existing job evaluation processes were very jobholder centred and task orientated, using long detailed job descriptions written by jobholders themselves and presented in person to the panel. In support of its broader objectives, the company introduced new job evaluation arrangements, key features of which were short job descriptions (little more than a page in length), focusing on the major areas of accountability of the job, written by managers for agreement by jobholders, and evaluated by small management panels, without jobholder presentation. The result was a significant contribution to the culture change objective.

A major point of caution should however be registered in this context. Job evaluation can only be one component of a whole set of initiatives needed to achieve culture change. There are many examples of cases where job evaluation has been used as the

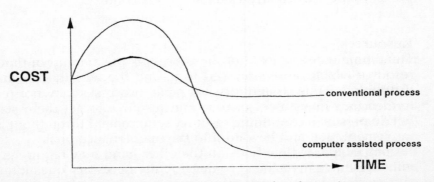

Figure 4.2   Comparison of cost over time for alternative processes.

only component of such change programmes, or too clearly at the leading edge, where the result has been rejection of a process which alone was seen to be too far away from existing culture and expectations.

Refining the process

Particularly for larger populations of jobs, or in situations where severe resource constraints apply and where efficiency of the process is paramount, more significant developments in the process are required. Some of the main processes which are now available are illustrated in Figure 4.3, on a chart showing the relationship between the speed or efficiency of the process against its sensitivity to individual job construction and detail.

Assume that the basic method of evaluation being used is a fairly conventional factor based method, in which points are allocated for various elements of job content and accumulated to give a total job size.

Benchmark evaluation

Most processes would begin at the bottom right hand corner of the chart, with evaluation of a benchmark sample of jobs, selected to give a representative picture of the larger population. The benchmark process is one of setting standards, establishing values, and putting the first pegs in the ground against which the rest of the evaluations can be tested. Each job is examined carefully, from first principles, to establish these basic standards. This process is thus very high on the sensitivity scale, but very low on speed and efficiency.

Panel evaluation of non-benchmarks

Following the benchmark setting, a similar panel process may be used to evaluate the remaining jobs. If so, progress is likely to be somewhat faster, since the benchmarks provide a starting point and a framework within which judgements can be reached more quickly. For this stage, it is quite common practice to develop 'rules of thumb', guidance notes, interpretations and so on, based on the benchmark evaluations, to guide subsequent judgements – though these can become the 'myths and legends' of tomorrow as noted in the last chapter. There is thus a little loss in sensitivity to match the gain in speed, since the standards, interpretations and reference points of the benchmark do constrain the judgements slightly – as of course they are intended to.

Generic jobs and ladders

For larger populations which may contain groups of similar jobs, the use of generic job descriptions to cover many jobholders in a particular job category is fairly widespread. If a series of generic jobs is produced to cover different levels of work, a 'ladder' is produced (e.g. engineer, senior engineer, principal engineer).

These produce a step-change in the efficiency of the process, since only one generic job need be evaluated to cover many individual jobholders. There is of course a significant loss of sensitivity to individual job detail, since these are smoothed out in the generic definition. There may also be equal value issues.

Classification

Taking the process a step further, it is possible to generate classification frameworks using the benchmark data against which individual jobs are directly assessed. Such approaches can be very rapid and easy to decentralise for large populations, and being underpinned by full job evaluation they have significant advantages over simple classification schemes developed from scratch without this underpinning. Of course they do represent a further loss of sensitivity to individual job detail, and find application where such sensitivity is not required – or indeed is positively not wanted, for example in a move away from individually defined jobs towards broader job categories in support of greater flexibility.

As illustrated in Figure 4.3, there is a fairly strong inverse relationship between speed on the one hand, and sensitivity on the other, a relationship which with conventional approaches it is

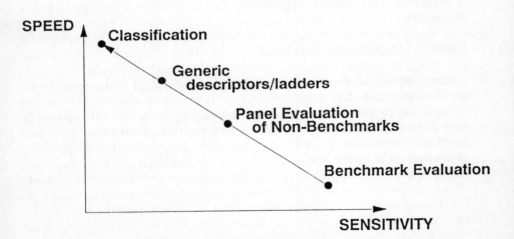

Figure 4.3 Job evaluation processes.

difficult to break. As described earlier, the appropriate positioning of the process on this spectrum needs to be chosen, taking into account the purpose, scale and diversity of the exercise, and the resources available.

Computer assisted processes

The development, during the second half of the 1980's, of computer assisted job evaluation processes (CAJE) now means that it is increasingly possible to break this efficiency-sensitivity relationship, and achieve processes which are both fast and efficient and sensitive to a wide range of job types and variations. CAJE approaches are discussed in detail in Chapter 9, but in the context of this discussion it is important to recognise that the computer provides assistance with the *process* and does not replace the need for a basic job evaluation *method* to underpin it.

Thus a typical computer assisted job evaluation exercise will begin with the evaluation, by conventional means, of a benchmark sample. This establishes the basic values and standards on which the computer model is to be built. Questionnaires are then constructed to elicit job information in simple processable form (e.g. multiple choice questions), and a mathematical relationship (algorithm) is built to relate job evaluation results to questionnaire responses using the benchmark sample.

The algorithm is then programmed into an appropriate software environment, so that for non-benchmark jobs, questionnaire data can be computer processed to yield an evaluation result. From this simple description, it is clear that the computer is not substituting for the job evaluation method, nor for evaluation judgements. Rather, it is enabling the values, judgements and standards which have been established in the benchmark to be reproduced consistently and efficiently. High sensitivity is maintained in a way that is impossible with comparably efficient manual methods like classification because the computer algorithm can handle multiple variables.

Computer assisted methods are rapidly gaining wide acceptance in the UK, and it is reasonable to forecast that during the 1990's a significant proportion of job evaluation processes in sizeable populations will use some form of computer assistance. This has certainly been the pattern in the USA where their introduction preceded that of the UK.

PART II: PRACTICE

5 The Nature and Purpose of Job Evaluation

As a working definition:

Job evaluation is a process for judging the relative size or importance of jobs within an organisation.

This brief statement has a number of important implications which are considered in this chapter.

- Job evaluation is a judgemental process.
- Job evaluation is about jobs.
- Job evaluation is about relativities.

The judgemental nature of job evaluation

Job evaluation is sometimes assumed to be 'scientific'. Superficially it may appear so, and certainly seems to employ some of the trappings of science – scales, numbers, precise definitions, calculations, statistical analyses and so on, but more careful examination shows that it is not, and can never be fully scientific.

In the first place, the concept of a 'job' – the thing that job evaluation is attempting to assess – is not a precise one. Some people view a job as a unit of organisation structure, a box on an organisation chart; others would see a job as a collection of tasks to be accomplished or accountabilities to be achieved; others again might see a job simply in terms of what a person does within an organisation.

Second, what do we mean by 'size' or 'importance' of a job within

THE NATURE AND PURPOSE OF JOB EVALUATION 41

an organisation? There cannot be a precise, scientific answer to this, since what is considered to be important will depend at least to some degree on the values which exist within the organisation.

It is particularly easy to forget the essentially judgemental nature of job evaluation when considering the various computer assisted processes which have been developed in recent years and which are rapidly gaining wide acceptance. Contrary to claims which are sometimes made, such approaches do not remove the judgement from job evaluation – they simply concentrate it. The computer system can only reproduce judgements and values which have been put into it at the start: their great value, of course, is that they can reproduce these judgements very quickly, efficiently and consistently. Computer assisted processes are dealt with in more detail in Chapter 9.

Acceptance of the essentially judgemental nature of job evaluation is not an admission of defeat, or of any fundamental flaw in the approach. It is simply a realistic recognition of the basic character of job evaluation, of which practitioners must constantly be aware.

Recognising that it can never be *fully* scientific, *fully* precise, *fully* objective, the skill is in designing a process which can yield *maximum* objectivity and reproducibility, with results which are *consistent* and *explainable*.

This is why job evaluation should be seen as a process, not just an isolated technique. Understanding job evaluation, and designing and implementing an effective approach is much more than considering just the basic measuring stick which is to be used.

Essential features of the process which are needed to refine the judgements, maximise objectivity and ensure consistency are:

- Information.
- Method.
- Process for applying the method.

Information requirements

The quality of judgements made about a job can only be as good as the quality of information available about the job – information which is both specific to the job itself, and about the context in which it operates.

Specific job information can be collected in a number of ways, and presented in a variety of forms, for example job descriptions or multiple-choice questionnaires. It is probably fair to say that over the years, this stage of job analysis has been the part of the job evaluation process which has been most neglected, and the quality and consistency of job information has often been poor. It is also a part of the process which meets much adverse reaction from employees and managers. Conventional written job descriptions are often considered to be too long and require too much resource investment to produce, compared with their perceived usefulness. There is also frequently a worry that they can present information in a variable way, unhelpful to consistent evaluation. Finally, and most fundamentally, there is a growing concern that conventional description of jobs can be restrictive on job design, and inhibit the development of the more flexible roles which today's organisations require.

Job definition and analysis is covered in detail in Chapter 8, together with consideration of how the approaches available are developing and changing in response to these problems, and to the needs of the organisations of today.

Beyond this specific job information, job evaluation also requires information and understanding of the context in which job operate.

Jobs, by their very nature, do not exist in isolation, but in the context of an organisation within which there will be complex working relationships, up and down and laterally across the structure. However good the specific job information, it is incomplete without such contextual information.

To give a simple example, consider the evaluation of a sales representative.

The job description or questionnaire may give excellent information on the accountability of the job for sales volume, for new business generation, for customer relations, and so on. It may also give details of the specific tasks undertaken, and the controls on the job's actions – for example the freedom the job has to vary prices or give discounts.

What it would probably not tell you are answers to questions like:

- What is the role of the area sales manager and how does this impact upon the job in question?
- If there is a technical service department, or a national accounts team, or a sales office support team, how do these affect the representative's job and activities, and how do they affect our view of the skills and responsibilities involved?
- What is the nature of the selling process? Is it direct to customers, or to distributors, or is it seeking to influence specifiers rather than direct purchasers – for example a building products representative influencing architects to specify, or a pharmaceutical representative influencing doctors to prescribe?
- Is selling largely a 'solo' activity or one involving extensive teamwork? For example in the selling of complex capital equipment, the sales representative is likely to be just part of a team comprising technical and design staff, contracts specialists and so on.

- How much of the sales is 'repeat' business, requiring servicing by the representative, and how much is real first-time selling?

Such issues are not just theoretical: they have a material effect on how one would evaluate the job of a sales representative. As a practical example, it is illuminating to track the way jobs of fast moving consumer goods representatives have changed over the last 10 or 15 years. Over this period the consolidation of retailers into fewer and more powerful buying units have changed the emphasis from direct selling by the representatives to the setting up of national deals by the national accounts staff, changing the role of the representative to one of local servicing of the national accounts. As a result, the way such jobs have been evaluated has changed significantly over this period.

While in principle such contextual information could be provided in a job description or questionnaire, this is not usually a practical proposition, especially given the increasing requirement for short, sharp statements of the basic essentials of a job and the rejection of long, narrative job descriptions.

In practice, such information and understanding has to be provided by the evaluators themselves. Thus the choice of evaluators is critical – an issue which is picked up in Chapter 9.

Job evaluation method

The second requirement to improve the quality of judgement is a *method* for actually assessing one job against another.

However good the information – specific and contextual – the results will probably not be very satisfactory if each evaluator is using a different basis or set of premises from which to make evaluation judgements.

However hard we may try as evaluators to take an unbiased view of jobs, we are all to some degree conditioned by our background and experience, and will have different views about what makes a job 'big' or 'important'. Some may value the requirement for technical and professional skills; others may put more weight on to jobs which control large resources; while others may see impact on sales as being the primary consideration.

What is required is an agreed method or set of criteria, used by all evaluators in the organisation, and which represent the values of the organisation as a whole. The method needs to provide the means of:

- structuring the judgements in a rational way.
- enabling objective debate about job size relativities.
- checking the consistency of judgements.
- recording and, if appropriate, justifying the judgements made, and why.

The job evaluation method is the core of the job evaluation process, and is dealt with in detail in Chapter 6. But it is by no means the whole story. The method only provides us with the basic measuring stick; just as important is the process by which it is applied.

Process for applying the job evaluation method

The third requirement to ensure high quality judgement in job evaluation is to ensure appropriate design and implementation of the process by which the basic method is applied. Even the best methods can yield dubious results if insufficient care is taken with the application process.

Most traditional job evaluation processes contain three important aspects, specifically designed for the purpose of improving the quality and reproducibility of judgements:

Use of benchmarks

Traditional job evaluation normally begins with the evaluation of a carefully selected sample of jobs, representative of the types and levels of job likely to be encountered in the full population. Benchmarking provides the means of establishing some basic reference points against which other jobs can be compared and their evaluations tested. It also provides the opportunity to 'translate' or calibrate the evaluation criteria in the method – which are necessarily expressed in general or conceptual terms since they must apply to a wide range of jobs – into practical real-life examples. Thus a rather obscure and theoretical definition of a particular level, say in a 'knowledge' factor scale, is translated/calibrated into 'the level of knowledge required for the buyer in the Warrington factory, the project engineer in central engineering or the area sales manager, West'. This gives necessary practical pegs in the ground in the process of turning theoretical statements into practical realities.

Use of panels or committees

Conventionally, job evaluation methods have been applied by one or more committees or panels, comprising members drawn from a variety of areas within the organisation, so as to ensure both a wide range of knowledge of how the organisation really works, plus the facility for arriving at a consensus view through debate and reasoned argument.

Review of results

When each job has been evaluated (and often at stages during the process) it is common practice to review the results which have emerged, to test the consistency of results and the relativities which have emerged. Where more than one panel is operating, say in a decentralised operation, such processes are particularly important to ensure consistency has been maintained.

As noted earlier, traditional processes are coming under increasing pressure and criticism for being time consuming and bureaucratic. In seeking ways to refine them and make them more efficient, it is important to recognise that the key features itemised above are not just there for the sake of it, but were seen to be the best available means at the time for improving and maintaining the quality of judgements.

In the newer processes which are emerging, the same needs have to be satisfied, but through more efficient means. This is why most modern processes still begin with benchmark evaluation to establish the basic standards and interpretations, and still end with review of results. The part that can now be replaced by other more efficient means (computers, frameworks, etc.) is the panel evaluation of the bulk of jobs in a population – since this is the most time consuming stage and the one in which the objective is largely to reproduce values and rule sets established through benchmarking.

Design and implementation of processes for job evaluation are considered more fully in Chapter 9.

The focus of job evaluation is jobs, and job relativities

While this may sound self-evident, it is important to stress that job evaluation only looks at jobs, and hence does not in itself determine pay levels, and takes no account of:

- Market pay requirements, pressures and differentials.
- Shortages of particular kinds of employees or skills.
- Individual performance, length of service or other characteristics.
- Business performance.
- Business economics and cost structures.

In the context of pay determination processes and the broader context of human resource management processes, it is essential to remember that job evaluation only addresses one facet – jobs – and must be used in concert with other related processes. Failure to recognise this has resulted in many of the problems identified in Chapter 2.

The ways in which job evaluation results are used in this wider context are reviewed in Chapter 12.

Finally, job evaluation is an exercise in relativities, not in absolutes. While consistent expression of job size in numerical or other terms within an organisation is essential, and between organisations may be helpful, to facilitate pay comparisons, the measures used are essentially empirical and designed only to express and quantify relativities.

The purpose of job evaluation

Most organisations undertake job evaluation in order to provide an input to their pay determination processes. However, this is certainly not the only use which the approach has, and many organisations seek additional outputs from it – or in a few cases alternative outputs, when the purpose is not pay driven.

As we have seen, understanding and clarifying what additional outputs are sought is an important consideration in designing the best job evaluation process, since different processes can provide different types of additional benefits.

Among the additional (or alternative) outputs often sought are:

Job clarification

Over time, jobs change, evolve and develop. It is surprising how many organisations may not be at all clear about what jobs they have, and how they are constructed. The job evaluation process, by providing a rigorous analysis of jobs and their relationships, puts a very useful spotlight on areas where there is lack of clarity, or simply lack of understanding about how jobs are really constructed.

Organisational analysis

Similarly, since job evaluation explores job relationships in some depth, it can, if properly done, provide an enormously valuable tool of organisational analysis. It does not in itself provide answers to how organisations should be changed to make them more effective, but it does provide very sharp insights into issues like:

* Lack of organisational clarity.
* Overlap between the responsibilities of jobs, or uncertainty about how the responsibility is allocated or shared.
* Overlayering of management structures.
* Apparent overlayering due to 'technical' hierarchies being represented as 'line' hierarchies (e.g. does the lawyer really report to the senior lawyer, as shown on the organisation chart, or is this simply a reflection of the level of work undertaken?).
* Gaps in the spread of responsibilities where no-one seems to be accountable, etc.

Many users of job evaluation gain great value from using job evaluation in this way, and find that it provides a powerful language for debate about jobs, job relationships and organisations. Some of the techniques available are reviewed in Chapter 14.

Management/career development

Again, since job evaluation can provide deep insight into job relationships and relativities, it can provide useful input into issues of career development, management development and succession planning. For example it can highlight areas of the organisation where there are large gaps between manager and subordinate, and where sideways or diagonal career moves will be required in order to provide for succession and career planning. Planning for such situations is of course increasingly important with the move to flatter structures with larger gaps between the layers.

As another example, we have seen job evaluation used within organisations to evaluate general management posts around the world, not primarily to control or determine pay, which may be locally determined, but to provide inputs to career development decisions and test the feasibility of moving people from one job to another.

Supporting changes in job structure/working practices

Existing pay and grading arrangements (whether based on job evaluation or not) may be seen to 'lock in' existing job construction, demarcation lines or working practices. Applying (or modifying) a job evaluation approach gives the opportunity to consider such inhibitions to change, and gear the process to support the changes. For example a move to greater flexibility in a production unit may be hindered by existing arrangements which treat 'operator machine A', 'operator machine B'...etc. as separate jobs. New or modified job evaluation arrangements enable reconsideration of the way jobs are defined, and may result, for example, in more broadly based definitions to embody the degree of flexibility which is required – with appropriate evaluations to match. These issues are explored in Chapter 8.

Supporting culture change

Since job evaluation reflects values and perceptions within an organisation about what contributes to job size – i.e. 'what matters around here' – it can be used to support culture change by careful control of the values which it reflects – and is seen to reflect. An example of this was described in Chapter 3, though it was noted there that job evaluation can only support such change, and should not be relied upon to lead the culture change process.

Aiding team building

There is a progressive move towards the integration of pay and conditions between employee groups within organisations, and frequently job evaluation is used to provide the logical underpinning to common arrangements. Apart from this 'technical' output, many organisations which have undertaken this have found great value simply from the process itself. In many cases, it has provided for the first time, a forum in which issues of jobs and relativities could be debated among different representative groups and management in a genuinely joint participative way, quite different from the adversarial context of the negotiating process. This can provide major inputs to the development of greater understanding and collaboration between previously separate groups.

Supporting decentralisation

While, because of history, job evaluation is often seen as a centralised process, it can be used to great effect to support the decentralisation of pay decisions to operating units or businesses. Many organisations wish to devolve pay decisions and pay management, but wish to ensure that there are processes in place which will provide a logical basis for these decisions across the organisation. Using a common job evaluation methodology, handled and controlled locally, and feeding into local pay decisions is one way in which many organisations have successfully achieved this balance.

6 Job Evaluation Methods

In this chapter we concentrate on the basic means of evaluating jobs – the underlying basis for evaluative judgement – not the processes by which the method is applied, nor the way in which the results are used.

Categorisation of methods

Job evaluation methods are commonly categorised into two types:

- *Non-analytical methods*, in which whole jobs are examined, without any breaking down into constituent parts or aspects.
- *Analytical methods*, in which jobs are considered using a number of criteria, factors or elements, with overall job size being an accumulation of these separate judgements.

While this is an important distinction, it is, to a degree, an oversimplification.

A further consideration is whether judgements are made by direct comparison between one job and another, or made by comparing each job with a set scale of some sort.

To illustrate this distinction by analogy, consider trying to rank 50 people in a room in order of height. Two approaches are possible. One approach is to line all the people up against the wall, and ask them to 'shuffle' until the shortest is on the left rising to the tallest on the right. This is analogous to evaluation by direct job–job comparison.

Alternatively, one could take a ruler, and separately measure each person in the room – which is analogous to evaluation of each job against a set scale.

(In practice of course, both in job evaluation or height measurement a combination of the two could be used. In our analogy this is like using a ruler to get a rough categorisation to the nearest couple of inches, followed by 'shuffling' for the fine tuning. Such combinations are widely used in practice in job evaluation).

In Figure 6.1, these two distinctions are shown together as a matrix.

| | **Means of Comparison** | |
	Whole Job (non-analytical)	By Factors (analytical)
Job–Job	Simple ranking Paired comparisons	Factor comparison
Job–Scale	Classification	Points factor rating

Basis of Comparison

Figure 6.1   Categorisation of job evaluation methods.

Across the top of the matrix is the distinction between non-analytical (whole job) methods and analytical (factor based) methods. Down the side is the distinction between direct job–job comparison and the use of scales against which jobs are individually compared.

Within the matrix we have categorised the commonly available job evaluation methods, the main characteristics of which are considered in the following sections.

The distinction between analytical and non-analytical methods has taken on a sharper focus in the light of equal value legislation enacted in recent years. This issue is explored in detail in Chapter 13, but in the context of this review it should be noted that the presence of an analytical job evaluation scheme which is not in itself discriminatory (and is not used in a discriminatory way) can form the basis of a defence against equal value claims. Non-analytical schemes are not accepted for such a defence, and the merits of the claim may therefore have to be tested more directly.

Methods using job–job comparison on a whole job basis

Simple ranking

This is the most straightforward method available, since it involves simply ranking a set of jobs in order of perceived size or importance, without any scales, numbers, factors, etc.

Its strength is in its simplicity, but therein also lies its weakness.

For a very small, uncomplicated organisation, where the relative importance of jobs is clearly discernible and unequivocal, then it can be perfectly valid. In practice many such organisations who would say that they do not have a job evaluation 'scheme' are in fact practising simple ranking by instinct – they just know which are the bigger jobs and which are the smaller ones.

In larger or more complex organisations the approach has a number of significant defects:

- Being non-analytical it cannot provide assurance of non-discrimination, nor defence against claims for discrimination.
- The results are impossible to explain, justify or defend, since the only basis is a blanket judgement – 'I think A is bigger than B' – without the means for recording why.
- Similarly, since there is no structured basis for the judgements, different evaluators with different perceptions may arrive at different rankings, without a language to express, debate and reconcile their different views.
- While the method enables ranking of order of perceived job size, it does not enable quantification of the differences between them. For example if ten jobs are ranked in order, are they evenly spread in size, or is there one very big one, two very small ones and seven middle sized ones or what? If job evaluation results are to be used as the basis for constructing pay and/or grading arrangements, some kind of quantification of the differences is important.
- Simple ranking is difficult when dissimilar jobs are being compared. Thus within a larger organisation, it may be feasible to rank all the accounting jobs in order of importance, and separately to rank all the engineering jobs for example. The

difficulty is in comparing accountants with engineers – and even more so, in comparing say the fifth largest engineering job with the fifth largest accounting job, without some structured basis for the comparison.
Some of these difficulties can be ameliorated by appropriate process design.

Thus for example, initial ranking of a benchmark of well-recognised jobs can provide a basic framework for ranking of other jobs. Nevertheless, the fundamental problems remain, and in practice the method only finds general application in relatively small, simple organisations where job relativities are well understood and accepted.

Paired comparisons

This is a refinement of simple ranking in which each job is compared in turn with every other job.

In each of these paired comparisons, the job judged to be larger is generally allocated 2 points, and the smaller one 0 points. If the two are judged equal, each is given 1 point. The points total for each job is then totalled, to give the rank order. Typically, individual evaluators make independent judgements, and the results averaged for the final rank order.

By forcing multiple comparisons, better results are usually obtained than from simple ranking, particularly when the population contains a range of different types of jobs.

However many of the disadvantages remain:

- It is still non-analytical from an equal value point of view.
- The result is still only a rank order. Even though a points score is given to each job, the scores only indicate order, and do not give any measure of the relative gaps between job sizes.
- It does not provide any framework or language for debate of relativities or the basis of them, or for communicating or justifying the results.

In addition, it can only be used for relatively small numbers of jobs, since the number of comparisons for larger numbers becomes unmanageable, even with computer processing. Thus a set of 50 jobs generates 1225 comparisons, 100 jobs require 4950 comparisons, while 200 jobs would need 19,900 paired comparisons. Thus it is not really practicable above 50 or 60 jobs.

Methods using job–scale comparison on a whole job basis – classification

Classification methods (e.g. IAM Office Job Evaluation, see Appendix 1) rely upon matching the content of an individual job to a series of job-level or grade definitions which have been established. Although the grade definitions may be expressed in terms of several different criteria, aspects or 'factors', these do not have separate scores or points attached to them, so the matching or slotting is essentially done on a whole job basis, choosing the grade definition which best matches the actual content of the job.

An essential difference in nature between classification and other forms of job evaluation is that in classification the structure of grades or job levels is set at the beginning, then individual jobs slotted into the framework. In contrast, most other methods examine individual jobs first, assign a score or rank order to them, then design the grade structure (if there is to be one) to accommodate the results in the most appropriate way. This is illustrated in Figure 6.2.

The principal advantage of classification is its speed and simplicity, especially for large populations, since once the framework is established, individual job slotting can be done very easily and quickly. It is also very amenable to decentralised operation, since it lacks the complexity of many other methods, and so users can be trained in its use very easily, with reasonable confidence that it will be applied consistently.

For these reasons it has been a very widely used approach, in one form or another, in many areas of both the public and private sectors in the UK, though in its more straightforward forms it is increasingly being questioned, and replaced or supported by other

Classification

DETERMINE GRADES ────► **ALLOCATE JOBS TO GRADES**

Other forms of job evaluation

EVALUATE JOBS ────► **DETERMINE GRADES**

Figure 6.2 The process of job classification.

methods, because of a number of disadvantages which it displays, as follows:

- Being non-analytical *it does not provide assurance or defence against equal value problems.*
- In itself *it rather begs the question of how the relativities which are embodied in the grades or classes themselves were arrived at in the first place.* If, as is common, these were arrived at on a simple felt-fair basis, then essentially the method is directly analogous to simple ranking, with all the disadvantages of that approach. The only difference is that in conventional simple ranking each job is ranked individually, whereas in constructing a classification structure each class or grade is ranked. It is thus equally difficult to express, debate or justify the relativities between the grades.

  More recently this problem has been addressed in a number of cases by using a more structured, analytical job evaluation method to underpin, derive or calibrate a classification frame-work, with excellent results. In such cases the evaluation *method*, i.e. the fundamental basis on which job evaluation judgements are made, is actually the underpinning methodology, and classification is really the delivery *process*.

- Like simple ranking, *it only works well in job populations which are highly homogeneous in terms of the nature of work, or which can be subdivided into groups, categories or families of jobs*, each of which is internally homogeneous.

  If one attempted to draw up single grade/class definitions to cover a wide range of jobs such as might be found in a typical medium to large sized enterprise, the definitions would need to be so broad, and contain so many alternatives, as to be woolly and useless. Division into categories or families of jobs is the most commonly used way of overcoming this, but as discussed under simple ranking, the major problem which this generates is the difficulty of calibration between families – unless of course the whole thing is underpinned by a more fundamental analytical job evaluation method, as noted above.

- *This commonly practised subdivision into job categories has in many cases produced a plethora of separate categories* – often associated with separate pay scales and/or negotiating arrangements. While this has enabled crisp definition of grades in each category, it inhibits the integration of pay arrangements which is a major feature of many organisation's pay strategies. For this reason, many such schemes are currently being dismantled in favour of approaches which allow for a more common, integrated view of jobs and rely less on segregation.

- *A related objection to such highly structured classification approaches is that they can lock in traditional separations or demarcations between jobs*, which may be no longer valid, or which may actually inhibit the development of the more flexible organisations required in the current environment. For example in the current office environment it is increasingly difficult to draw the line between traditional 'clerical', 'typing' and 'data processing' jobs; in many works environments there is the requirement to develop multi-skilled production teams in which traditional craft and operator distinctions are becoming increasingly blurred; in operating a complex chemical or process plant, the distinction between an 'operator' and a 'technician' may no longer be at all clear – or indeed wanted.

- A final difficulty with many classification systems is that *they are susceptible to drift*, because the process of allocation of jobs to classes/grades is not structured. The more the job population is categorised into highly specific job families, each with its own set of grades, the more this drift can be controlled, but then the problems of categorisation as noted above become more of a problem. In designing a classification method it is therefore usually necessary to strike a balance between over-categorisation on the one hand, and over-vague generalised descriptions, susceptible to drift, on the other.

Despite these significant disadvantages, classification is still a widely used and valuable method for large populations, where speed, simplicity and decentralisation are essential requirements, and where the problems of over-categorisation are not significant because the population is highly homogeneous in nature.

In more refined forms, where it is used as the delivery process for an analytical method, it is particularly valuable.

Methods using job–scale comparison on a factor basis – Points Factor Rating

Introduction
Methods of this type fall into the category usually referred to as points factor rating.

The basis of such methods is the breaking down of a job into a number of factors which are considered to contribute to job size, allocating points to a job under each factor heading using numerical scales, and accumulating the separate factor scores to give a total job size.

Points factor rating methods may be 'off the shelf' schemes in which the factors, scales and weightings are already determined, or 'tailor made' in which the scheme is designed from scratch to suit a particular set of circumstances and a particular range of jobs. In practice, the distinction between these is not always very great: most 'tailor made' schemes come out with similar factors, weightings and ultimate results.

The steps usually involved in building a points factor rating scheme are as follows:

- Determining factors.
- Developing scales for each factor.
- Establishing a rank order for a sample of jobs.
- Weighting the factors to give the required rank order for the sample.
- Testing on a wider sample.

These steps are considered in more detail below.

Determining factors

This is usually done by analysis of a sample of jobs, representative of the population, and from this the identification of those factors which are seen to differentiate between jobs of different levels and hence contribute to job size.

While the way that factors are expressed and the number of factors chosen will vary significantly, most factor sets which emerge from such a process typically fall into the following categories:

Input factors

These relate to the level and type of input required in order to do the job, and may include aspects like:

*   Skills (manual and mental).
*   Qualifications and/or experience.
*   Technical/professional knowledge.
*   Interpersonal skills.
*   Team leading/building skills, etc.

Output factors

These are intended to assess the level and scale of responsibility carried by the job, and are often expressed in terms of factors like:

*   Responsibility.
*   Decision-making authority.
*   Responsibility for resources (people, assets, money, etc.).
*   Responsibility for results (output, sales, profit, etc.).

Throughput or processing factors

These relate to the use of knowledge and skills in doing the job, and turning the input into output, and typically include aspects like:

* Mental effort.
* Problem solving.
* Originality/creativity.
* Initiative.
* Judgement.
* Concentration, etc.

Physical factors

Where these are relevant to the types of jobs being evaluated and considered to be comprehensible elements, a range of factors may be developed to take account of issues like:

* Physical conditions and environment in which the job operates (e.g. temperature, light, fumes, exposure to weather, noise, dirt, etc.).
* Physical effort required, either by heavy work, repetitive actions, or working in confined spaces, awkward positions, etc.
* Dangers and hazards presented by the work.

Although they may not be presented in this way, the factors in most points rating schemes fall into these general types – and in practice bear a great similarity to each other. It is important to note that the choice of factors, and the relative balance of factors of different types, is – or should be – a reflection of the values which the organisation has, or wishes to have. Thus if the factors are predominantly of a 'knowledge, skills, experience' type, this will reflect a predominantly input based culture.

Conversely, if the factors are loaded towards responsibility, authority, results, then this will support or reflect a strong output orientation. Within this balance of emphasis in constructing the factors, certain issues require particular attention:

Equal value: If the set of factors is loaded towards those which typically characterise traditionally 'male' occupations, – for example an over-emphasis on factors to do with lifting, pushing, pulling, etc., – then the scheme is likely to be seen to incorporate sex bias. While this is also an issue for factor weighting, the choice of factors, the way they are expressed and the balance of them are also important considerations. These issues are explored in Chapter 13.

Factors which are organisationally restrictive: As described in the earlier chapters on the challenges to job evaluation, most organisations are undergoing major structural change and development. For factor based job evaluation methods to be robust and accommodate organisational change, the factors should not be specific to, or make assumptions about, any particular organisational model. For example:

- Factors which explicitly relate to the position of a job in the structural hierarchy (e.g. number of levels down from the chief executive) will not work if the structure is delayered, or may lock in old organisational assumptions.
- Factors which relate to control of resources will emphasise this aspect. While such factors may be relevant, excessive loading towards them will maintain a concentration on resource control as a means of progression, at variance with much current organisational thinking and development, and can be seen to be encouraging empire building.

Communication of values through factors

Apart from the 'technical' aspects of selecting factors outlined above, they also present an important form of communication to employees, if the basis of the factor scheme is generally known or communicated. Essentially the factors used are saying to the employee, 'these are the things that matter round here', and so great care needs to be taken that the delivered message is in line with the intended one. There is no point managers trying to promote a sharper output-orientated culture if the job evaluation factors are all about inputs. Equally, it makes it difficult to develop a culture which values technical excellence (as for example in a research environment) if people's jobs are evaluated using factors which predominantly value position in hierarchy and resources controlled.

Developing scales

Once the factors have been determined, it is necessary to develop a rating scale for each, so that a job can be allocated a score for the degree to which that factor is judged to be exhibited in the job.

Scales may be quite short, including only 3 or 4 levels, or they may involve 10 or more levels. The different levels may be simply expressed (high, moderate, low, etc.), may involve detailed descriptions for each point on the scale, or may simply be expressed as a rating scale (say from 0 to 10) with little description of the various levels in between. If a careful factor weighting process is used (see later in this chapter) the relative lengths of the scales should not matter too much. However, in some simple schemes where each factor is given the same weight, then the relative lengths

---

Factor 6 : contacts

This factor considers the requirement in the job for contacts inside and outside the company. Contacts may involve giving and receiving information, influencing others, or negotiation. The nature and frequency of contacts should be considered, as well as their effect on the Company.

Level 1 : little or no contacts except with immediate colleagues and supervisor. (10 points)

Level 2 : contacts are mainly internal and involve dealing with factual queries or exchange of information. (20 points)

Level 3 : contacts may be internal or external and typically require tact or discretion to gain cooperation. (30 points)

Level 4 : frequent internal/external contacts, of a sensitive nature requiring persuasive ability to resolve non-routine issues. (40 points)

Level 5 : frequent internal/external contacts at senior level or on highly sensitive issues, requiring advanced negotiating/persuasive skills. (50 points)

Level 6 : constant involvement with internal/external contacts at the highest level or involving negotiation/persuasion on difficult and critical issues. (60 points)

Figure 6.3 Example of a factor scale from a points factor rating scheme.

do matter – since 'high' on a 0–10 scale scores twice as much as 'high' on a 0–5 scale and so is effectively weighted twice as much.

An example of a typical factor scale is shown in Figure 6.3.

Establishing a rank order for a sample

Following development of the factors and scales, it is common practice to undertake a first rough weighting of the factors, but in order to go through a more detailed weighting process, a rank order needs to be established for a sample of jobs, using some means which is independent of the factors which have been developed. Factor weightings can then be fine-tuned to reproduce the rank order which has been set.

Typically a sample of jobs, representative of the population as a whole, is selected, and a ranking of these developed. The means available to accomplish this ranking include:

- Simple ranking on a felt-fair basis.
- Use of existing grade relativities for the sample jobs: this clearly demands that in the sample selected, existing relativities are felt to be appropriate.
- Use of existing pay relativities – again assuming that for the sample, these provide an appropriate foundation for building the weightings.
- Use of market pay relativities for the sample jobs.
- A paired comparison exercise on the sample.

Of these, probably the most widely used is the paired comparison approach.

It is clear from considering these alternatives that this stage is something of an Achilles heel for points factor rating schemes, since the factor weightings need to be built on the results of this ranking step, and all of the means available for conducting this step have some practical or conceptual problems associated with them.

None of them of course is an analytical approach, and while points factor rating methods are accepted as being analytical in nature, it is perhaps not generally recognised that they are built fairly directly on a non-analytical foundation.

Thus simple ranking to provide the foundation carries with it all the problems associated with that approach, and discussed earlier. In particular, it only produces a rank order, with no indications of size differences, is difficult to handle in a heterogeneous population, and in that it lacks any framework or language it may produce a rank order which includes bias of one sort or another, particularly sex bias.

Paired comparison improves the technical quality of the results, but is still an unstructured basis, open to bias, and only yields a rank order, and for a reasonable sample is a major exercise in its own right.

Use of existing grade or pay relativities makes the assumption that these are 'right' in the first place. In that job evaluation is often introduced to check this or to establish new, more supportable relativities, there is a conceptual as well as practical problem here, with the risk that the logic can become dangerously circular. There is also a very real danger that existing biases will simply be preserved.

These problems also apply to the use of market pay to give the ranking – plus the added difficulty of actually measuring market pay with any confidence (in all but the most homogeneous markets), and the fact that market pay variations are driven by many other factors than simply job size.

Weighting the factors

As noted above, this is often a two stage process, with initial rough weightings being established on a 'felt-fair' basis, followed by refinement using the benchmark sample.

For this second step, common practice is to evaluate each sample job on the factor scales which have been developed and then use the statistical technique of multiple regression to relate these results to the rank order which has been developed. This produces factor weightings which provide the best correlation between the cumulative factor scores and the rank order which has been set. In simple terms, it provides a means of reproducing the initial rank order most accurately by the use of the factors: this illustrates the importance of that first step of setting the rank order as discussed earlier.

In practice, this is usually an iterative process, involving refining the factors, the way the levels are expressed, as well as the weightings, so that a workable set of relationships is obtained.

Testing on a wider sample
Before applying the method as developed above to the full population, it is normal (and sensible) practice to undertake a wider testing, to ensure that the results obtained on a broader sample of jobs are judged to be reasonable, and if not, that the factors themselves, or their weightings can be adjusted accordingly.

Points factor schemes – general observations
Points factor methods are widely used in the UK, since they do offer significant advantages over the simpler non-analytical approaches.

In particular, they provide a more structured framework and language, through the factors for debating, rationalising and communicating evaluative judgements about relative job size. As we have seen, they are inevitably based on a much less analytical foundation, but provided the processes for defining factors and weights are carried out rigorously then a high level of objectivity can be incorporated.

Simple points factor schemes can of course be put together quite quickly, if the steps of factor weighting and testing as described above are omitted, and weights allocated on a largely arbitrary basis. While the resulting schemes may have the semblance of an analytical approach, it is questionable whether they add much in reality to the simpler ranking or classification processes, since their construction lacks the necessary basis and rigour.

To do the job properly in designing and testing a points factor plan is a significant operation, so it is common practice to engage consultants to help with such developments, based on their experience of building such methods in other organisations. Often, consultants may offer both ready made and tailored methods. In this context much stress is often made of the merits of tailor made schemes to reflect the particular values or characteristics of the organisation, though it has to be said that in practice many 'tailor made' schemes do bear a remarkable similarity to each other – not surprisingly since there are some strong commonly held values and attitudes to what makes a job important, across different organisations. There is also the reality that these 'tailor made' schemes tend to draw on a 'bank' of already tested factor and level definitions, altering the wording for new organisations/clients to meet particular cultural requirements.

Single factor or skewed schemes

Whereas in most points factor methods, the attempt is made to achieve a balance between the different types of factor described earlier, some approaches have been developed which concentrate on just one factor or factor type. While these are often presented as quite different approaches, it is important to recognise them as a specific case within points factor rating, in which all the emphasis is placed on one factor or skewed to one set of factors.

It is worthy of note that the earlier attempts to arrive at single factor approaches tended to concentrate on 'output' type factors, whereas current developments in this area typically focus on the 'input' factors of knowledge and skills. This reflects the shift in emphasis and fashion in thinking over the last 20 or 30 years from a structural, 'scientific' view of organisations and management to a much more people-centred emphasis. It is a pity that in the search for simple solutions or artificial distinctiveness, a pendulum effect seems to occur, with an over-emphasis in one direction being replaced with an overswing in the other. Methods which value one aspect of a job to the exclusion of others seem to be missing the point that in reality jobs are a mix of inputs and outputs – that is how they work – and need to be considered from both angles. Organisations in the nineties are operating in an environment that is intensely competitive, both in terms of business results, and in their demands for high quality people and specific skills, so methods of valuing jobs will need to maintain a sensible and practical equilibrium between input/people and output considerations.

Examples of single factor schemes with an output emphasis include:

Time span of discretion method

This was an approach developed by Elliott Jaques when working with the Glacier Metal Company in the 50's and 60's, to evaluate jobs on the basis of the 'time span of discretion' – i.e. the longest period of time for which a jobholder can exercise discretion about his or her work without supervision.

It was based on a hypothesis that this factor correlated with the requirement for skills and the difficulty of the job, and with people's general perception of job hierarchies and relativities. Although appealing, the concept was difficult to apply and few practical applications were ever developed.

Decision banding

Again, in this method a single factor is used, consisting of six levels or decision bands, each of which describes a different level of decision-making required of the job. This ranges from policy decisions in the top band through to defined decisions in the lowest. It was developed by TT Paterson in the 1970's and has been quite widely used outside the UK. See Appendix 1.

Ranking methods for branch structures

Organisations containing relatively large numbers of jobs of basically similar content but of different scale have often sought a quantitative ranking technique to determine pay and pay differentials. Examples include multiple branch structures like retail stores, where sometimes pay scales for managers are developed in which pay is related to the sales turnover of the store. Although this may not be described as job evaluation, in fact it is a single factor method of assessing relative job size in order to derive pay levels – i.e. a form of job evaluation. Like other single factor approaches, its problem is one of oversimplicity. For example one store may be situated in an affluent area, with no local competition, while another of the same turnover serves a poor neighbourhood and is next door to a direct competitor. Simply assessing on turnover fails to recognise these differences in job content and size.

Knowledge/skill based schemes

In the last few years a variety of approaches have been developed which assess jobs against a number of skill factors, each with an appropriate rating scale. Often the rationale for doing this has been to support multiskilling and the technical upgrading of the workforce. Usually, care is taken not to present these as job evaluation methods but as a different approach, more attuned to today's flexible, skill based organisations. Examination, however, often reveals the same essential features as any other points factor job evaluation scheme, except that all the factors are to do with input. So, far from providing a radically new approach, they are simply job evaluation under a new label, with the severe limitation that output factors are ignored. As discussed at greater length in Chapter 3, valuing jobs without regard for the output expected from them presents some difficult questions and potential conflicts to any enterprise, since all are required to generate some kind of output and to do so in an increasingly competitive environment.

Methods using job–job comparison on a factor basis – Factor Comparison

Background to Factor Comparison

In factor comparison, jobs are evaluated by comparison with each other against a number of factors, rather than on a whole job basis.

It was originally developed in the United States in the pre-war period by Benge and co-workers, with the objective of overcoming some of the difficulties associated with points factor schemes, particularly in the areas of the choice and weighting of factors.

Factor choice

Based on careful analysis of a wide range of jobs, and of existing points factor schemes, they concluded that at least 200 potential elements of job content could be discerned, each differing in detail from the others. Choosing a manageable number of such detailed elements is clearly difficult, so the factor comparison method was based on the idea of grouping (rather than choosing) these detailed elements into a relatively small number of more general and comprehensive factors. In the early examples, the factors used were:

*   Mental requirements.
*   Skill requirements.
*   Physical requirements.
*   Responsibility.
*   Working conditions.

Factor weighting

A fundamental difficulty with points factor schemes is the weighting of the factors. This is both a practical difficulty, and a conceptual one, in that the fixed-scale, fixed-weighting framework of points factor methods assumes a constant weighting between factors for all jobs. In factor comparison, explicit judgements were made job-by-job about the relative contribution which each factor made to the total job size, eliminating the need for blanket weighting, and allowing each job to be considered individually.

Basis of factor comparison methods

The detail of the factor comparison method is well documented in the literature, and since it is now little practised in its original form, we will not give a detailed description here. However, since it forms the basis for important later developments it is important to outline the principles involved.

The main steps in the process are:

- Selection and analysis of a sample of benchmarks or 'key jobs'.
- Taking each factor in turn, each member of an evaluation committee then ranked the key jobs under that factor. This produced separate rankings under each factor heading, so that for example the job ranked as having the highest mental requirement may be much lower down the ranking for, say, physical requirements. In its original form, individual evaluators undertook these rankings separately, and repeated the process a week or two later, and then all the results were summarised, and differences discussed and reconciled.
- The next critical step was for the evaluators to make a separate judgement on how each job's total weight was reflected in each of the chosen factors – i.e. how much is attributable to mental requirements, how much to physical requirements, etc. In its initial form, pay rates and relativities were used to provide a numerical scale for this, and the key jobs were selected so that their pay rates and relativities were considered appropriate and uncontentious. A subsequent development – Turner's Per Cent Method – enabled numerical scales to be developed without reference to existing pay rates.
- There then followed a process of reconciling the two sets of judgements – one of the rankings of jobs by factor, the second of the relative importance of each factor by job. This enabled the drawing up of numerical factor scales which reflected the relationships (both ways) which had been determined for the key jobs. An example of such a 'step rate scale' drawn from Benge's work is shown in Figure 6.4. From the basis of their derivation, these factor scales differed significantly from conventional points factor rating scales in a number of respects. They were not necessarily of the same length or spread – this was determined purely by the relationships established – and there was no fixed weighting between them. Also since the scales were for comparison of jobs rather than sizing against an absolute scale, the numbering patterns that emerged were typically based on geometric progressions (i.e. each number being a percentage increase over the previous one) rather than the simple arithmetic scales typically used in points factor rating – reflecting the reality that comparative judgements are related to the relative difference being judged, not its absolute size. Since

job evaluation is essentially an exercise in relativities, this was an important feature.

Other jobs were then evaluated by comparison with the key jobs against each factor, to yield a total job size.

Mental	Skill	Physical	Responsibility	WC
5	5	10	10	3
6	6	12	11	4
7	7	14	13	5
8	8	17	14	6
9	9	21	16	8
10	10	25	18	10
11	11	28	20	12
13	13		22	15
15	15		25	19
17	17		28	22
20	20		31	
23	23		35	
27	27		38	
31	31		43	
36	36		48	
41	41		54	
47	47		61	
53	53		68	
61	61		76	
70	70		85	
81	81		95	
93	93		106	
104	104		119	
			133	
			143	

Figure 6.4   Step-rate scale.

While the factor comparison method as originally conceived was very sound conceptually, it had the major problem of being very time consuming and complex to set up. On this basis, in today's environment it is not widely used. However it did form the basis for the job measurement methodology described below.

The Hay Guide Chart Profile Method

This is now the single most widely used method worldwide, and we include it in this section because it was a development from the factor comparison approach outlined above. Undoubtedly some of the reasons for its success and widespread use are that it combines the sound conceptual basis of factor comparison with the ease in use of points factor approaches.

The original factor comparison approach and its later derivatives – the Per Cent Method and the Profile Method – established the use of per cent based step rate scales, and the principle of examining the balance between factors in a job – the profile. Hay combined this approach with descriptive scales in the form of a Guide Chart for each factor, which made the process of evaluation significantly more straightforward.

In the early days of the method, specific Guide Charts were built from first principles for each application, but as a result of using the method in a wide range of organisations, patterns and relationships emerged which resulted in the more standardised form of today's Guide Charts.

As in the original factor comparison approach, the Hay method of today uses a small number of broadly based factors, applicable to all jobs (Know-How, Problem Solving and Accountability – plus, if appropriate, factors to cover physical requirements and environment).

To provide greater focus, each factor is examined in terms of two or three elements or facets, for which the Guide Charts provide descriptive scales, together with a numbering pattern for each factor, based on a geometric progression. The 15% step interval in this progression provides the basic building block for job–job comparison by factor, and the allocation of a numerical value to each judgement. As in the original factor comparison, judgements are also made about the balance between the three basic factors in each job (the profile). Thus the method maintains the concept of judging the 'shape' of the job, and recognises that the three factors will have different relative importance in different types of job – rather than relying on fixed factor weightings.

While it is thus essentially a development of factor comparison, it is as straightforward in use as simple points factor rating. Thus a job is considered against the scales and definitions of each Guide Chart which provides a numerical 'score' for each factor. Fine tuning of job–job comparison is aided by use of the 'step difference' concept, and the three individual factor points are added to give a total job size. A separate profile judgement is made (against well established criteria for different types of jobs), and compared with that which the three factor judgements have generated, and any differences examined: this gives an important check on the consistency of evaluation.

A more detailed summary of the Hay method is given in Appendix 1, together with summaries of other proprietary methods.

7 Job Evaluation Processes

Introduction: process design

The range of job evaluation methods available has remained relatively stable for some time – there are after all only a limited number of perspectives which can be taken on the basic factors or criteria which determine job size, and a reasonable consensus as to what these are, or at least the range from which they should be selected.

The area in which there has been the most substantial change in recent years is in the processes by which job evaluation is applied, and it seems likely that this change and development will continue throughout the nineties. As discussed earlier, it is in the process area that traditional job evaluation approaches have met with most criticism – whether for their inefficiency and bureaucracy, or for their restrictive influences on the way jobs are defined and viewed – and this has to a large degree spurred the development process.

The traditional job evaluation process is already well documented. Indeed it is almost too well documented, since it comes across as a fixed, prescriptive process from which little variation is possible. For example, in most texts on the subject there are implicit assumptions that the process will be managed by a steering committee; that a job description for each post is the only vehicle for presenting job information; that a job evaluation committee is the only way in which job evaluation judgements can be applied, etc.

While in a particular case these approaches may be the most appropriate, in other circumstances they will not. Thus the exercise may be managed by means other than a steering committee; questionnaires or generic role definitions may replace conventional job descriptions, and expert systems may replace, at least in part, the evaluation committee.

As a result of the process developments which have taken place along many different channels, it is no longer appropriate simply to consider 'installing' or buying in a predetermined process package. In the current environment, the process must be designed, step by step, to achieve what is required of it.

The general process design criteria were outlined in Chapter 4, i.e.

- The purpose of the exercise – what is wanted from it.
- The scale of the job population in question.
- The diversity of the range of jobs to be covered.
- The resources (time, money, people) available to do it.
- A range of considerations of culture, expectations, history, change, etc.

In this and subsequent chapters, we examine the job evaluation process step by step, to identify the range of options available for each, and the characteristics of each of them.

Establishing the objectives and overall shape of the process

Clarification of objectives

The first step in designing and implementing a job evaluation process is to clarify the objectives which are to be met, so that the broad shape and framework of the process can be established. While this may seem self-evident, in practice it is a step which is often glossed over, which can easily result in inappropriate process design.

In clarifying the objectives, it is important to recognise that job evaluation is just one component of pay management, which in turn is part of a broader set of human resource management processes whose direction is driven by business needs. Thus it is necessary to establish a hierarchy of objectives for the exercise as follows:

- *What features of the business, its current circumstances and future strategies need to be reflected and supported?*
  For example, if the business is attempting to decentralise and devolve operational power to individual business units, it would be counter-productive to design a highly centralised job evaluation process.

- *What are the main features and future directions of overall human resource policies and strategies to be reflected?*
  For example, if there were a strategy to move towards establishing single-status employment with common terms and conditions, it would indicate the need for a common job evaluation process, not one divided between different employee groups. Or, if the need were to develop more fluid organisations, and encourage job flexibility, it would be extremely unhelpful to initiate a job evaluation process which involved asking every employee to produce a job description focusing on detailed description of tasks and duties undertaken.
- *Within these human resource management strategies, what pay policies are sought?*
  For example, it is important to establish the relative balance which the organisations wishes to achieve between paying for job size, for performance achievement or, say, for skill acquisition, so that the job evaluation process can be designed to give the appropriate focus, and degree of emphasis.
- *What is the starting point?*
  Except in a start-up situation, pay is not a 'green field' issue. Before introduction/modification of job evaluation arrangements, people are already being paid. In order to design job evaluation processes which are practical and aid the transition from where you are now to where you want to be, it is critical to understand in some detail the starting point, i.e. how current pay/grading procedures work, the strengths which should be retained and the weaknesses which need to be overcome.
- *Finally, what specific requirements need to be satisfied by the evaluation exercise itself, in terms of costs, timescales and resource demands?*

Balancing costs and benefits
Introducing new or changed pay arrangements almost inevitably incurs costs in two areas:

- The cost of developing the new arrangements, in terms of internal resources, and if used, external consulting fees.
- The direct payroll cost of assimilating from one structure to another. Some of this cost is immediate – since normal assimilation arrangements involve no decreases in individual pay but may involve some increases (to individuals whose jobs are 'upgraded'). Further costs may be incurred over time if, for example, the new structure provides more pay potential in the form of longer pay scales.

An important issue in designing the most appropriate job evaluation process on which to build the new structure is to balance these costs against the benefits which are sought, ensuring that there is a net benefit to the organisation: if there is not, then why do it?

Thus, if the motivation for introducing new pay arrangements based on job evaluation is simply one of 'tidiness', then the benefits may be quite small, so the implementation costs for the process must be kept correspondingly small. If more significant benefits are the aim, greater costs can be tolerated.

In many cases, organisations face a range of possible options, each with different cost/benefit characteristics and balances. It is important to analyse these carefully, in order to select the one which gives the most appropriate balance.

A particularly important example of this is being faced by many organisations in the current environment. In the past, and notably in the 1970's when incomes policy meant that promotion was the only means of getting a pay rise above the voluntary norm, grade structures were frequently quite finely divided, so as to show small distinctions between jobs at different levels. This was consistent with the emphasis placed on job size, and lack of emphasis placed on performance in many traditional pay structures. Many organisations are now investigating the practicality of much coarser grade structures – often involving around half the previous number of grades – to reduce the focus on fine job distinctions and enable greater focus on performance, and individual development, so as to encourage greater flexibility. These are desirable aims in the current climate, but it must be recognised that they are aims with potentially significant costs attached. Assimilating to a coarser grade structure will almost certainly generate immediate costs, and the wider pay bands which each grade is likely to have will generate potential future cost, unless pay progression can be carefully managed and controlled.

These costs can only be justified in business terms, if they are offset by real, tangible benefits deriving from greater flexibility – for example greater productivity. Simply adopting broader grades because it is fashionable is likely to prove an expensive luxury. In such circumstances, an organisation may need to choose between high cost–high benefit solutions involving substantial changes to the way jobs are defined, organised and structured, low cost–low benefit combinations, or a range of possibilities in between.

While these may seem to be issues of pay structure, performance management or even manpower planning, beyond the scope of this book, it is in practice impossible to divorce them from job evaluation process design, if the most appropriate approach is to be determined.

Managing the process

Having determined the objectives to be achieved, and the general shape of the process needed to achieve these objectives, the next step is to determine how the process is to be managed, in particular the degree of participation or involvement by employees or their representatives in the management and conduct of the process.
This will depend upon two key factors.

The first of these is the existing pattern of employee relations practice in the organisation, and hence the expectations there will be about participation and involvement. A job evaluation process which is too far out of step with existing practices (in whatever direction) is liable to cause problems of cultural 'fit' and acceptability.

The second factor is the degree to which the job evaluation exercise forms part of a broader objective to change the existing employee relations pattern and practices which exist. As noted earlier, job evaluation should not be expected, on its own, to generate such changes, but can be used as an important supporter and facilitator of change within a wider set of employee relations initiatives. Thus, adopting a more participative approach to job evaluation can be an important component in building a more participative employee relations climate, if that is the broader requirement. Similarly, many organisations have found joint participation by different employee groups has given major benefits in promoting better collaboration between these groups. Conversely, if the requirement is to help reinforce managerial accountability then a more clearly management-led process may be indicated.

In this context, it is critically important to establish and clarify the difference between participative job evaluation and negotiation. Participative job evaluation (if used) involves the various parties involved reaching joint decisions relating to relative job size. Individual evaluators are selected from different groups but are not there to 'take sides' or negotiate results for the specific benefit of their particular interest groups. They are there as members of a team of evaluators, aiming to achieve a consensus view on job size relativities. Once these results have been arrived at, a process of more traditional negotiation may follow to determine the pay levels to be attached to different job sizes or grades, or on other features of the pay structure.

Such joint activity may be unfamiliar to some organisations, in which all debates on pay or grading follow the traditional adversarial style of negotiation. In such circumstances, it can be used to great effect to provide a basis on which genuinely participative processes can be built.

In order to reinforce the distinction between evaluation and negotiation, some organisations have different people on the evaluation committee and on the negotiating body, so that there is no confusion of role.

In determining how to manage the process, it is important to determine at the outset:

- What is to be negotiated.
- What is to be determined jointly and participatively.
- What is to be the subject of management decision and communication.

Examples of the range of options which may emerge from such considerations include:

- *Full participation of employee representatives in the management and conduct of the exercise.*
  If this approach is adopted, it is likely that a joint steering committee would be established to manage the process, and evaluation would be conducted jointly. Almost certainly, pay levels would be negotiated, following evaluation.
- *Management led process, but with joint participation in the evaluation stage.* Establishment of pay levels following evaluation may or may not be negotiated.
- *Fully management led and conducted.* In this case, it is unlikely that pay would be the subject of negotiation, but would also be determined by management.

There are many variations on these themes.

Communications

As part of the planning stages, the requirement for communicating with employees about the exercise needs to be established.

The nature, content and methods of communication adopted will depend to a large degree on the way the process is to be managed, as outlined in the previous section. However, in all cases, planning communications requires making decisions on what is to be communicated, to whom, by what means and when.

What is to be communicated

The categories of information which typically need to be communicated are:

- The nature of the exercise, its purpose and objectives.
- The methods and processes to be used.

- What is required of people to make the process work (e.g. writing job descriptions, completing questionnaires, meeting implementation deadlines).
- Progress on the project.
- The results, their effect on pay and the implications for individuals.

In any particular case, it is important to determine at the planning stage the openness there is to be about each of these categories of information, and the amount of detail which is to be communicated.

Except in cases where job evaluation is simply being used as a 'back-room' input to a purely management-driven pay setting exercise, most organisations, wisely, provide fairly full information about the methods and processes used, the objectives and about progress. A more sensitive issue is usually the question of disclosure of results, and the form this should take. At one extreme, full details of evaluation results may be given to individuals – including, if a factor based evaluation method has been used, detailed breakdown of the result by factor. At the other extreme, there may be no information given about the raw evaluation result, simply the out-turn in terms of pay and/or grade.

The arguments for and against these options, and the many possibilities which exist in between, are complex and often heated. Proponents of total openness argue that it builds greater trust in the whole exercise, and that there is no reason to keep anything hidden. Conversely, it can be argued that giving detailed evaluation results focuses unnecessary attention on what is essentially a means to the end. This argument has more force in circumstances where the evaluation result is used to allocate jobs to grades, or where the attempt is being made to re-focus the emphasis in pay arrangements away from detailed job size issues and towards performance. The decision is also heavily influenced by the existing practices of the organisation and the expectations of its employees. If openness is the norm, then apparent secrecy about job evaluation results can lead to suspicion and levels of trust in the organisation will drop.

Because of this, it is impossible to generalise about the degree of disclosure which is most appropriate. However, in reaching a decision on this, two points are worth bearing in mind:

- *In general, it is easier to increase openness over time, rather than decrease it.*
- *The amount of detail given to individuals about job evaluation results needs to be matched by their ability to understand it.*

There is no point disclosing detailed factor and point breakdowns, if people do not have sufficient knowledge of the evaluation method to understand their significance – indeed in some cases it can be positively damaging and cause unnecessary disruption. Hence if full disclosure of results is planned, this needs to be preceded by an appropriate programme, educating employees about the methods used and the significance of each element of the process. The more detailed the disclosure, the more substantial this programme needs to be. It is also a programme that will need to be repeated as new people join the organisation to ensure consistency of understanding.

To whom is communication required?

In most cases there is not a single 'audience' within an organisation to which communication can be addressed – there are usually several different audiences, each with its own expectations and requirements. The detailed content and methods used for communicating with each of these may need to be differently geared, while maintaining a clear consistency of message throughout. General information about the methods and processes used is likely to be fairly common across the different audiences; what will vary is the emphasis. Audiences which may need to be considered include:

Managers

The emphasis in communicating with managers about a job evaluation exercise is likely to be on the purpose and objectives of the exercise, and how it relates to broader human resource plans and business needs. Communication will need to clarify managers' own role in managing the process, and should provide them with enough information to answer questions and concerns about it, raised by those who report to them.

Employees themselves

Frequently, the major concerns of employees, when job evaluation is being undertaken, are about what it will mean for them – in terms of pay, grade and status. These are highly sensitive issues, and if not addressed carefully can lead to unnecessary fears or inappropriate expectations. Such concerns are often more about the way evaluation results are to be used, rather than just job evaluation itself, and the communication programme needs to address these carefully. A useful technique is to try to anticipate the questions which employees might raise, and try to answer them. Inability to do so usually indicates a gap in thinking through how the whole process is going to work, which should be addressed before the event.

Employee representatives, trades unions and staff association

While these bodies represent employees, and hence mirror the requirements and concerns noted above, they may need to be considered as a different audience. Their perspectives (whether as company based representatives, or as local or national officers) may be slightly different from those of the individual employee, since the canvas on which they are operating may be broader, and involve a somewhat different mix of considerations.

Specific employee groups

Within the organisation there may exist particular groups of employees with specific concerns and requirements to do with the job evaluation process. For example there may be professional groups (engineers, scientists, accountants, lawyers, IT professionals, etc.) with particular issues about the impact of job evaluation on career development. In the craft area there may be specific issues about multiskilling and how job evaluation is to deal with this; in the clerical/administration area there may be particular issues about the impact of information technology on jobs, and how this is to be considered, etc.

In planning the communications programme it is worthwhile considering whether any such groups exist, and whether more focused communication with them is required.

How communication is to be conducted

As a general principle, communication about job evaluation should build on and integrate with communication processes which already exist within the company. Thus, for example, if communication is normally handled through regular briefing groups, department meetings or whatever, then every attempt should be made to build on these, and supplement them where necessary.

A second general principle is that communication on job evaluation is usually most effective when it involves line managers in the process and is not purely driven from the personnel function. Clearly the lead in determining the content and methods used may well come from personnel specialists, but involvement of line managers in the delivery process can help tremendously in building ownership and presenting job evaluation as a 'real life' issue, not simply a technical exercise. In any event, managers will eventually become involved in the communication process at the stage when employees come to them with questions and concerns. If they feel outside the process, or simply do not have the necessary knowledge, then their response is unlikely to be constructive. Much better to build them in to the process from the start.

Of course, if this approach is taken, then it is critically important that a consistent message is provided: a situation where different interpretations are given in different places is untenable. A variety of methods can be used to ensure this consistency, including:

- Provision of a briefing 'kit' to managers.
- Preparation of booklets covering the main facts about the method and process, often supplemented by a list of typical questions and answers.
- Videos or slide presentations which enable the core content to be presented consistently, followed by discussion.

Other communication vehicles which exist may also be used in support. For example company newspapers can provide a useful medium for giving short progress reports during a long job evaluation exercise.

When to communicate

The main stages at which communication is required are at the start and finish of the exercise. At the start, the emphasis is on communicating the objectives of the programme, the methods to be used and what is required of people to make it happen. At the end, the focus is on the results and their implications. In an exercise of moderate size, these two phases of communication may be all that is necessary. In larger exercises, where many months may elapse between announcing the intentions and delivering the results, it may be appropriate to avoid long silences by periodic, short, progress reports – for example using the company newspaper, or specifically designed bulletins.

Appeals

At the planning stage, it is also worth establishing the approach which is to be taken to appeals – not least because this is also connected to the views taken on communications and involvement.

In this context it is essential to distinguish between appeals and re-evaluation of changed jobs. The latter is an aspect of maintenance and is covered in Chapter 10. In contrast, the appeals process (if there is to be one) allows jobholders the opportunity to appeal against the result of job evaluation, not because the job has changed but simply that they consider the result to be wrong or inappropriate.

The detail of appeals procedures will depend very much on the pattern of employee relations practices and procedures already in place in the organisation, and the degree of involvement in the job evaluation process itself. Thus, for example, in a purely management driven evaluation process, there may not be any appeals procedure at all.

If there is to be one, particular features which need to be considered include:

What is to be the subject of appeal?

For example, is the appeal to be against

- The raw evaluation result.
- The resulting grade (if used).
- The resulting pay.

This depends very much on what is decided in terms of disclosure of results. For example if only grade and pay are disclosed, then appeals against the raw evaluation result would not be feasible.

Grounds for appeal

The grounds for appeal need to be carefully spelled out, to avoid appeals which simply say 'I don't like the answer' without justifying why.

Some organisations allow appeals on the grounds that inadequate job information was provided in the first place. Others take a harder line and argue that it was the jobholder's responsibility to make sure the job information was adequate before signing it off. Most procedures allow (or indeed require) appeals to be made on a comparative basis – i.e. citing comparator jobs which the jobholder believes bear an inappropriate relativity to his/her own – with reasons.

Of course for this to be possible reasonable information on relevant comparator jobs needs to be available. This may be because results are generally published, or provided on request.

Who is to hear the appeal?

Typically this may be:

- The original evaluators.
- A sub-group of the original evaluators.
- Either of the above, supplemented by 'independent' members.

If the third option is selected, every care must be taken to ensure that the additional members are fully trained in the evaluation method.

Processes which rely entirely on 'independent' evaluators who were not part of the original process are generally to be avoided. Unless there is some link with the original process, it is impossible to revisit fully the reasons behind the original evaluations and test their validity, and there is a risk that independence simply becomes ignorance.

8　The Definition and Analysis of Jobs

Introduction: job analysis and job evaluation

In order to evaluate the relative size of jobs, it is first necessary to gather and analyse the relevant facts about each job, and to present these facts for evaluation in a way which is appropriate to the evaluation process used. For conventional committee based evaluation processes, the job information is likely to be presented in some kind of job description format; if a computer assisted evaluation process is to be used, then the vehicle for presenting job information will be a multiple choice questionnaire.

This process is usually referred to as job analysis, the approaches to which are covered in this chapter.

At the outset, it is important to separate the processes of job analysis and job evaluation, both conceptually and practically.

Job analysis is – or should be – an analytical process involving gathering facts, analysing and sorting these facts, and re-assembling them into whatever consistent format has been chosen. Whereas job evaluation involves making judgements about the relative size of jobs, the emphasis in job analysis is factual rather than judgemental. Some critics argue that this cannot be achieved, and that the process of job analysis inevitably involves judgement in determining which facts to present, and how they are presented. Similarly, there are often fears that people who are 'good with words' may present job information in a more favourable light, thereby influencing the final evaluation result. There may be an element of truth in these concerns if job analysis is conducted in an undisciplined way, but the process can be designed and conducted in such a manner as to minimise these potential problems, and yield job information which is genuinely factual and objective.

The process to help the quality of the job analysis process and ensure objectivity and factual content includes the following commonly used features:

- *Approval of the job description or questionnaire by both jobholder and supervisor* – whichever one has provided the information.
- *Use of a standardised format for the job description, or a common questionnaire*, to make sure that the same kind of information is elicited for each job, and that it is presented in a consistent form.
- *Involvement of job analysts, trained in the techniques involved.* In the past, it was common practice for job analysts actually to prepare job descriptions for approval, based on interviewing the jobholder or boss. While this gives high quality results, fewer and fewer organisations are able to provide the resources necessary for this approach. Much more common is the provision of job information directly by the jobholder or boss. In these circumstances, trained job analysts can still be used to great effect, by acting as helpers and advisers to jobholders/bosses, and providing a quality assurance review of the information provided. This is a much more efficient approach, and can be used to great effect with both job description and questionnaire forms of analysis.
- *In a conventional evaluation process, the evaluators themselves can make a major contribution to ensuring the quality and consistency of data provided.* A well-conducted evaluation process considers jobs in their organisational context, and examines job relativities directly. Evaluators are therefore in a good position to identify cases where job information is contradictory, where it is ambiguous, or simply unclear. Evaluators should always be encouraged to refer back for clarification any job for which the data provided gives an inadequate basis for evaluation. In computer assisted processes this facility is not available, so additional care needs to be taken with the quality assurance of the questionnaires themselves, and review of the results which emerge.
- *If job analysts are used, it is common practice for these to be different people from the evaluators.* This can help separate the factual from the judgemental and avoid any compromise or confusion between the two processes.

In practice, given the kind of steps outlined above, and reasonable attention to the process, job analysis can be objective and factually based, and in our experience, the worries often expressed about 'persuasive' job descriptions influencing results are largely overstated.

However, the quality of job analysis in many organisations is not of the required standard to ensure high quality job evaluation. It is the first part of the process to 'slip', with job information being presented in a variety of forms, descriptions gradually increasing in length but decreasing in quality, or simply not being updated and maintained. To some degree this is not helped by the time required for conventional job description preparation, and the understandable reluctance of jobholders and supervisors to devote this time. One of the particular advantages of computer assisted processes is that multiple choice questionnaires are much quicker to complete. In this context, the claim is sometimes made that such questionnaires are inherently more accurate or objective than conventional job descriptions, since they ask for the same information from all jobholders in precisely the same way. In our experience of both approaches, this claim is overstated.

However carefully framed are the questions, there will always be a degree of judgement on the part of the jobholder/boss in answering them, just as there is in the presentation of information in narrative form. The real value of questionnaires is in their efficiency, not their 'accuracy'. Indeed in practice, quality assurance of questionnaire responses is a critical requirement for effective computer assisted processes.

Job definition or job description?

When embarking on a job evaluation exercise, there is great temptation to rush straight into the job analysis phase, send job description forms or questionnaires out to everyone, wait for the responses – and hope for the best. This will almost certainly not produce a satisfactory outcome, and leave many problems of job definition for the evaluators to sort out. Inadequate attention to setting up the job analysis phase is liable to add very considerably to the workload placed on the evaluators, and will probably leave many situations unresolved.

The first consideration is whether jobs are simply to be described, exactly as they exist now, or whether they are to be defined in a way more appropriate to the current and future needs of the business. Most standard works on job evaluation stress that jobs should be described 'as they exist now', and until recently this has been the accepted wisdom in the job evaluation field, compatible with the typical use of job evaluation to hold a mirror up to the organisation as it currently exists.

In many circumstances, this is still the requirement, and jobs are described in terms of their current content and construction.

However, in a growing proportion of cases, the rate of organisation change is such that examining jobs as they stand is more a reflection of history than of how jobs need to be constructed to meet the needs of the business. Hence evaluating their current content does nothing to support the organisational change, and may even inhibit it.

To illustrate, a manufacturing unit may currently contain the following jobs: hopper and mixing operator; raw materials assembler; packaging service operator; fork lift truck driver; extruder operator; slitting machine operator; raw material tester; machine cleaner; shrink wrap packaging operator; warehouse operator, finished goods; raw material stores attendant; label printer; blow moulding machine operator; waste disposal operator.

To date, these jobs have probably been defined separately, each with its own list of tasks and duties. If there is an existing job evaluation scheme in place, they will have been evaluated individually, and graded accordingly.

It is likely, in the current environment, that the business in which these jobs exist is seeking greater job flexibility in order to increase productivity from the unit. Such flexibility means that the members of the production unit operate as a team, not simply sticking to their own closely defined job. Introducing a new job evaluation scheme in which the jobs continue to be defined in their current, separate form will do nothing to support this change, and is more than likely to inhibit it. This is a good example of a case where 'job evaluation' per se may well be blamed for inhibiting flexibility, whereas in reality it is the way jobs are defined which can inhibit – or support – the changes required.

So in this example, how should the jobs be defined – and indeed how many 'jobs' are there? Total flexibility of operation would require just one job to be defined – in terms of the full range of operations in the unit, and the skills necessary to carry them out. In many cases, this degree of flexibility is impracticable. Individuals in the team may not be prepared – or in some cases able – to acquire all the skills needed to operate across the full range of activities. Or, from a business perspective, the additional productivity gains from total flexibility may not justify the costs involved in achieving it.

Hence in practice, the appropriate and realistic level of flexibility needs to be determined, and the 'jobs' which this implies defined accordingly. This requires study of the nature of the operations, the workflow, plant layouts, etc., and so there is no standard answer as to the outcome. However the following examples illustrate the kind of results which such study might indicate.

One possible outcome might be to define say three *levels* of job (or two, or four...) differentiated by the range of tasks expected to be undertaken at each level, and/or the skills necessary to cope with these. Where there is the need to encourage flexibility by enabling people to acquire the necessary range of skills, the levels may be defined predominantly in skill terms, and individuals placed in a level according to the skills they have acquired. The onus then of course is on managers to ensure that the skills which have been acquired (and paid for) are used appropriately.

In different circumstances it may not be necessary or feasible to seek flexibility right across the unit, but instead to increase flexibility within defined areas of the operation – for example in the raw materials area, the machine area and the packaging area. In this case it would be better to define jobs of 'raw materials operator', 'machine operator' and 'packaging operator', with the necessary range of tasks and skills defined for each. Again, two or more levels of job may be defined in each area to allow for different ranges of tasks and skills.

The above example illustrates the point that in a changing organisational environment, simply describing 'what is' may not be the best approach to analysing jobs, and that job analysis is not simply a descriptive exercise, but one which requires careful examination of the nature of work, of jobs and of changes in these. Simply writing 12 job descriptions for the jobs listed in this example would not address the needs of the operation – and its people – and would probably be counterproductive. Hence an important decision at a very early stage is whether jobs are to be described 'as is', or defined in terms of developing requirements. Of course, if the latter course of action is adopted, great care must be taken to ensure that what is defined is practical, realistic and actually in the process of happening.

Defining theoretical jobs, or ones based on a 'blue sky' vision of how we would like the organisation to operate – but which we have little chance of achieving – is clearly inappropriate. As examples of this, we have seen many cases where jobs have been defined (and ultimately paid for) in terms of total flexibility, when in practice only a small percentage of individuals have, or are prepared to acquire, the skills needed to operate that way, and in any case the business only needs a proportion to achieve that level. The result is that the business pays for skills which it is not getting – and doesn't need – and from the employee's perspective there is no differential reward for having taken the trouble to develop skills over and above colleagues who have not bothered.

What is meant by a 'job'?

Jobs or roles

In order that jobs can be satisfactorily described or defined, it is important to reach a view on what is meant by 'a job' in the context of the organisation concerned. This may seem like a pointless question, one so obvious it is not worth raising. Indeed, in the past it probably has not been raised very often in the process of setting up job evaluation. After all, we all know what a job is, don't we? Or do we?

Many of the issues surrounding this question have already been explored in Chapter 3. To summarise, in the past, jobs have been considered very much as units of organisation structure, definable in terms of their specific accountabilities, tasks, duties and position in the structure. While this is still valid for many jobs in many organisations, there are a growing number of cases where it is not. The demand for greater organisational flexibility and the wish to make best use of the abilities of people, without constraining them in rigidly defined jobs, have produced the need, in many areas, to define jobs differently, and more in terms of flexible roles.

A vital consideration in planning the job analysis stage is to determine the way in which jobs are to be viewed, so that they can be described in a compatible and supportive way. This may of course be different for jobs in different parts of the same organisation. For example in a manufacturing and selling company, jobs like those of plant manager, sales representative, chief accountant, personnel manager, etc. may be largely definable in classical 'job' terms, since the organisation's requirements from each are clear and well specified. On the other hand, jobs of production operators, project engineers, R&D scientists and technicians, in the same company may be more appropriately defined in 'role' terms, to reflect the inherent flexibility which is required, and the close relationship between the level of work actually undertaken and the skills and competencies of the jobholder to do it. The distinction of course is not a sharp one: in many of today's organisations, the requirement for people to engage in team activities and projects may affect the way we describe even the most structurally definable jobs.

Individual or generic jobs

Closely related is the question of whether jobs are to be defined individually or generically. At the extremes, the answer is probably clear : there is for example only one national sales manager, so an individual description is appropriate. Conversely there may be five shift supervisors on rotating shifts, doing exactly the same job on the same plant, just on different shifts – a clear indication for a single description for all five. But there are many situations where it is less clear, and requires investigation.

For example, the company may employ a hundred secretaries. Does this mean there are a hundred separate jobs, or a much smaller number of generic secretarial jobs? If the latter, how many different generics need defining, and what is the basis on which they are differentiated? Techniques for analysing generic jobs and job ladders are considered later in this chapter.

Source of information

A further question which needs to be settled early in the job analysis stage is who is going to provide the job information. The issue here is not so much who is actually going to write it down, but who is going to provide the basic source of information about the job.

The choice is essentially between the jobholder providing the information or his/her manager.

Traditionally, it has been most common for the jobholder to be the primary source of information, either completing a job description or questionnaire directly, or with the help of a job analyst, for agreement with/approval by the boss. This approach has a number of important benefits, including:

- The person closest to the job, and hence in the best position to know how it really works, is the jobholder.
- Obtaining the information from the jobholder means he/she is directly involved in the process, and can identify with, and have ownership of, the information which is provided to the evaluators.
- There is less chance of jobholders appealing against an evaluation result on the basis that 'you didn't describe my job properly'.

However, this approach is only really suitable when the emphasis is on describing (and subsequently evaluating) jobs as they currently stand. If, as discussed in the previous section, the emphasis is more on job definition, particularly in a changing organisational context, then it is more appropriate for the primary source of information to be the manager. Of course in both cases it is normally important that both manager and jobholder agree the description/questionnaire content before it goes forward for evaluation.

Over the last few years, there has been a general trend towards using managers as the source of job information, rather than jobholders. This has been driven partly by the rate of organisational change as discussed above, but also by a change in emphasis in some organisations towards placing the responsibility on managers to specify the jobs for which they are accountable. One major manufacturing company for example recently moved away from jobholder-written job descriptions to manager-written ones, as part of a broader initiative to reinforce managerial accountability. As in most such cases, this change was not made in isolation, but as one of a number of changes all supporting the same objective – for example adopting a much shorter description format, emphasising major accountability areas rather than detailed tasks, and changing the evaluation method to one with greater emphasis on accountability and output factors.

If job definition is to be carried out by managers rather than jobholders, an important consideration is the level of management at which it is to be done. This will depend upon the nature of the organisation, the level of the job, and how heavily layered the structure is. In general, in selecting the managers responsible for providing the job information, a balance needs to be struck between their being close enough to the job to know it in detail, and being at a level where they are seen to be genuinely responsible for the jobs reporting to them, not simply providing day to day guidance and work scheduling for example. The same is true, of course, in defining the level of manager who should approve job information when this is provided by jobholders.

The purpose and uses of job analysis

Our primary focus in this book is the use of job analysis in relation to job evaluation. However it is necessary to recognise that job analysis is fundamental to a wide range of human resource management processes, and that some kind of job description, or specification is necessary as an input to:

- Organisational analysis.
- Recruitment.
- Succession planning and career development.
- Performance management.
- Recruitment.
- Competency and skill analysis.

While these may present somewhat different requirements in detail and emphasis, all require the same common understanding of jobs and their content.

A problem in many organisations is that these processes have, in the past, been seen as separate issues, and often dealt with by different specialists within the company. The result may be that there are several different job descriptions in existence for each job, each geared to a different purpose. All too often, the job description produced for job evaluation is written purely for that purpose, and filed away and forgotten as soon as the evaluation is complete. This situation is not only inefficient in terms of the effort required to produce several different descriptions, but also confusing to all concerned. It also misses the opportunity for job analysis to provide a real input to how work is conducted and managed, and not just be a sterile paper exercise just geared to getting an evaluation result.

Hence, in determining the process and form of job analysis, every effort should be made to bring together these requirements into a single – or at least an integrated – approach. The role blueprint concept outlined in Chapter 3 is an illustration of how a comprehensive view of jobs can be adopted, bringing together a wide range of uses and requirements.

Presentation of job information

Job information can be presented for evaluation in a wide range of forms. The major options available are described in the following sections.

Conventional job descriptions

The traditional vehicle for presenting job information is the job description. In practice, these come in a variety of shapes, sizes and forms, but whatever detailed format is adopted, the following general principles should be applied.

Analysis not lists

The format should encourage an analytical approach in which the key facts about the job can be expressed clearly, and not lost in a mass of detail. Simply listing tasks and duties is not a helpful approach to job analysis.

Consistent format

Whatever format is adopted, it should be applied consistently to all jobs in a given population. This helps ensure that the same type of facts are presented for each job, and helps evaluators use the descriptions efficiently, since they will know where to look for particular pieces of information, rather than searching through various different formats.

Sometimes, different detailed formats will be adopted for different job populations within an organisation (e.g. different formats may be used for management jobs, for clerical and for manual) if it is necessary to gear the format closely to the particular job group's needs. However, there should still be a broad consistency in the formats used if the same evaluation method is to be applied across the different job groups.

While it is relatively easy to control the use of a consistent format when job evaluation is initially being introduced, the discipline often lapses over time. After a few years, one frequently finds job descriptions being presented in all sorts of forms – from scrappy notes through to erudite essays on the critical importance of the marketing function (but failing to say what this particular marketing job actually does)! Without being too bureaucratic about it, it is well worth controlling job description format over time, to ensure continued quality and consistency.

Concise format

Jobholders often worry that if the job description is too short, then vital facts will be left out and the job will be undervalued. Evaluators often worry that if the job description is too long, the vital facts will be buried in detail and the wood will not emerge through the trees.

To be effective, job descriptions should be concise, concentrating on the essential facts and not concealing them in detail and padding. If the evaluators themselves are knowledgeable about the organisation, there is no reason for descriptions to exceed a few pages in length, and in many cases a one or two-page description is perfectly satisfactory. Examples are discussed later.

Facts not judgements

The description should present the facts about the job, not judgements about it. The difficulty of drawing this distinction has already been pointed out, but every effort should be made to do so. For example:

> 'This job requires a very high degree of skills in dealing with people' is a judgemental statement – inviting responses like 'who says so?' or 'in comparison with what?' or 'what do you mean by very high?'.

Much better to give the facts about the job, e.g.:

> 'The job involves supervising 65 people on a high speed packing line'.

or

> 'Successful project completion requires bringing together the work of several subcontractors plus the internal electrical and mechanical departments'.

or

> 'The jobholder sells products into a market where

there is major overcapacity and where margins are
continually under pressure'.

All of which may lead the evaluators to judge that there is a
requirement for a high level of interpersonal skills.

The format of job description adopted can help or hinder in this
respect. Generally, formats which directly mirror the evaluation
factors tend to encourage judgemental statements. For example if
an evaluation factor is human relations skills, then a job description
section with the same title may encourage the kind of judgemental
observation given in the above example. In practice, an evaluation
judgement on this factor takes into account a range of pieces of
information about different aspects of the job, which the evaluators
must weigh in reaching a view about the job in the round, and these
pieces of factual information will be gained from several different
parts of the job description.

Keep it simple

There is often a misconception that for a job description to be
effective and well received by evaluators, it has to be couched
in flowery language and presented in 'literary' style. Jobholders
often worry that if they (or their bosses) are not 'good with words'
the jobs will be undervalued. This is sometimes keenly felt in
departments whose stock in trade is not words, but deeds and
where the process of preparing documents like job descriptions is
not a familiar one.

Long experience working with evaluators in all kinds of environments demonstrates that these fears are largely groundless. Evaluators are not marking literary style or even grammar: they just want
the basic facts about a job, simply and straightforwardly stated.
Indeed they are more likely to react against long flowery essays, full
of jargon and buzz words than they are to be impressed by them.

Why write 'maintain the ongoing operations of the department
and its constituent parts within the parameters indicated by the
periodic, rolling budgetary planning cycle and associated documentation', when you could simply say 'stay within budget costs'.
Many people feel they cannot use nice simple words like buy, sell,
make, do, find out, help, etc., and feel obliged to lapse into a style
of English they would never use if you stopped them in the street
and said 'Tell me about your job'. Most evaluators in our experience
would prefer simplicity to 'style'.

Examples of conventional job description formats

The detailed format adopted needs to reflect the particular requirements of the organisation, the job to be covered and the job evaluation process and method which are to be employed. Hence the range of formats in practical use is enormous. In the following sections we illustrate this range with examples of formats which have been widely and successfully used – recognising that there are many detailed variations on the themes illustrated.

A widely used approach which meets the general criteria outlined above, and which helps achieve an analytical approach is to divide the description into five main sections, as follows:

- Purpose.
- Principal accountabilities.
- Dimensions.
- Organisation.
- Nature and scope (this section may be in narrative form, or further structured as described below).

Purpose

This should provide a short statement of WHY the job exists. The purpose statement should be confined to a single sentence except perhaps in the small number of cases where a job genuinely has a dual role. If this discipline is not observed, there is a tendency to get into the detail of how the job operates, thus obscuring the simple question of 'WHY'?

Writing a useful purpose statement is perhaps the most difficult and analytical part of the whole process. Often jobholders (and their managers) do not think in these terms, since they are more concerned, day to day, with the many tasks, duties and activities involved, and may seldom stop to think, 'Why?'. In writing the purpose, it is often helpful to consider questions like:

- What part of the organisation's/unit's total purpose is accomplished by this job?
- What is the unique contribution of this job that distinguishes it from those around it?
- What would not get done if this job did not exist?

Although difficult, this analytical process is useful, since it helps with focus and clarity, and if there are any ambiguities, or misunderstandings, forces these to be addressed before evaluation, and not simply glossed over.

Examples of typical purpose statements are given in Figure 8.1.

For a production shift supervisor:

> To supervise a shift production team in the granulating plant so as to achieve output targets within set safety and quality standards.

For a personnel director:

> To develop and implement personnel policies and practices which will support the achievement of the company's business aims.

Figure 8.1   Examples of typical purpose statements.

Principal accountabilities

These are statements of the continuing end results or outputs required of the job. They answer the question 'What are the main areas in which this job must get results in order to achieve its purpose'? The main characteristics of principal accountabilities are:

- Taken together, they represent all the major outputs expected of the job.
- They focus on results and outputs, not detailed tasks and duties – they focus on WHAT is required, not HOW.
- Each one is distinct from the rest, and describes a specific area in which results are to be achieved.
- They suggest (but do not state explicitly), measures or tests which could determine whether or not they are being met.
- They relate specifically to the job in question, not to the broader organisational unit.

For most jobs, between four and eight principal accountabilities are sufficient to cover the major areas of results involved. Less than this probably means something is missing: more may mean that individual tasks are being listed.

The distinction between a task and an accountability is crucial in this form of job description. For most jobs, even those which are very simple and highly structured, the number of individual tasks which could be written down is vast, and the result would not be a job description but an instruction manual. Tasks and duties essentially describe HOW the job is done, whereas the emphasis in accountabilities is WHAT is to be achieved. Thus, any one accountability statement may be made up of large numbers of specific tasks and activities.

For example, a principal accountability for a materials manager might state:

- Control the purchasing of raw materials and packaging to ensure that production requirements for quantity, quality, cost and timing are met.

If we were to try to write down all the activities that contribute to this – the meetings, negotiations, letters, reports, forecasts, etc. – it could fill many pages, but would not really add much to our understanding of what was required of the job. Indeed it would probably cloud the issue in a welter of detail.

Using principal accountabilities instead of task lists clearly helps achieve a more concise and focused approach. But it also has the advantage that while tasks and activities may change rapidly as methods evolve, the basic areas of accountability are likely to be much more stable – only changing as the basic nature of the job changes. The need to re-describe the job is thus much less frequent.

Similarly, properly written accountability statements enable a high degree of flexibility to be written into a job, in a way which task lists preclude. This is vitally important in the current organisational environment, with increasing requirements for job flexibility. Many of the criticisms of conventional job description, in terms of inhibiting organisational change and flexibility, can be overcome by proper use of principal accountabilities, rather than task description. A further advantage, valued by many users of this approach, is that it focuses on output rather than input. Tasks are essentially inputs – means to the end, not ends in themselves – whereas accountabilities clearly state the output requirement.

Typically, accountability statements are written in the form 'Do something, in order to achieve a stated result/or to a stated standard'. Using this form emphasises the action requirement and the purpose of the action, and makes it harder to 'fudge' the real accountability with woolly or ambiguous descriptions.

The approach may not always be called 'principal accountabilities'. In some cases, alternative headings are used – for example key results areas, major activities and results, etc.

An example of a typical set of principal accountabilities is given in Figure 8.2.

Principal Accountabilities

1.   Formulate and get agreement to Company marketing plans which meet Company objectives of growth, market share and profitability.

2.   Develop and recommend pricing policies and discount structures which enable the achievement of company profit targets.

3.   Ensure that marketing plans and objectives are met within agreed levels of expenditure and take corrective action as necessary.

4.   Monitor continuously market trends, technological developments and competitor activities in order to contribute to business decision-making.

5.   Ensure that all promotion, publicity and advertising activity is in support of Company objectives and within agreed expenditure levels and promotes an image which befits the Company.

6.   Organise the timely provision of market data and plans to the Sales Function personnel to assist them to set and meet their sales targets within the marketing framework.

7.   Develop and maintain a marketing department structure which is staffed with people who know what is expected of them and are capable of meeting departmental and individual objectives.

Figure 8.2   An example of the principal accountabilities of a marketing manager.

Dimensions

(Sometimes called 'Statistics', or other headings). It is usually convenient to collect together relevant numerical data in one place in the description. The nature of this data will depend on the job in question, but might include:

- Financial statistics (costs, budgets, incomes, turnovers, etc.).
- People statistics (numbers supervised or influenced).
- Other numerical data, e.g. number of customers, locations, invoices processed, tonnes of product manufactured, etc.

It is usually best if the data in such a section is presented just as data, without explanation of how the job affects it: that will come clear elsewhere in the description.

To avoid long lists, only *relevant* data should be included. On the other hand, the data should not just focus on things *controlled* directly by the job, but include relevant items that the jobholder may influence or be involved with. For example, for a factory accountant, the dimensions should probably include total factory costs: it is relevant to the job to know these, even though the job does not directly control them.

Examples of typical dimensions are shown in Figure 8.3.

- For a Plant Manager:

    - Sales value of production: £30m (92 budget)
    - Staff managed: 3 shift supervisors
                                                               140 shift operators
    - Production expenses (including labour costs):   £2.6m
    - Raw material costs: £15m

- For a claims office manager in an insurance company:

    - Number of staff: 24
    - Number of claims: 11,000 p.a.
    - Number of investigations: 3500 p.a.
    - Average value of claims: £600

- For a technician in an analytical laboratory:

    - Number of analytical procedures used: 20
    - Number of samples processed: average 50 per week

Figure 8.3   Example of dimensions.

Organisation

In order to understand how the job fits organisationally with those around, it is helpful to have a section for an organisation chart, which should show at least the job, the boss, any other jobs reporting to the same boss, and any subordinates which the job may have.

While it is normal to stick to direct reporting lines, in more complex matrix structures it may be appropriate to include important functional/project or other relationships with a short explanation.

An example of a typical organisation chart is shown in Figure 8.4.

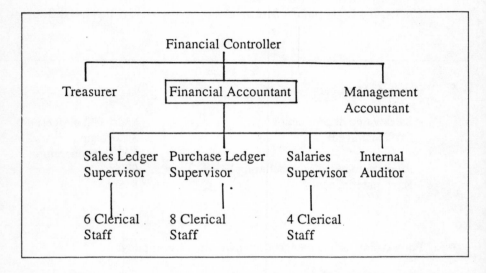

Figure 8.4   Example of an organisation chart from the job description for a financial accountant

Nature and scope

While the above four items provide the core information about the job, it is often necessary to provide some more detail about the context in which it operates, particularly important features, some outline of how it is accomplished, etc. In other words, some 'flavour' on the bare bones provided in the first four sections.

In the most traditional forms of job description this was often done in an unstructured narrative section variously headed Nature and Scope, Background Information, Job Context, etc.

The advantage of the narrative approach was that it gave the writer the necessary flexibility and elbow room to pick out and elaborate on relevant aspects of the job. Thus, for a production job the section might focus on outlining the processes used and the products made; for a personnel job, on the industrial relations climate; for a sales job on the nature of the market and competitors; and so on. Certainly a well-written Nature and Scope section in narrative form can provide excellent insights into the job, its content and context.

However, its major disadvantage is that it requires good analytical skills to prepare, if it is not to be over-long, rambling or missing vital aspects. It is thus very much reliant on trained job analysts to do the actual drafting, based upon interviewing either jobholder or boss. This was common practice in the 70's, but, as noted earlier, its use has decreased since then, because the process is heavy on time and resources.

It is much more common in today's environment to ask the jobholder or boss to prepare the description, with any involvement from job analysts being limited to input of advice, and perhaps overall quality assurance. Narrative form job descriptions prepared by the jobholder/boss are extremely variable in quality, and for this reason have progressively been replaced by more structured formats.

In these formats, which vary considerably from company to company, and may need to be tailored for specific job groupings, it is common to keep the basic sections of Purpose, Principal Accountabilities, Dimensions and Organisation, but to replace the narrative Nature and Scope with a series of sections drawn from a list which might include:

- Job context.
- Decision-making authority.
- Assignment, review and approval of work.
- Supervision of others.
- Knowledge, skills and experience.
- Contact with others – internal, external.
- Major problems.
- Physical conditions.
- Plant, equipment and tools used.

Such structured description formats are often accompanied by brief guidance notes, explaining the kind of information required in each section, plus – sometimes – short briefing sessions. Given such assistance, descriptions of satisfactory quality can be produced by jobholders/bosses without particular skills or experience in job analysis.

'Short form' descriptions

Where evaluation is to be conducted by people with a good understanding of the jobs concerned, of the organisation and its operation, some organisations are now using a much shorter job description format, comprising basically the four main sections of Purpose, Principal Accountabilities, Dimensions and Organisation. Sometimes this may be supplemented by a very short (one paragraph) section in which specific features may be highlighted. Given knowledgeable evaluators, this can provide a very focused and efficient approach, and one which sharply emphasises accountability and results.

Examples of narrative form, structured form and short form job descriptions are included in Appendix 2.

Generics, ladders and families

Generic jobs

In many traditional approaches to job analysis and evaluation, there was an implicit focus on the individuality of jobs. Unless a job was clearly the same across a number of jobholders (e.g. a team of five shift supervisors, or a group of territory sales representatives), the tendency was to treat each 'post' as an individual job, and to look for differences, rather than similarities.

In recent years, the trend has been to question the validity and usefulness of this approach, and as a result the use of generic job descriptions has grown. A generic job description is one covering a group of jobs which are essentially similar, though some fine detail may vary.

The main reasons for this trend have been:

Process efficiency

In many traditional processes, vast amounts of time (and trees) were spent in producing, and evaluating, piles of individual job descriptions for engineers, secretaries, technicians, etc., only to find that the real differences between the jobs was very small and not significant from an evaluation point of view. With the increasing pressure to reduce the time and resources spent on job evaluation, many organisations have begun to use generic job descriptions in appropriate cases.

Job flexibility

Quite apart from the drive for process efficiency, the increasing requirement for building flexibility into job definition has encouraged the growth of generic approaches. If, for example, a group of technicians are carrying out broadly the same kind of work, but on different projects, defining the role generically gives greater flexibility as people move from project to project, without having to go through the unnecessary task of re-writing and re-evaluating the job each time – only to get much the same answer.

While generic descriptions can make a useful contribution to improving efficiency and gaining flexibility, their use needs to be handled very carefully. Implicit in the use of a generic description is the assumption that the specific 'posts' covered are broadly the same. This assumption needs careful testing to make sure that genuine and significant differences are not simply steamrollered into a common generic statement. Similarly it needs to be recognised that in most organisations some jobs are individually constructed and need to be treated as such: only a proportion are likely to be amenable to generic treatment.

For specific generic descriptions which do not form part of a 'ladder' or 'family', conventional job description formats can usually be used, with minimal amendments required.

Ladders and families

It frequently becomes apparent when analysing a job group to arrive at a generic statement that while the nature of work carried out may be basically the same, there are significant differences in the level of work undertaken. For example, in the case of technician jobs noted above, analysis may well indicate that some jobs are typically required to undertake more difficult, more important or bigger projects, or carry out more sophisticated tests and experiments than others, and this would demand higher levels of skill, experience and technical knowledge from the jobholder.

In a group of secretarial jobs, all may cover the same range of activities, but the emphasis in some may be on providing a straightforward, efficient typing and filing service, while others are expected to be much more involved in organising meetings, carrying out administrative duties, answering correspondence without reference, and so on. In such cases, a single generic approach to the group would be over-simplistic, and fail to recognise differences which are real and apparent – not least to the jobholders themselves.

The solution is often to define a series of levels to form a ladder or family of generic roles. This approach has been used extensively over the years in technical and professional areas, but is increasingly being used across a range of functions as the requirement for flexibility demands that jobs are more generically defined, while still recognising the need to distinguish between levels of work.

The levels or rungs in the ladder are often described using a fairly conventional job description format. The disadvantage of this approach is that major aspects of the jobs at the different levels are the same or very similar. Thus for example, the purpose and principal accountabilities for the different levels may be virtually the same, while the remaining job description sections may not give the necessary focus for distinguishing the levels clearly. What can result is a set of descriptions for each level, requiring much searching to 'spot the difference'. This is not very helpful, either for

	Technical accountability/leadership	Assignment Leadership	Setting Objectives	etc.
Level 1	Accountable for applying established techniques within a defined area or specialisation.	Carries out defined experiments and procedures as part of a research investigation.	Determines day to day procedures within overall experimental design.	etc.
Level 2	Accountable for providing specialist expertise in a defined discipline.	Undertakes well defined research investigations in a specialist area, or particular parts of a multi-disciplinary investigation.	Determines experimental programme to meet defined objectives.	etc.
Level 3	Accountable for developing the company's body of knowledge within a defined discipline.	Leads significant research investigations in the area of specialisation.	Plans and programmes research investigations including inputs from other areas of specialisation.	etc.
etc.	etc.	etc.	etc.	

Figure 8.5   Extract from Scientist ladder, expressed in terms of levels and differentiating factors.

job evaluation or if the ladder descriptions are to provide a useful input to career development processes.

A better approach is to focus directly on the factors which differentiate between the levels, and express each level in terms of these factors. The example shown in Figure 8.5 is in this format, which may of course be supplemented by a common set of Purpose and Principal Accountability statements.

This format can be used for job evaluation purposes, and for linking directly to career development issues. The approach is particularly helpful in supporting a move to increase job flexibility and get away from highly specific individual job definitions. The job population is first divided into families, and each family analysed into a series of levels as described. Within a family, the differentiating features are expressed in terms relevant to the family and in the language of the family. Job evaluation is then used to evaluate the levels, so as to provide the cross-family relativities which are needed to build the framework for company-wide pay structures.

Role blueprints

This concept was introduced in Chapter 3. In practice, it is really an extension of the family and level approach described in the previous section.

The differentiating factors which emerge from the process described above fall typically into two categories:

- Those relating to the kind and level of output required from the role.
- Those to do with the technical knowledge, skills and experience required to deliver this level of output.

These clearly correspond to the 'output' and 'skill' areas in the role blueprint concept.

It is therefore simply a matter of extending the range of factors to include the behavioural competencies, in order to complete the picture of the role. While these competency factors may not affect the size of the role, they help to characterise it fully, and enable the role blueprint to provide a comprehensive starting point for selection, career development and performance management, as well as pay structure.

Job family questionnaires for computer assisted evaluation

This is also a refinement of the family and level approach to defining and describing jobs.

A limitation of the approach in 'generics, ladders and families' is that it assumes the family is homogeneous, and that jobs or roles

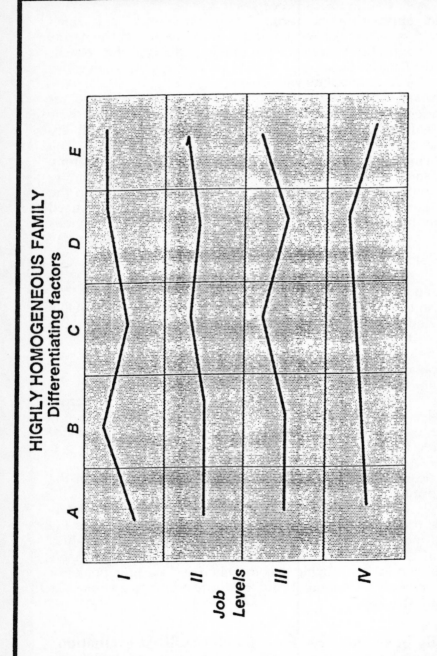

Differentiating factors and levels for a highly homogeneous family.
Typical level definitions can be read across.

Figure 8.6   Highly homogeneous family.

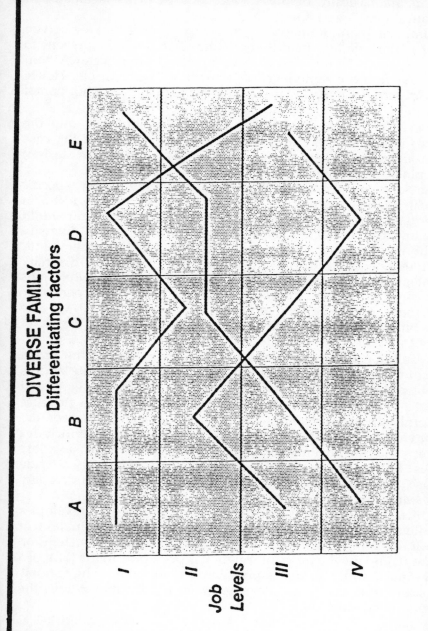

Figure 8.7   Diverse family.

Differentiating factors and levels for a diverse family.
Different jobs have different factor/level combinations.

within it are basically of the same character. This is illustrated schematically in Figure 8.6.

The implicit assumption in the generic approach is that for a given level of job or role, all the differentiating factors will be present to the same degree. In other words, for a given level of factor A, you will always find the same level of factor B, of factor C, etc. Hence generic descriptions can be 'read across' as shown by the horizontal lines on Figure 8.6.

However, in many cases this is an oversimplification, and the range of jobs within a family is more diverse. Consider the case of a group of professional engineering jobs, engaged in design, development and project work.

Some jobs may be deep specialists, providing highly specific technical inputs to projects. They would justify a high level on differentiating factors to do with technical specialisation, but would be at a low level on factors to do with project integration, diversity of technology or supervisory requirements. On the other hand, project engineers in the group would rate highly on diversity and integration but relatively low on specialist depth, while jobs supervising the drawing office might rate highly on supervisory requirement, but low on the other factors.

This situation is illustrated schematically in Figure 8.7, where different jobs show different factor combinations.

One solution to this problem is further to subdivide the broad family until homogeneous ladders result – i.e. define separate ladders for project jobs, for specialists, for supervisors, for development jobs, etc. In practice, this is cumbersome, and can also produce unhelpful barriers. Frequently in such circumstances, career development is not simply up a series of parallel ladders, but includes sideways and diagonal moves as people gain experience in a variety of roles. Rather than parallel ladders, what is wanted is a 'wide staircase' or a 'scrambling net' which can accommodate diversity of roles and career paths between them.

In these circumstances, a useful approach is to develop a computer based job family model, in which any combination of the differentiating factors can be processed to give a consistent job size result, and in which job information is presented in the form of a questionnaire which focuses directly on the differentiating factors.

Typically, the process for developing such a model includes the following main steps.

- *From study of the range of jobs within the family, the main factors which differentiate between jobs at different levels are determined.* This is normally done by an 'expert' group drawn from the family itself. Frequently, the number of factors which emerges is between 6 and 10, depending on the diversity within the family.

- *For each differentiating factor, the levels at which it may be present are defined, again usually by the expert group.* These first two steps are very much the same as would be used for the development of a simple ladder or framework of generics.
- *The factors and levels are then expressed in questionnaire form,* with each factor being a question, and the levels representing the range of responses to that question.
- *A benchmark sample of actual jobs is then selected and evaluated using a conventional job evaluation process,* to provide the basic values and standards on which the computer model is to be built.
- *The questionnaire is also answered for the same sample jobs, and a mathematical algorithm built* to relate questionnaire responses to evaluated job size, and programmed into a suitable software environment.
- *After further testing of the questionnaire and algorithm, the model is then available for use with any other job in the family.* For these jobs, the job analysis requirement is simply to complete the job family questionnaire, which can then be computer processed to yield directly an evaluation result – subject of course to appropriate quality assurance checks.

The job evaluation aspects of this process are considered in some more detail in the next chapter. In the context of this discussion on job analysis, the important features of the job family questionnaire as a job analysis instrument include:

- *It is specifically geared to the requirements of the family concerned,* and focuses on the particular differentiators which are important in that family.
- *The questions can be expressed in the language of the family,* and represent the values of the family.
- *Close links can be made into processes of competency analysis and career planning.*
- *Any combination of the factors which may be present in a job can be reflected,* so considerable diversity of role within the family can be accommodated.
- *It is short, focused and very easy and quick to complete.*
- *From a job evaluation viewpoint, computer processing is very efficient,* and since the model is underpinned by conventional evaluation, it yields results which are compatible with other jobs in the organisation which may have been evaluated conventionally or using generics.

The limitation of the approach is of course that it can only be used for jobs in the family for which it was designed. A complex organisation would need a number of families to cover most of its jobs, though frequently the approach is used for one or two major families on which specific focus is helpful, with alternative (but compatible) approaches being used for the remaining jobs.

Though it can be applied to any defined family, it has found particular application in such areas as:

- *Technical/professional/knowledge worker environments* (e.g. scientists, engineers, technicians) where conventional job analysis/ evaluation approaches present particular difficulties.
- *Clerical environments*, where as in the above case there may be large numbers of jobs which although similar in nature are quite diverse in detail.
- *'Branch' type jobs* (e.g. bank managers) where again there may

---

QUESTION 4

INFORMATION HANDLING

Please tick the box which best describes the job:

❏   1.   No responsibility for the processing of data.

❏   2.   Responsible for checking data, and referring errors for correction.

❏   3.   Responsible for maintaining, checking, updating and deleting information held in files or systems of predetermined format.

❏   4.   Responsible for extracting information from files or systems and compiling reports in standard format.

❏   5.   Responsible for gathering information from a variety of established sources and compiling reports within an agreed framework.

❏   6.   Responsible for compiling special and one-off reports, using data from a range of sources, involving non-standard information retrieval and report formats.

❏   7.   Responsible for identifying new sources of information and/or the setting up of new administrative procedures, systems and reporting formats.

Figure 8.8   Extract from a job family questionnaire for a group of clerical and administrative jobs.

be large numbers, and a range of particular factors/factor combinations which contribute to overall job weight.

An extract from a typical job family questionnaire is given in Figure 8.8.

'Universal' questionnaires

A more commonly used approach to computer assisted job evaluation is to gather job data through a single questionnaire, used for all jobs in the organisation, or at least for a broad spread of jobs. The job evaluation aspects of this are described in the next chapter: here we focus on the questionnaire itself.

Although such questionnaires are sometimes called 'universal', this only means that they are used for all (or most) jobs in a particular organisation or job group. They are not – or should not be – 'universal' in the sense of standard questionnaires applied to any organisation. At the very least, they need to be tailored to the particular organisation, the range and types of jobs to be covered, and to focus on those aspects and values which are considered to be important in the organisation concerned.

Compared with job family questionnaires, universal or general questionnaires are normally longer – typically containing around 30 questions – since the range of possible differentiating factors will be much greater in a diverse job population.

For the same reasons, the questions themselves are inevitably more general and less sharply focused than in the job family approach.

However, the major attraction of universal questionnaires is that they provide the means of gathering job data efficiently and consistently, using a single instrument applicable to all (or most) jobs in the organisation, in a form amenable to computer processing. The questions themselves are usually of two types:

- Multiple choice questions, in which the respondent chooses a statement from a list which most accurately describes a particular aspect of the job.
- Questions which ask directly for a number to be entered – e.g. number of people supervised, value of budget controlled, etc.

An extract from a typical universal questionnaire is given in Figure 8.9.

Questionnaires may be completed by the jobholders themselves, for approval by the supervisor/manager, or by the boss – or in discussion between them. Trained questionnaire analysts can provide a useful input to this process by helping to ensure that questions are fully understood and answered in a consistent way.

Q6   Internal contacts

Select the level that best describes the most common way in which the job must liaise with others.

(Internal means within the company and includes remote sites/headquarters, etc.)

1.   The job involves no need for contact outside the particular work group and its management.

2.   The job involves infrequent contact with others, and the contact is for the purpose of exchanging job related information, which needs to be done accurately and effectively.

3.   The job requires frequent contact with people outside the department in order to provide or obtain information. There is a need to express oneself clearly. The job requires courteous behaviour in face-to-face dealings with other employees.

4.   The need to express oneself clearly is an important part of the job, and jobholders will typically have had specific training in communications skills or will have been selected because they possess these skills. The importance stems from a requirement to create a favourable impression on others as well as communicate information effectively.

5.   The job requires you frequently to seek cooperation from, or influence others. The jobholder must develop relationships and persuade others to help resolve problems. The ability to listen to others and to develop a mutual understanding is an important requirement of the job. This level usually includes jobs which allocate, monitor and review work of other employees, or jobs which have regular and significant dealings with colleagues in a variety of different locations.

6.   The job requires you to motivate subordinates or colleagues where the degree of motivation and commitment achieved will directly impact upon the results of the department.

7.   The job requires highly developed communication skills for dealing with sensitive, or potentially controversial interpersonal situations. The jobholder must create behaviour change in people and/or obtain the cooperation and commitment of subordinates/colleagues. This level is usually required for positions responsible for the development, motivation, assessment and reward of other employees.

Figure 8.9   Typical question from a universal questionnaire.

Typically, the questionnaire should take no longer than an hour or so to complete, which represents a major time saving over the preparation of a conventional job description.

Whatever process is adopted for questionnaire completion, it is critical to build in appropriate quality assurance processes to ensure consistency. Experience shows that the quality of evaluation results which emerge is directly proportional to the care taken with quality assurance of the data input. While most computer systems for processing the job data to give evaluation results contain a variety of consistency checks, these can only indicate inconsistency of response between questions within a job. They can never pick up situations where a job's responses are consistently over or under-rated. Some form of involvement of trained questionnaire analysts in the process is one of the most effective ways of building in the necessary quality assurance.

The questionnaires themselves may be paper based, for subsequent batch processing through the computer, or can be on-screen for direct entry of the responses – though quality assurance may be even more difficult in the latter case.

9 Processes for Applying the Evaluation Method

Setting standards – benchmarks

The first stage in the job evaluation process is often to evaluate a benchmark sample of jobs, to provide a framework of basic standards, interpretations and reference points against which other jobs can be judged.

Exceptions to this include:

- Where the population is small and does not warrant a separate sampling and standard setting stage.
- Where a benchmark sample has already been used in the development of the method itself. In such cases, many of the observations below on benchmarking apply to this earlier stage.
- Where job evaluation is not being used to evaluate individual jobs, but for example to provide a framework of job size to a pattern of flexibly defined roles. In such cases, although the population of people may be large, relatively few roles may be defined and not warrant separate sampling.

It is important to separate the benchmark stage both conceptually and practically from the process used for evaluating subsequent jobs. Once standards have been established through the benchmark, they can be applied to the remaining jobs by a wide variety of processes, both manual and computer assisted: these are described in the later sections. The focus in this section is the process for evaluating benchmark jobs.

The nature and purpose of benchmarking is sometimes misunderstood. On one hand it is often regarded as simply doing the first few evaluations, with no more significance than that. This understates their importance in setting standards, values and reference points. In a similar vein, some people worry that making explicit comparison of subsequent jobs with benchmarks is somehow 'cheating' and that each job should be done completely from first principles, without regard for relativities. Again this is missing the point that job evaluation is an exercise in relativities, and that benchmarks are there to help evaluators achieve consistency of judgement.

At the other end of the spectrum, benchmarks are sometimes misinterpreted as providing the only evaluations which can be used. For example, if a benchmark area manager job is required, people sometimes worry that if the smallest area is chosen to provide the benchmark, then all the others will have to come out the same and hence be undervalued. Of course this is not the case: the benchmark only provides the reference point against which the others can be tested. If they are genuinely bigger, then they should be evaluated as such.

How many benchmarks?

The proportion of jobs to be selected as benchmarks will depend on:

- The range and diversity of jobs to be covered, in terms of job level, function and organisational unit.
- The overall size of the population of jobs.
- The nature of the subsequent process for evaluating non-benchmarks.
- How 'tight' a framework is needed to set and maintain standards for subsequent use.

In general, between 10% and 30% of the total number of jobs is typical (though this may of course be a very much smaller percentage of the number of *people*).

Selecting benchmarks

The purpose of the benchmark is to provide a sample of jobs, which is representative of the levels, functions and organisational units in the full job population.

A useful technique to assist in this is to draw up a matrix as shown in Figure 9.1. Down the left hand side is shown the level of the job: this clearly cannot be precise, since the purpose of the job evaluation exercise is to determine the levels of jobs! Nevertheless it is usually possible to use existing grade or some other measure

Existing job grade or level.		FUNCTION/DEPARTMENT				
		Branch Ops	HQ Admin	Marketing	Customer Services	etc. . . .
	A	*		*		
	B		*		*	
	C	*	*			
	D	*		*		
	E		*		*	
	F	*		*	*	
	etc.		*		*	

Figure 9.1   Matrix to assist benchmark selection.

of perceived level to do this. It does not matter if it is not quite right, since all it will affect is the choice of the sample, not the final results, so all that is needed is a rough guide to likely job level. Across the top, the functions, departments or units are listed – depending on how the organisation is constructed. Actual jobs can then be listed in the matrix, and a sample selected which gives reasonable coverage across both dimensions.

The first cut at this usually produces far too large a benchmark, and the initial selection may need to be reviewed several times to get a manageable number which is still representative.

This provides the spread of jobs to be selected. Useful criteria to apply in this process are that benchmark jobs, wherever possible, should be stable, well understood, representative of the mainstream of jobs in the organisation, and uncontentious regarding their content. Clearly it is not always possible to meet all of these criteria. In a rapidly changing organisation, jobs in some areas may be far from stable, or be so new as to be not well understood. Nevertheless, if they are representative of important parts of the organisation, they need inclusion.

In general, actual jobs are used to provide benchmarks: in some circumstances, synthetic jobs may be included – for example where benchmarks are required to represent a new organisation which is being developed, but is not yet fully in place – though great care needs to be taken in doing this to ensure that the jobs are realistic.

In general, the benchmark selection should broadly reflect the distribution of jobs across the levels and functions – i.e. areas with many different jobs should be well provided with benchmarks. In addition, it is worth ensuring that the top and bottom levels in the population are sufficiently represented, to ensure that the limits of job size are fully explored, and that in the subsequent phase there is little need to extrapolate too much beyond the job size range reflected in the benchmark.

Using the above approach, the sample which usually emerges is a scattered distribution across the population. In some circumstances it may be appropriate to supplement this scatter by deliberately selecting some related 'strings' of jobs, so that detailed relationships can be explored in the benchmark evaluations. For example, if there is believed to be a significant issue about the relationships between sales representative, senior sales representative and area manager, then it may be worth including all three in the benchmark, to establish guidelines and standards which can be applied in other areas.

Analysis of benchmark jobs

Because they are to be used to establish references and values, particular care should be taken with the analysis of benchmark jobs. Typically, a conventional job description format is used to present the job information, even if the subsequent process for non-benchmark jobs is to use multiple choice questionnaires and computer processing.

Ideally, trained job analysts should be involved in the analysis of benchmark jobs – not necessary in actually drafting the descriptions, but certainly providing advice and input, and carrying out careful quality assurance of the descriptions which are produced. If internal resources are insufficient, they may be supplemented in this activity by external consultants.

Benchmark evaluations

Having selected the basic evaluation method to be used, the critical process issue at the benchmark stage is who should carry out the evaluations. In principle, benchmark evaluations could be conducted by:

- An external consultant.
- An internal specialist.
- A panel of HR specialists.
- A management panel with members drawn from the main areas of the business.
- A participative panel comprising managers and employee representatives and/or trade union representatives.

Each of these has a different balance between efficiency, adequate reflection of the organisation's values, and accurate reflection of the real content of jobs. At the benchmark stage – unlike subsequent stages of evaluation – efficiency of the process is not usually the major consideration. The scale of the benchmark exercise is usually relatively modest, and it is to a large degree a once-off exercise. The major requirements are to ensure that the organisation's values are properly reflected, and that the jobs used to demonstrate these values are properly understood and reflected.

For these reasons, benchmark evaluation purely by an external consultant generally provides the least satisfactory balance of characteristics. Being external, the consultant will have very limited knowledge of both the values of the organisation, and of the detail of jobs and relationships beyond what is in the job description. The exception is where the primary requirement is not the establishment of internal pay arrangements, but is purely to evaluate jobs to enable external pay market comparisons.

The internal specialist suffers many of the same problems, though to a lesser degree, assuming that the specialist has reasonable knowledge of the organisation and its values. Nevertheless, it provides only a single perspective and does not allow for debate about relativities between different jobs and functions.

This can be improved by the use of a panel or committee of HR specialists, but this approach still lacks the direct input of people closely involved with the jobs concerned, and like any 'specialist' approach may cause problems through lack of ownership of the results.

In most cases, some kind of panel or committee drawn from a variety of functions is to be preferred. Whether this is a management-only group or a participative one is less an issue of technical quality, more one of broader employee relations requirements as discussed earlier.

If a panel or committee is to be used, the size is usually between four and eight people. Less than this may make it difficult to get the necessary coverage, while more can be unwieldy and slow down the reaching of conclusions.

Panel members should be selected so that as individuals they bring knowledge and experience of particular areas of the company plus as broad a perspective as possible. Collectively they should be able to provide informed views across the whole organisation. Selection should be on the basis of getting the right people on the panel – not just those who happen to be 'spare'.

The panel should be thoroughly trained in the use of the chosen method. Where external consultants are used, they would normally train the panel and provide technical leadership and guidance during the benchmark phase. Normally a chairman is appointed to manage the business of the panel.

Evaluation judgements should be reached on a consensus basis – not by voting or 'negotiating'. It is important that panel members do not see their role as 'representing' a particular area or interest group, in the sense of arguing every issue for the benefit of their area or group. They should aim to reach joint decisions based on reasoned debate, not by bargaining or horse trading.

A useful approach for panel evaluation is for the members, having read the job description, to debate the content of the job thoroughly before evaluating it. A high proportion of disagreements about an evaluation arise from different interpretations of the job itself. Debate before evaluation can usually avoid this.

In some organisations, the information in the job description is supplemented by the jobholder or manager attending the panel to present further background or answer questions. In practice this is becoming less common, even for the benchmark phase, since it can add significantly to the time required, and in many cases merely duplicates information in the job description. However, the panel should be free to ask for supplementary information when it needs it, and to refer back any job information which they consider inadequate, unclear or contradictory.

When all jobs in the benchmark have been evaluated, the panel should review the overall relativities, and reconsider any jobs which may appear inappropriately placed. Great care needs to be taken to ensure that this is not just a 'tidying up' process: any changes made must be clearly justified and considered from first principles.

Recording results and rationales

As well as maintaining careful record of the benchmark results, the panel should also record the reasons leading to each evaluation judgement – often referred to as a rationale. The purpose of the benchmark is not just to arrive at a set of evaluations: it is also to establish principles and guidelines to aid the subsequent evaluation process, whatever that may be – hence the need to record why the results were arrived at, as well as the results themselves. If relatively conventional processes are to be used for post-benchmark evaluation, it is fairly common practice to summarise the principles emerging from the benchmark stage in some form of written guidelines, or reference manual.

Post-benchmark evaluation – traditional approaches

Continuation of the benchmark process
Traditionally, post-benchmark evaluation has essentially been a continuation of the same kind of panel process used for the

benchmark. In its most straightforward form, this may simply be the same panel carrying on to do the remaining jobs following the benchmark, then reviewing the resulting total rank order.

There are two main advantages to this approach:

First, through the panel process, it enables debate and analysis of the organisation and the relationships between jobs. While some of this is possible at the benchmark stage, it is limited by the fact that the benchmark is only a sample in which many organisational relationships simply may not be demonstrated.

Evaluation of the full population of jobs in the panel provides the means for detailed organisational consideration. Many users of job evaluation gain substantial additional added value from this aspect of the process. Some of the techniques which can be used for this are described in Chapter 14.

Second, the facility to use the panel process to assist with team building and joint collaboration is maintained. This may be particularly important when job evaluation is being used as a component of harmonising pay and conditions across several employee groups. Some users of job evaluation in this context report that the benefits obtained from the process in terms of collaboration and joint working were at least as valuable as the actual evaluation results which emerged.

Set against these advantages, the major problem with this approach is that it can be slow and demanding on resources – both for job description preparation and for actual evaluation. While the rate of progress is certainly faster than at the benchmark stage – because basic guidelines and references have already been established – this aspect is a significant disadvantage of the traditional process, especially for large job populations.

Nevertheless, it may be the preferred approach for small to medium sized job populations, where the investment required to build more structured approaches (as discussed in subsequent sections) is not justified – or where the additional benefits of organisational debate and analysis or of team building are considered to justify the time and resource needed. In such circumstances, traditional approaches are used widely, and are likely to continue to be used, particularly when techniques for streamlining the panel process are used, as described in the following pages.

Streamlining the conventional process

In recent years, much effort has gone into simplifying and streamlining the conventional job evaluation process, so as to reduce its time and resource demands, while maintaining its main strengths.

Some of the techniques used to achieve greater efficiency include:

Streamlining job analysis

Major gains in efficiency can be achieved by streamlining job analysis, both in the time taken for job analysis itself, and in the panel time needed to consider the information presented to it. As described in more detail in the last chapter, significant streamlining can be achieved as follows:

- *Considering carefully what jobs actually exist before job analysis and job evaluation begin and whether these are to be defined very individually or more collectively.* If these issues are left for the panel to sort out, much time can be wasted both in unnecessary job description preparation and in panel debate. In any case, the job evaluation panel is not the right place for these issues to be sorted out, and much time can be wasted because of this, since problems or areas where there is lack of clarity need to be referred back thus extending the process still further.
- *Shorter, more focused job descriptions require less time to prepare – and to read.*
- *Where appropriate, use of generic job descriptions and ladders can cut down the number of jobs to be considered*, and hence the panel time required.
- *Many organisations have dispensed with, or at least significantly reduced, the involvement of jobholders/managers 'presenting' jobs to the panel*, relying more on the job description and only asking for supplementary information when the panel considers it is necessary can reduce the time taken per job enormously. With satisfactory job descriptions and knowledgeable evaluators, there should be no loss in real quality through this.

Using smaller panels

Post-benchmark jobs are sometimes evaluated by smaller sub-groups of the main benchmark panel. This increases the speed of debate and also reduces the time demand on individual evaluators. Often, this is organised on function, unit, or department lines – once the essential cross-functional or inter-unit relativities have been established through the benchmark, a small focused panel working systematically through a function can achieve considerable improvements in efficiency, consistent with quality. It can also enable very focused organisational debate on the job relationships within the area being considered, though of course the facility to consider cross-functional organisation issues is reduced. Sometimes there is cross-functional representation in the process to avoid too introspective a view – or the same requirement may be satisfied by the presence of an HR specialist or consultant on each sub-group.

When this type of approach is used, it is fairly common for

the full benchmark panel to meet following all evaluations to review the total picture and identify any significant divergences from benchmark standards which may have crept in.

Evaluation by specialists

A further continuation along the same lines is for post-benchmark evaluation to be carried out by an HR specialist or small group of two or three such specialists.

As long as the benchmark process has ensured that broad company values are represented, that cross-functional relativities have been debated and thrashed out, and that there is ownership of the standards adopted, then the disadvantages of specialist evaluation noted earlier are much less applicable. Essentially the specialists are then simply applying the principles set by the benchmark. Consistency of application of these principles is usually high in such an approach. Again, final review by the benchmark panel can be built in if it is seen to be appropriate. Obviously in this approach, any of the 'team building' aspects of the panel process are lost. It may still enable organisational analysis, though from a 'specialist' perspective, not involving direct inputs from, and debate between, managers or staff directly involved in the areas concerned. In practice, this approach is quite often used, not for the initial implementation of job evaluation, but for subsequent maintenance, when efficiency and consistency are more important than organisation debate or team building.

Decentralisation of job evaluation
In the past, job evaluation was often set up as a highly centralised process, very much in line with the emphasis on using it as a control mechanism, as outlined in earlier chapters. Not surprisingly, such centralised approaches are now often seen as bureaucratic, unresponsive to the needs of particular business units or operations, and slow in their response to job and organisation changes.

Progressive decentralisation of business control is widespread in all sectors of the economy. This requires similar devolution of control of pay, and in turn of job evaluation processes as an input to pay.

In the extreme case, devolution of pay responsibility to units may be total. In such cases, each unit operates, in effect, as a separate organisation, and chooses its own pay arrangements, job evaluation method and process, etc. Inter-unit comparisons, relativities and so on are not issues, and so processes do not need to be set up to consider them. In practice, this extreme degree of decentralisation is not the norm, except, for example, for subsidiaries of a holding company where business control is largely one of financial performance and capital allocation, and there is little integration of pay or other human resource management processes.

More commonly, decentralisation is less complete, and this needs to be reflected in the job evaluation processes adopted. Typically, the degree of decentralisation which needs to be built in varies according to the level of jobs in the organisation; the frequency with which people typically move from one part of the organisation to another; and the degree to which inter-unit comparisons are relevant. Thus in a multinational company, the top jobs in each country may be evaluated centrally at an international level, senior management jobs evaluated at country level, middle management and professionals at divisional/business unit level, and clerical/manual jobs at site level. Whatever arrangements like this are adopted, it is important that they mirror the nature of the organisation's structure and management processes, and the way in which real business control is decentralised.

As well as reflecting the real structure of the business, decentralisation of the job evaluation process enables significant spreading of the workload involved in job evaluation, and can produce a much more responsive and less bureaucratic approach, both in initial implementation, and perhaps more significantly in the subsequent maintenance phase. One of the criticisms of over-centralised processes is the time taken for re-evaluation of changed or new jobs: local evaluation can give a much faster response, as well as one which is more sensitive to the local situation, organisation and emphases.

However, decentralisation of the process presents its own problems in terms of establishing – and maintaining over time – common evaluation standards. Within the context of conventional evaluation processes, some of the approaches used in practice to achieve consistency include:

Central standard setting/benchmarking

A common technique is to handle the initial benchmark stage on a central basis, so as to establish a framework of common standards which can then be applied by each of the decentralised units.

Typically, a central panel convened for this purpose would comprise representatives from each of the units, who in many cases would then go on to lead the subsequent evaluation process in their own units. The benchmark sample would be selected to include jobs from each of the units concerned. This kind of process is good for setting initial standards: it is less satisfactory for maintaining standards over time, since it can become bureaucratic and slow the process down, or can degenerate into 'second-guessing' or duplicating work done locally.

If a central panel is not used, other mechanisms can be employed to ensure an agreed benchmark starting point. For example, results from separate unit benchmarks can be pooled and reconciled before proceeding, or if external consultants are used, their presence on separate benchmark panels can be used to ensure consistency of standards.

Common process standards

As well as using common reference points in the form of benchmarks, adoption of the same – or at least compatible – evaluation processes can do much to assure uniformity of approach: for example compatible approaches to job analysis, panel membership, evaluator training and methods of panel operation.

Exchange of panel members

In some organisations, each unit's panel contains one or more members drawn from other units, to give an external perspective. In other cases, a member of the central HR function may be involved in the panel processes of all units, or the same role may be fulfilled by external consultants.

Overall review of results

Where possible, an overall review of all units' results is useful. However, in large populations it may simply be impossible (or unacceptably time consuming), and testing for uniformity of standards may need to be limited to a sampling exercise.

Periodic audit

Even when common standards have been adopted at the initial implementation stage, they can soon drift apart over time. Periodic audit, both of process and results, gives an important contribution to maintaining standards. This and other maintenance aspects are considered in Chapter 10.

In this context, it is worth commenting on what is meant by 'common standards'. In a multi-unit organisation, jobs of the same title and superficially similar content may appear in several units – e.g. accounts clerk, production supervisor, management accountant. But the weight of these jobs may in fact be different between units, due to different content, different organisational context, etc. Care needs to be taken that 'common standards' is not too simplistically interpreted, since if there are real differences between jobs, then these should come through in the evaluations.

Finally, it is important to note that the degree of decentralisation of job evaluation process which can be achieved by the above methods is limited. For application in an organisation with up to, say, ten decentralised units, the processes described can work well. Where the need is to decentralise much further – say to twenty or thirty sites or area operations, or even more so, to possibly several hundred branch operations – they become difficult to operate, or extremely cumbersome. Even the training requirement for such numbers of separate panels is a daunting prospect, but a basic essential if the chosen evaluation method is to have a chance of being used consistently.

Hence in these circumstances, more structured approaches are generally used, either simplified classification processes developed from the underlying evaluation method, or computer assisted processes. These are described in the following sections.

Post-benchmark evaluation – structured approaches

Requirements for simplified processes

Particular indicators for a simplified more structured approach to post-benchmark evaluation are:

- When the job population is large.
- When the time and resources available for job evaluation are limited.
- When the primary requirement is to grade jobs, and other objectives such as organisational analysis are very much secondary.

An additional indicator, which reinforces the need may be:

- When there is the need for a high degree of decentralisation of the process, particularly to a large number of units, while maintaining consistency of application.

In the past, when these circumstances existed, a process of simple 'slotting' of jobs against the benchmark evaluations was sometimes adopted. However in its basic form, without any kind of structured framework, individual slottings were difficult to rationalise and justify, and it was difficult to ensure consistency of application. Many of these problems can be overcome by building classification-type processes on the results of the benchmark evaluations.

Simple classification

Where the job population is highly homogeneous, a simple classification framework can be developed from the benchmark evalu ations by considering:

- What kind of jobs were evaluated at different levels in the benchmark sample?
- Why were some jobs evaluated similarly, while others were evaluated differently? In other words what are the main differentiating features between jobs as demonstrated in the benchmark sample?

From such an analysis, a simple classification framework can be constructed, which specifies the types of job to be found at each level or grade, together with their principal distinguishing features.

Jobs are then graded directly using the classification definitions, a process which is very rapid, and requires only minimal training, and hence can be heavily decentralised. The advantages over 'standard' classification methods are that the framework and definitions are specifically tailored to the job population, and that the whole framework is underpinned by full analytical job evaluation. Thus the relativities between the grades or levels can be set on a logical basis, and the relationship with jobs elsewhere in the organisation where different processes may be applied can be logically based.

The major limitation of this approach as described above is that – in common with all simple classification processes – it is only satisfactory for highly homogeneous populations and there can easily be equal value implications. If the range of jobs to be covered is wider, then the classification definitions inevitably become more woolly and broadly stated, or are complicated by many 'either/or' statements. For the process to work well, the definitions need to be crisp and unequivocal, which is difficult in a varied range of jobs.

In practice, even job populations which may seem homogeneous at first sight can contain a surprising variety of jobs, each type requiring different definitions of the various levels/grades which exist. Take for example a population of 'clerical' jobs – an area where classification methods have been widely used. In most environments, there is significant diversity of content (as well as size) in such a population. In a financial services organisation, for example, clerical jobs providing direct customer services may be totally different from those engaged in central or 'back-office' administration, and the grading criteria would need to be expressed in totally different terms. In a manufacturing organisation, clerical jobs administering physical and financial transactions may be quite different from those engaged in the processing of data, or the provision of secretarial services.

Hence an important refinement of the simple classification approach is job family based classification as described in the next section.

Job family classification

In this approach, the difficulty referred to above is overcome by using grade/level definitions specific to particular job groups or families. They can thus be made crisp, unequivocal and clearly focused on the major differentiating factors which apply in each family of jobs. Because each separate family classification is underpinned by common job evaluation, the whole framework can be made internally consistent and each family clearly related to the others through a logically based common grade structure.

Typically the process to develop and apply such an approach involves the following main steps.

- *Selection, analysis and job evaluation of a benchmark sample of jobs using conventional methods and processes.*
- *Analysis of the benchmark results, and the rationales behind them, to determine a framework of job families.* Within each family, the nature of work is common, but the level is different between different jobs. It is important to note that job families do not necessarily mirror the organisation structure in terms of functions or departments. Within a broad clerical population, for example, there may be a group of jobs whose focus is on the recording and analysis of data. Some may be in the marketing department working on sales statistics; some in the factory on production statistics; some in personnel, working on personnel records, etc. Because the nature of work is similar, such a group may be considered as a job family, even though it extends right across the conventional organisation structure.
- Further analysis within each family, to establish the levels of job which exist, and the main characteristic at each level.
- Development of a common grade structure, using the benchmark evaluations, which links across the levels within each family.
- Documentation of the framework of families and levels in a form which can be used for grading all other jobs in the population.

Other jobs are then directly graded by comparison with this framework, in a two step process: Into which job family does the job most clearly fall, based on the kind of work undertaken?

Which level definition within the selected family most closely matches the content of the job?

- Guidance is usually included in the documentation on how to deal with jobs which may have aspects spanning more than one family. For the small proportion of jobs which really do not fit the framework, conventional job evaluation can be carried out, using the same method which underpins the classification framework.

- Training to use the approach is minimal, since the documentation can be framed in language familiar to users, not in the jargon of job evaluation. Hence very high levels of decentralisation can be achieved, without extensive training and with highly consistent results.

The approach described has found particular application in large, dispersed clerical populations – in some cases involving decentralisation of application to many hundreds of locations – and produced results which were consistent and accepted, and which have stood the test of time. Because high levels of decentralisation are possible, the speed of applying the process can be very great, once it has been developed – for example involving the grading of literally thousands of jobs in a matter of weeks.

Finally, the underpinning by conventional job evaluation enables the organisation to manage logically the relativities between the jobs covered by this process, and other job groups (e.g. management jobs) where the same basic method may be applied by more conventional processes.

Job family classification and generics/ladders

Superficially, the process described above has many similarities to the use of generic job descriptions or role definitions as considered in Chapter 8. However, although many of the steps in the process and many of the considerations are similar, it is important to recognise a fundamental difference between the two approaches.

In the case of the job family classification process, what is produced is a framework describing types or characteristics of jobs against which actual jobs are tested and matched. Hence some form of individual job data usually needs to be prepared – often in the form of a brief job description or questionnaire – to provide the basis for the matching.

In contrast, the jobs or roles described in a framework of generics are the jobs, so no *job* matching process or individual job description is involved. However there may need to be separate processes for ensuring that all holders of a generic job accept that that is their job, and in the case of generic ladders that people are appropriately allocated to the various levels. In this latter context, considerations of skills and competencies associated with each level can provide useful input, thus providing link between these aspects and the job evaluation process.

Computer assisted job evaluation (CAJE)

Basis of computer assistance

Probably the most significant development in job evaluation practice which has taken place since the mid-1980's has been the introduction of computer assisted processes.

The driving forces behind these developments were explained in Chapter 4: in short, the need to improve radically the efficiency of the process, and to cut through the bureaucracy, paperwork and 'cottage industry' so often associated with traditional evaluation processes.

While the structured classification based processes outlined in the previous section can give enormous efficiency gains over traditional panel processes, in practice they are largely limited to fairly homogeneous populations of jobs, if 'force fitting' of jobs into categories is to be avoided. For large populations containing a wide range of job types, manual classification can be cumbersome, or insensitive to real job differences. It is in these circumstances that computer assisted job evaluation (CAJE) processes are proving invaluable.

At the outset, it is important to recognise that CAJE techniques are essentially forms of job evaluation *process*, and are not in themselves job evaluation *methods*. In other words, they do not provide the basic 'measuring stick' or set of values on which one job is judged against another. What they do provide is an efficient and consistent means of applying and reproducing the evaluation criteria and values which have been chosen. Hence they are not 'black box' solutions, and should not be seen as replacing the need for human judgement in the evaluation process. Their strength is that they enable these judgements to be replicated quickly and consistently – but the judgements must be made in the first place.

Types of computer assistance

The types of computer assistance available fall into two broad categories:

- Software systems which support and help increase the efficiency of conventional evaluation processes, by providing data management, storage, sorting and retrieval facilities to the evaluators.
- Processes in which evaluations are generated by the computer, based upon questionnaire responses. This is the category of approaches most commonly understood by the term 'computer assisted job evaluation'.

Just as for manual processes, computer aided techniques need to be selected, designed and adapted to satisfy particular sets of requirements. As for manual processes, the most appropriate approach to computer assistance will be determined by the purpose of the exercise, the size and diversity of the population involved, the resources available and the culture of the organisation.

Even within a single organisation, different job groups may present quite different process requirements. For example there may be a small senior management group for which the facility for organisation debate is an important requirement from job evaluation; a large clerical population distributed between many branches for which efficiency and consistency are primary requirements of the process; and perhaps a group of professionals where the need is to link job evaluation and pay to career progression and competency.

Computer systems which provide a single 'packaged' solution are unlikely to be able to meet these different needs, and the risk is that they may be applied inappropriately, or applied only to a part of the organisation making it difficult to achieve compatible evaluations between job groups – a growing requirement as pay arrangements are harmonised.

Ideally, computer systems should therefore provide the flexibility to respond to a range of process requirements; yield results which are compatible, whatever process options are chosen; and contain these options within the same software environment.

While many CAJE systems have been developed – mainly by the larger management consultancies – most tend to focus on a particular process option. The major exception is the HayXpert system, developed by Hay Management Consultants. For this reason, we will illustrate the range of CAJE processes which are possible by reference to HayXpert, recognising that other systems may provide similar facilities in some of the categories described – particularly in the questionnaire area.

HayXpert is a flexible software environment, within which a range of related and compatible process options can be operated. It is built upon a database, which enables the storage, sorting and rapid retrieval of job and related information, and is equipped with a wide range of output and reporting facilities. It is designed so as to provide both computer support to conventional evaluation processes, and to accommodate questionnaire based CAJE processes through four modules described below. In addition to these four job evaluation facilities, modules can also be provided for job pricing, salary administration and competency analysis.

Support to conventional evaluation process

QED Chart

This facility provides on-line support to conventional panel based evaluation processes using the Hay Guide Chart Profile method of evaluation. It enables the storage and retrieval of job description information and evaluation notes as well as the evaluation results themselves. 'Electronic guide charts' are built in, which calculate scores and flag up inconsistencies. Flexible report generators can provide on-screen and printed outputs in virtually any form, including organisation charts, and jobs can be coded in whatever way is appropriate to the organisation, to enable selective sorting and retrieval.

One of its most important facilities is the ability to call up on screen full information about any comparator job or set of jobs, so that the evaluation of the job under consideration can be fully tested in relation to others, plus the ability to compare any particular evaluation with those of its boss and subordinates, so as to examine each evaluation in its organisational context. This provides enormous help in ensuring evaluation consistency without having to bring a trunk full of paperwork to each panel meeting. Indeed, used to its full potential, the system enables a totally paper-free evaluation process.

The application of this type of system is in circumstances where panel based processes are preferred (for example because the organisation debate and/or team building aspects of panels are valued), but where greater efficiency is required. It also finds application in multi-panel processes, where the ability to cross

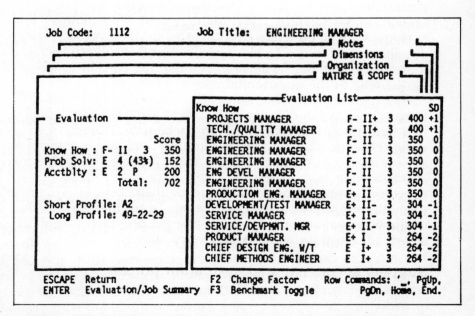

Figure 9.2   Sample screen from QED Chart showing the facility to compare an evaluation with the full evaluation list, by factor.

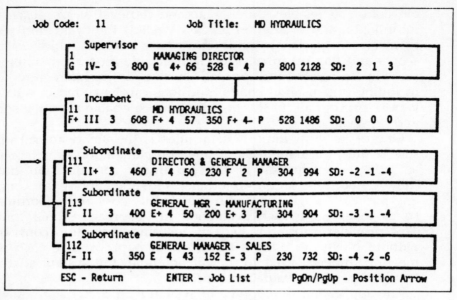

Figure 9.3   Sample screen from QED Chart showing the facility to compare an evaluation with those for jobs above and below it in the organisation.

reference and to compare with common benchmarks can give major improvements in consistency of standards.

Figures 9.2 and 9.3 illustrate typical screens from the QED Chart system.

Comparison

This facility provides support to the more structured 'slotting' or classification processes described in the previous section. As pointed out there, one of the limitations of classification processes, even when underpinned by full benchmark evaluation, is that they rely essentially on whole job comparisons, and hence are largely restricted to highly homogeneous populations, or ones which can easily be divided up into homogeneous families.

Comparison provides the means of accommodating a number of simplified slotting factors, derived from full benchmark evaluation. These factors can be expressed in language relevant to the jobs and the organisation – not in job evaluators' jargon – and so can be used by line managers or others with limited job evaluation knowledge. In addition, the software enables direct comparison with evaluated benchmark jobs. Hence the approach represents a halfway house between simple classification and full evaluation, providing the speed and ease of use of the former, combined with at least some of the sensitivity of the latter through the use of simplified factors.

In practice, the approach typically involves the following stages:

- Selection, analysis and evaluation of a benchmark sample by conventional means.
- Analysis of the benchmark results to determine the framework of simplified 'slotting' factors.
- Determination and definition of the factor levels.
- Programming into HayXpert.
- Testing with line managers/users.
- Quality assurance on resulting evaluations.

The Comparison software provides a split-screen display in which the slotting factor levels are shown on the left hand side, with benchmark examples on the right. An example screen is illustrated in Figure 9.4. The facility is provided to 'go behind' this basic information for more detail of the factor levels and the specific benchmark jobs should this be needed.

Evaluation is then carried out by direct slotting, factor by factor using these displays. The computer then generates the job size or grade directly. All the data management and reporting facilities of QED Chart are incorporated to help administer the process.

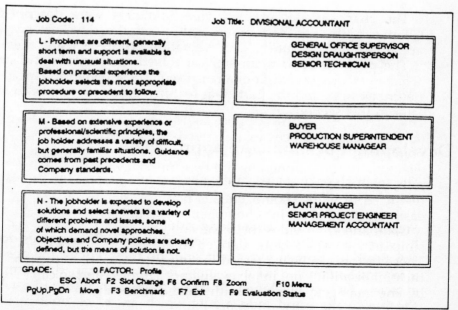

Figure 9.4 Sample screen from the Comparison facility of HayXpert® showing part of a typical factor scale, with benchmark examples.

As for manual classification, this type of approach is suitable for large populations where the primary requirements are for rapid and efficient grading, and for devolution of operation to line managers or other non-evaluation specialists. Unlike simple manual classification or slotting, it can deal with much more heterogeneous job populations.

Questionnaire approaches

In the above techniques, evaluation judgements are made for each job by evaluators; the computer provides the means for doing this more efficiently and consistently. In questionnaire methods, the computer itself generates the initial evaluation from questionnaire responses entered into it.

Using HayXpert, two broad types of questionnaire approaches are possible:

- *Job family questionnaire*: short, focused questionnaires designed to evaluate jobs within a group or family where the nature of work is broadly similar, but the levels are different.
- *'Universal' questionnaire*: a single questionnaire designed to cover all (or most) jobs within an organisation. The title 'universal' should not be construed as meaning a standardised question-naire for all organisations : it is 'universal' within the organisation for which it has been developed.

The characteristics of these questionnaires were described in Chapter 8. In this section we will cover the development and application of computer aided evaluation processes using them.

The principles and main steps involved are basically the same, whichever form of questionnaire is used. These common aspects are described first, and the particular features of the two types covered later in this section.

Developing questionnaire approaches

The main steps involved in developing and setting up a question-naire based CAJE process are:

Step 1: Establish the underlying values
It was noted at the start of this section that CAJE processes do not substitute for human judgement, nor do they replace the need for a job evaluation *method* of some kind to underpin the computer system which is developed. The first stage is therefore to establish the basic values and judgements which are to be built in to the computer model.

The best way of doing this is to select a benchmark sample

of jobs, and evaluate them by conventional means, as described earlier in this chapter. The issues involved in benchmark selection and evaluation are basically the same as they would be to initiate a manual evaluation process. After all, the computer system is simply trying to apply benchmark evaluation standards to subsequent jobs, just as evaluators would be doing in a conventional process.

The results of this benchmark evaluation provide the dependent variable on which the mathematical algorithm, which is the basis of the computer system, is to be built. When using HayXpert software, the benchmark evaluation may be carried out using the Hay Guide Chart Profile Method, using a tailor-made method for the particular organisation concerned, or using an evaluation method which already exists within the organisation.

Alternatives to benchmark evaluation to provide the dependent variable do exist, but are generally less satisfactory. These include:

Simple ranking (or paired comparisons) of a benchmark sample

As discussed in Chapter 5, these methods are less satisfactory in that they only provide a rank order basis, and do not indicate the magnitude of the gaps in job size or weight within the rank order.

Existing grade

Using this as the dependent variable assumes that all is well with the existing grade arrangements, at least for the sample jobs. This must be questionable, especially since job evaluation is usually introduced to establish new grading arrangements because the existing ones are deficient in some way.

Existing pay

Using existing pay levels has the same deficiencies as existing grade, plus the potential difficulty in ensuring equal value considerations are met. If existing pay arrangements contain discriminatory elements, then these will become locked in to the evaluation algorithm. It then becomes a nonsense to try to use a job evaluation scheme developed on this basis to ensure that Equal Value requirements are met.

Market pay

Algorithms based on market pay are potentially even more flawed from an equal value perspective since they will embody any existing discrimination which is present in the market. In addition, it is very difficult to assess 'market pay' with any precision.

But most fundamentally, algorithms based on market pay confuse the two quite distinct issues of job size and market price. Market price is a function of many economic factors of supply and demand, which have little to do with job size or weight. Secondly, market price is variable, as the supply and demand conditions change in the relevant job market. Hence if this basis were used, there would be the need continually to adjust the algorithm to take account of changes in market relativities.

Step 2: Develop and test the questionnaire

The characteristics of job family and universal questionnaires were described in Chapter 8. In both cases, the questionnaire needs to be developed/refined so that it elicits the information required for evaluation. The questions themselves, the number of levels and the language in which they are expressed need to be appropriate to the range of jobs to be covered, and the organisation in which they exist.

Generally, universal type questionnaires are tailored, rather than being developed from scratch each time, drawing on a databank of questions/question types which have been demonstrated to work well. In the case of job family questionnaires, it is more likely that these are built from first principles, in conjunction with members of the family concerned, to ensure that the specific differentiating factors between jobs in the particular environment, are captured and reflected.

Once the first draft questionnaire has been established, it is normally tested and refined to ensure that it is understood and capable of being answered easily and consistently.

Step 3: Questionnaire completion for benchmark jobs

The questionnaire is then completed for the benchmark jobs. Completion may be by jobholder, manager, analyst, or a combination of these. Whatever process is adopted, careful quality assurance of the questionnaire responses is essential, to ensure that the questions have been consistently interpreted, understood and answered.

Step 4: Build and test the algorithm

Steps 1 and 3 have generated two sets of data about each benchmark job – a conventional evaluation or ranking, and a set of questionnaire responses. The next step is to build a mathematical relationship between these two sets of data (the algorithm) such that evaluations/rankings can be calculated directly from the questionnaire responses. Depending on the requirement, the algorithm may be designed to produce a full evaluation factor by factor, an evaluation total, or simply a grade.

In practice, algorithm development and testing is usually an iterative process, which may involve refining both the algorithm itself and in some cases the questionnaire until it works well and evaluations can be predicted with confidence from questionnaire responses.

Step 5: Program into software

Once the algorithm is running well, it can be programmed into the software package which is to be used to handle subsequent evaluations. Apart from the requirement to calculate evaluations from questionnaire responses, the software needs to provide a database for storage, administration and retrieval of evaluations and job and data reporting facilities. The software normally also contains facilities for testing consistency of results. In the case of HayXpert, all the basic facilities described earlier as functions of QED Chart are provided when using questionnaire methods.

Standard evaluation models

The above steps describe the typical process for developing computer evaluation models based directly upon the particular organisation's values and judgements about job relativities.

In some cases, systems are offered containing ready-made models, which remove the need for initial benchmark evaluations (or at least reduce the need substantially, if a small benchmark is used for calibration purposes), and where questionnaires are largely standardised, requiring only minor tailoring. Such systems have the obvious attraction that they come largely ready to use and hence the cost, time and resources needed to develop them are significantly reduced.

Their disadvantage is of course that they are not built upon the organisation's values and judgements, and hence give a largely external perspective on job size and relativities. In this context it is necessary to recognise that a similar process to that described above has to be gone through to develop a standard model: the difference is that the basic standards and evaluations used to underpin the model are external and not specific to the organisation.

In judging the applicability – and acceptability – of standard models, the balance must therefore be drawn between these considerations. Thus if a standard approach is adopted because the costs and resources needed to develop a tailored model cannot be justified, then it must be recognised that the downside is the acceptance of externally supplied values and judgements. One set of circumstances in which this conflict does not arise is if the purpose of job evaluation is principally to help make external market pay comparisons. In such circumstances then application of the same external values as are used to analyse market pay data is a perfectly valid approach.

Application of questionnaire approaches

The last section outlined the development of CAJE systems based on questionnaires. This section deals with processes for their application.

In principle, the process simply involves completing a questionnaire for each job and processing through the computer to yield a job size or grade. However, in practice, great care needs to be taken with the application process to ensure satisfactory results. In particular, careful quality assurance of both input data (questionnaires) and output (evaluations) is needed if the results are to be worthwhile. Experience demonstrates that the quality of results produced is directly proportional to the care taken with these aspects.

Particular features of the process requiring consideration are:

Who completes the questionnaire?

The issues here are broadly the same as for any other form of job analysis, and were discussed in Chapter 8. Whether jobholder or manager completes the questionnaire, the critical requirement is that there is an effective approval process. Simply asking managers to 'sign off' dozens of questionnaires may be insufficient if the result is that some just literally 'sign off' without paying sufficient attention to the actual responses they are approving.

Normally the straightforward approval processes need supplementing by specific quality assurance processes.

QA processes for questionnaire responses

Ideally such processes should emphasise quality *assurance* – i.e. building in quality at source, rather than retrospective quality control. After all it is a little disconcerting for a jobholder to complete a questionnaire, have it approved, and then be told to alter it after the event because he/she 'got it wrong': much better to provide guidance and assistance during the completion/approval process to ensure consistency of interpretation. A variety of detailed processes can be used for this, including the use of trained questionnaire analysts to advise and counsel jobholders and managers during the completion/approval process, or to complete the questionnaires directly, drawing on inputs from jobholders/managers.

Processing of questionnaires

Many CAJE software systems allow for either direct entry of responses using on-screen questionnaires, or batch entry of the results from hard-copy questionnaire forms. In general the latter is much more common, since it is more amenable to the application of

QA processes, and less liable to generate distortions through people playing 'computer games' as can occur with direct entry methods.

Review of results

Review of the final results, and the relativities which they represent, is an essential step in any job evaluation process, whether manual or computer assisted. While every care may have been taken in the design of the system, and in assuring the quality of the questionnaire inputs, it is still critical to review the overall picture to see if it makes sense and that the relativities are appropriate.

Most CAJE software systems have some inbuilt consistency checks to help in this process.

For example, HayXpert provides the facility (illustrated in Figure 9.5) to test the consistency of responses to individual questions. In the illustrated screen, the ticks in the central boxes indicate the 'expected' level of response to a particular question, given the responses to the other questions. A tick significantly away from the centre indicates an unusually high or low response – which may indicate an unusual job, or simply an inappropriate response to the question concerned.

Consistency check screen from HayXpert®. Ticks in the central column indicate 'expected' responses to the questions. Ticks away from the central column indicate higher or lower responses than expected.

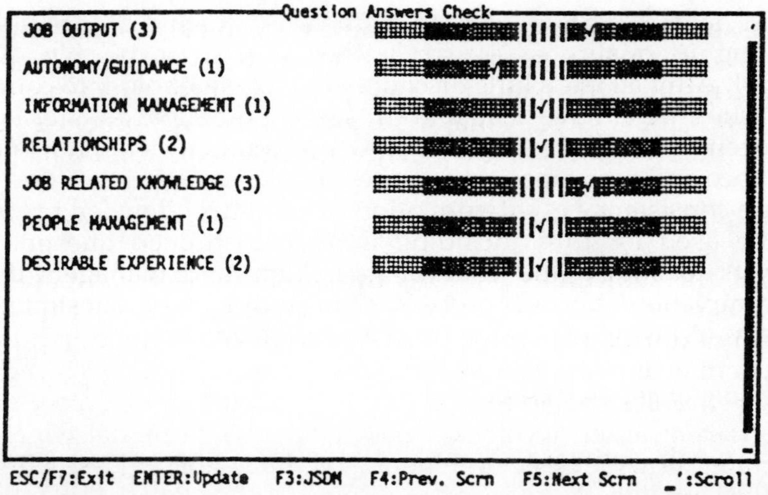

Figure 9.5   Consistency check screen from HayXpert®.

While such inbuilt checks can identify inconsistency *within* a questionnaire, they cannot pick up consistent over- or under-rating. This must come back to the judgement of evaluators through the examination and testing of resulting relativities.

In this context again we would reinforce the fact that CAJE systems do not remove the need for judgement, but inform and assist that judgement process.

When and why to use CAJE processes

Computer assisted processes – particularly those based on question-naires – represent a major addition to the range of job evaluation processes now available and their use is significant and growing rapidly. However, as with any other specific process, they do not represent the solution to all job evaluation process requirements. In this section we outline the circumstances in which they are likely to be the preferred option or at least where there are strong indicators for considering them seriously.

Efficiency

A major attraction of CAJE processes is their efficiency, both in job analysis where questionnaires are much less time consuming to produce than conventional job descriptions, and in the evaluation process itself. Hence CAJE processes are particularly appropriate for large populations, or where time and resources for job evaluation are at a premium.

Maintenance

The issue of efficiency is not limited to initial implementation. Many large-scale conventional job evaluation processes generate a high resource demand for maintenance, through re-evaluation of changed/new jobs. A major advantage of CAJE processes is the ease with which these maintenance requirements can be met.

Decentralisation and consistency

One of the difficulties with decentralisation of conventional pro-cesses is to ensure consistency of evaluation standards. This can be done, but it usually involves significant efforts on training different groups of evaluators and implementing audit/checking procedures. CAJE processes enable consistency to be built in much more easily, since decentralised groups work with the same model which will generate the same basic evaluation standards and values, wherever they are applied.

Against these major advantages must be set the fact that CAJE processes largely remove the stage of panel debate about each job – apart from the benchmark, and final overall review. Where this debate is valued within the organisation, then its value needs to be weighed against its costs and resource implications, in considering whether CAJE or conventional approaches are more appropriate.

Job family model: particular characteristics

The above comments apply mainly to CAJE processes of the 'universal' questionnaire type.

The job family model approach has particular characteristics, beyond simple efficiency and consistency, which make it a powerful approach in some circumstances. The essence of the job family approach is that it focuses on the highly specific differentiating factors which distinguish one level of work in the family from another. These factors, and the issues involved in deriving them, map very closely on to the skills and competencies which are required at each level and the career development routes through the levels. Hence the approach is particularly powerful in circumstances where issues of job size, competency and career development are closely related, and where it needs to be recognised explicitly that the nature and level of role actually undertaken depends both on the demands of the organisation and the capability of the person in the role. These issues were explored more fully in Chapter 3.

Job family modelling has found particularly important application in a wide range of 'knowledge worker' environments, where the characteristics described above typically apply – for example clerical and secretarial populations, engineers, scientists, IT staff, and other technical/professional groupings.

The second important feature of the approach in such cases is that while the questionnaires focus on factors specific to the family, the model is underpinned by conventional job evaluation through the benchmark, enabling a consistent view of job size to be taken between families, or with groups of jobs where more conventional evaluation processes have been adopted. Job family modelling thus provides the means of combining clear focus on the relevant issues within a family, with a common underpinning of job size values across the organisation.

Computer assisted job evaluation – myths and misconceptions

Despite the fact that computer assisted processes have only been around for a few years, a surprising number of myths and misconceptions have grown up around them – often deriving from excessive claims made by the proponents of particular packages.

First there is the claim sometimes made that CAJE systems are 'totally accurate'. If by this it is meant that every time a particular set of questionnaire responses are entered the same answer always results then the claim is valid – but that is rather a limited definition of accuracy. As explained earlier, the validity of results from a CAJE approach is dependent on the care which is taken with a wide range of process and quality assurance features. Providing this care is taken, CAJE processes can provide a major input to ensuring consistency of evaluation even when operated in decentralised circumstances.

On the other hand, concern is sometimes expressed that CAJE is just a 'black box', mechanistically producing results, and hence inappropriate to something as complex, sensitive and important as people's jobs. Of course these techniques can be applied in 'black box' mode, in which case these fears are justified, but in most cases they are not applied in this way. Properly applied, the questionnaires and computer models are based on careful consideration of the values of the organisation and the particular factors and features which are felt to be important in that environment. Final review of results generated by the computer ensures that these values have been reflected in a sensible way. Indeed, at its best, the development of computer assisted models – especially job family models – involves more fundamental exploration of these values and principles than is often produced by the simple manual application of conventional job evaluation.

A related 'black box' concern is that people don't understand what is happening inside the black box. In response, one could ask how much people really understand about what is going on inside the conventional job evaluation committee room. Properly explained, the process is actually a simple one, and one in which a high degree of involvement can be built at critical stages. Essentially the process is one of establishing standards through a benchmark, and building a model which will reproduce these standards and apply them to the answers to a questionnaire. In this sense it is entirely analogous to the conventional process in which evaluators process facts through a 'mental algorithm'. In other words the conventional evaluator is saying: 'Given this set of facts about the job, and given the conclusions we reached on the benchmark, the evaluation is...'. This is just what the computer is doing.

Involvement of people in the benchmark evaluation and final review processes means that the process can, if required, be handled on as 'open' a basis as conventional evaluation.

The final misconception, with which we began this description of CAJE, is that it removes the need for human judgement. Once the nature of the process is understood, the fallacy of this view is clear. The great value of CAJE processes is their ability to help, inform, and improve the efficiency and consistency of judgement – not to remove it.

10 Maintenance Requirements

However good the job evaluation process that has been applied, its continuing quality will depend directly on the care that is taken to maintain it.

Particularly in the current environment, organisations and the jobs within them are changing and evolving constantly. If the evaluation of jobs does not keep up with these changes, the whole process can decay, and be seen to represent an outdated, historical and therefore irrelevant view of the organisation. It is fair to say that one of the most common causes of the failure of job evaluation is lack of adequate maintenance, and with today's rate of change, the failure can be rapid. Conversely, a well maintained process can last virtually indefinitely. Given the investment of time, money and resources in the application of job evaluation, it is surprising how often poor maintenance allows the value of the investment to decline.

As with maintenance of a physical asset, maintenance of a job evaluation process requires both primary maintenance and preventative maintenance.

Primary maintenance

The basic requirement is that as jobs change, they are re-evaluated. This should not be confused with appeals, and care should be taken to distinguish re-evaluation processes from appeals procedures. An appeal is when the result of a job evaluation is challenged, by the jobholder, or his/her supervisor or representative on the basis of disagreement with the result or its relativity to others: in contrast, a re-evaluation is an updating of the evaluation of a job when some significant change has occurred in its content.

One of the difficulties in setting up maintenance processes, is to define what is meant by a 'significant' change, justifying re-consideration of its evaluation. Virtually all jobs are changing all the time, as new techniques are employed, new working methods are adopted and so on. If every such change means that the job has to be formally re-evaluated, the risk is that the whole process will simply become congested, and require excessive time and resource to consider changes, only a small proportion of which turn out to be significant. Apart from the resource requirement, in these circumstances there is the risk that the cases genuinely requiring reconsideration may get lost in the mass of more trivial changes.

To a large degree, this is a function of how jobs are defined in the first place. If they are defined in terms of very specific and detailed tasks, then there is a greater likelihood of constant requests for re-evaluation as the detail changes, and the growth of an attitude along the lines of 'It's not in my job description, so I won't do it unless the job is re-evaluated'. Frequently, an excessive re-evaluation workload is symptomatic of this kind of attitude to jobs, which needs addressing at source.

Hence the first requirement to minimise trivial and unnecessary claims for re-evaluation is to ensure that jobs are defined in such a way as to allow for an appropriate level of flexibility and change to be accommodated, in the context of the organisation as a whole.

The second approach, adopted by many organisations, is to have some form of agreed 'filtering' process prior to formal re-evaluation. This should not be a complicated process, otherwise it is adding to the resource requirement, not reducing it. In many cases, a specialist in the HR function undertakes such screening. Sometimes such an individual has the power of veto, if he/she considers the claim does not warrant consideration; in other cases it is an advisory function, and if both jobholder and manager still wish to proceed, then it goes forward for re-evaluation.

The re-evaluation process itself typically mirrors the original evaluation process, whatever form that took. If this is some kind of panel or committee process, then it is common practice to calendar meetings some time in advance, so that individual submissions can be appropriately scheduled, and delays minimised. Where such meetings are relatively infrequent, it is common practice to apply any changes with effect from the date that the change took place rather than from the date of re-evaluation. If computer aided processes are used, re-evaluation can be undertaken as and when required, not needing panel meetings to be scheduled.

It is impossible to say how frequently re-evaluation events should take place, since this will depend on the size and stability of the job population in question. Typically there will be a steady low-level requirement to accommodate the general rate of change, with periodic peaks following significant reorganisations or business changes. Certainly, if the re-evaluation load is considered 'excessive', then primary attention should be given to re-orientating the way jobs are defined, the attitudes to jobs, and the way the results of job evaluation are used in determining pay.

In many cases, the requirement to re-evaluate a job will simply be initiated by the jobholder and his/her manager, or be the direct result of a clear re-organisation. What may be more difficult to pick up are the more subtle changes which occur over a period of time – often years – and which if ignored can result in inappropriate evaluations. A useful trigger to identify such changes is the annual appraisal process, if there is one, at which the opportunity can be taken to take stock of the job and consider whether material changes have occurred in its accountabilities, its scale of operation, its skill/knowledge demands, etc.

Evaluation drift

Drift of evaluation standards over time is a constant problem for many organisations. In many cases this is a result of pressure being put upon the evaluation process by inflexibility in the pay structure. Inability to reflect performance or market requirements in pay are the most frequent cause of this pressure, as discussed in earlier chapters.

However, even if these pressures are minimised, there is still a tendency for evaluations to drift over time – almost always upwards. Not surprisingly, most requests for re-evaluation arise because the job is believed to have got bigger: not many people (or their managers) apply to have their job re-evaluated because they think it has become smaller! Some practical hints to help minimise evaluation drift are given below.

When a job is being re-evaluated because it has gained responsibilities or resources, the evaluators should ask where these resources or responsibilities have come from. If they are genuinely new to the organisation there is no problem. If, as is more likely, they have been acquired from another job elsewhere in the organisation, then the evaluators should consider the job which has lost them as well as the one which has gained.

Where the basis for re-evaluation is the need for new skills or knowledge, evaluators should consider whether these are additional skills or simply replacement ones. The nature of knowledge and skills required in most jobs is continually changing, but as new skills are added, old ones can be forgotten. Since the basis of job evaluation is the job *requirement*, the issue is whether the total requirement for knowledge and skills has genuinely increased, remained at the same level (though different in nature), or actually diminished. This is a particularly important issue in considering the effects of information technology on many jobs. Although the requirement for keyboard/terminal skills for example may have increased, the need for knowledge about often quite complex paperwork systems may have decreased. Thus while the skill requirement for some jobs has undoubtedly been increased by the growth of IT, equally certainly the total skill requirement in others has diminished.

Many cases for re-evaluation represent incremental change – something has grown or been added, while much of the job remains the same. Quite reasonably, evaluators will typically focus on these changes, to see in which aspect of the evaluation factors or criteria the changes should be reflected. Thus, for example, if the job was previously evaluated on a skill factor at level 5 and the argument is that more skills are needed, then clearly the tendency would be to go to level 6 on that factor. However, it is also important to step back from the incremental change and ask: 'If this job were being looked at for the first time, would we put it at level 6 in comparison with other jobs in level 6'? If this is not done, incremental changes can easily produce creep in evaluation standards. The way that factor scales are defined can have a bearing on this: for example the 'step difference' concept on which the Hay Guide Chart Profile method is based provides a valuable means of testing whether an incremental change is significant or not. A well established framework of benchmark standards also provides a strong basis for testing the significance of such changes.

Preventative and planned maintenance

The above comments have concentrated on the direct maintenance requirement of re-evaluating jobs as they change. For the best results, however, this should be supported by a planned maintenance programme incorporating the following features:

Design for maintenance

The best place to begin consideration of maintenance requirements is in the initial design of the whole process. Too often, maintenance issues are dealt with as an afterthought which can result in processes being established for the initial implementation, which later prove difficult to maintain. Reference has already been made to the need to define jobs in a way which is compatible with the degree of flexibility and change anticipated. Similarly, the evaluation process itself may facilitate, or hinder, maintenance. For example, a highly centralised evaluation process may just about be acceptable for initial implementation but may prove unworkable for subsequent maintenance. Undoubtedly, one of the major appeals of computer aided processes is their ease of maintenance. Although the resource required to implement them may be greater than that for conventional approaches, this can very quickly be recouped over the maintenance period.

Periodic audit of results

Re-evaluations occur sporadically by their nature. While every effort should be made (as outlined above) to test out the effect of changes on relativities, inevitably the focus is relatively narrow and the broader perspective can be lost. An important feature of planned maintenance is periodically to audit the full set of evaluations, to check that it still represents sensible relativities, and that the changes which have been made are consistent. Frequency will clearly depend on the stability of the population and the quality of the ongoing maintenance processes, but in general a fairly brief annual review is a better approach for picking up problems at an early stage, than leaving it for several years by which time the cumulative effect of any problems may require more substantial effort.

Process maintenance

As well as periodic checking of results, it is also important to maintain the necessary quality standards in the process itself. Frequently the first step in the decline of a job evaluation system is neglect of the process itself. Once the first flush of enthusiasm surrounding initial implementation is over, it is very easy for sloppiness to creep in, and ultimately affect the results themselves. For example:

- Decline in the quality of job descriptions – or in the worst cases, absence of job descriptions.
- Decline in recording evaluations and rationales.
- Inadequate training of new or replacement evaluators.
- Benchmarks which are out of date, no longer representative, or simply not used.
- Evaluation meetings being badly organised, too infrequent, or just never happening.
- Evaluation meetings being too frequent, dealing with too many apparent changes – indicating lack of control in the whole process.

Periodic audit of the process as well as the results is a good way of monitoring process quality – and again, 'little and often' is better than leaving it until major reconstitution is required.

Maintenance of 'standards'

The way in which reference standards are expressed will depend upon the nature of the evaluation process adopted, but whatever their form they should be regularly examined to make sure that they are up to date and still relevant to the current organisation. For example:

- In a conventional panel based evaluation process, the reference standards are probably expressed in the form of benchmarks. Both the evaluations of the benchmarks and the selection of benchmarks should be reviewed regularly to ensure their relevance and usefulness.
- In a classification-type process, or one heavily reliant on generic descriptions or ladders, the definitions used, and particularly any examples quoted, should be reviewed similarly.
- In a computer assisted questionnaire based process, the standards are embodied in the computer algorithm, based on original benchmark evaluations. This should be tested periodically to ensure that it reflects any changes in the underlying values of the organisation.

PART III:
APPLICATIONS

11 Grading

To grade or not to grade?

In some job evaluation processes, particularly those involving some form of classification approach, a grade structure is determined at the outset, and individual jobs allocated directly into a grade, or at least into a job category or level which equates to a grade. In such cases, whether to use grades or not is not an issue – grading is an inbuilt assumption.

In other approaches, particularly analytical points based methods, the raw evaluation result is simply expressed as a number of points. In such cases, the first decision is whether, for pay structure purposes, individual evaluations are to be used or whether they are to be grouped together into grades.

For example, a points based job evaluation method might produce the following results for five jobs:

Job A	333 points
Job B	342 points
Job C	344 points
Job D	353 points
Job E	366 points

In an 'ungraded' approach these would be treated differently for pay purposes, each job being allocated its own unique pay level or pay range. In a graded structure, they may be grouped together as a single grade, with a common pay level or pay range.

There is no standard answer as to which is 'best', and both

approaches are used in practice by different organisations, or in many cases in different parts of the same organisation. The issues to be considered in reaching this decision include:

Administrative convenience

In the past, this was frequently used as an argument in favour of a graded structure particularly for large populations, since it undoubtedly requires fewer and simpler calculations and pay administration procedures than individual pay ranges. However now that most pay administration systems are computerised, there is really little weight in this argument, and the decision need not be based on pure administrative convenience.

Communication

Especially in large populations, it is undoubtedly easier to communicate the results of job evaluation and its implications for pay in terms of grades than in terms of raw points. Thus, for example, it is a relatively easy matter to communicate to the holders of jobs A to E in the above example:

> 'As a result of evaluating your jobs, your jobs are all
> in Grade 5, for which the pay range is x to y'.

Assuming that the grade structure was reasonably constructed, then jobs in the next grade up or down would typically be seen as clearly different, requiring only limited explanation of relativities. In contrast, in an ungraded structure it would be more difficult to explain, say to Jobholders A and B why their pay ranges were slightly different without fairly detailed explanation of the evaluation method and the reasons why Job B was evaluated 9 points higher. This distinction, of course, pre-supposes that a fairly high degree of disclosure of results is planned. If job evaluation is used purely as a management tool to help set pay levels with limited disclosure of anything other than the final implications for pay, then there is much less weight in the argument.

Individualism versus collectivism

A graded structure may be seen to reinforce a more collective view of jobs and roles than an ungraded one. Thus it may tend to communicate the message 'You are a Grade 6' rather than 'You are the Superintendent of the Machine Shop in the Leeds factory'. This may be undesirable if the aim is to increase individual identification with a specifically defined job. Conversely, it may be appropriate if the aim is to support identification with a particular level of work –

say in a professional/technical ladder, or in a skill based progression designed to increase flexibility of role and reduce identification with a particular job. This is linked to the next consideration.

How jobs are defined

If jobs are designed and defined as 'one-offs', each with a unique purpose and areas of accountability, then an ungraded structure which reflects this uniqueness is probably to be favoured. In contrast, if the emphasis is more on flexibly defined roles, then a grade structure which reflects the different levels of role which can be distinguished is probably more appropriate. Not surprisingly in this context, ungraded structures have mostly been applied at management levels, where jobs have typically been more structurally (and hence uniquely) defined. However, the issue is not simply one of pure job size: the nature of the role is what matters.

As an example, a major manufacturing company undertook the evaluation of all its jobs at middle and senior management levels and their equivalents in technical/professional roles. The structures adopted were ungraded for the line management jobs in the operating businesses to reinforce individual accountability. However a grade structure was developed for senior jobs in their technical and R&D units, since this was seen better to reflect the requirement for flexibility in an essentially project based environment, and avoid any tendency for constant re-evaluation of the detail of jobs as the project mix changed.

Performance orientation

Derived from the 'collectivism v individualism' issue, it is sometimes argued that an ungraded structure better supports a performance orientation since it promotes recognition of the job–person–performance relationship, which may get blurred in the more collective environment of a grade structure. This is only true up to a point, and depends essentially on how performance is defined for the particular jobs in question. If performance can (and should) be defined mainly in terms of achievements against specific targets or objectives, then the argument holds water. If, on the other hand, performance is expressed more in terms of the demonstration of appropriate levels of skill, knowledge or competencies, then the argument is reversed, and a graded structure may be seen to be more appropriate. Hence the argument that an ungraded structure better supports performance orientation is only really true for senior line management jobs, where performance is most likely to be objectives-driven.

Pressure on job evaluation

In ungraded structures the direct relationship between the detailed individual job size and the pay range adopted means that there may be increased pressure on the evaluation process as individuals try to get a few more points. The degree to which this is true will depend very much on the relative emphasis which job size is seen to have in the broader pay determining processes. Thus if little regard is given to individual performance in determining pay then, as discussed in earlier chapters, the only way for the individual to increase his/her pay is the job evaluation system. Clearly in such circumstances there will be pressure if the effect of getting a few more points is seen directly in pay. In a graded structure, there will be less general pressure of this kind, but it becomes concentrated at the grade boundaries, where the 'prizes' are correspondingly greater.

In practice, there is probably little to choose between the generalised pressure in an ungraded structure and the concentrated pressure in grades. If pressure on the evaluation system is a real problem, then the issue is much more fundamental than that of grading or not, and requires examination of the broader basis of pay determination and the relative role and emphasis of job evaluation within it.

Status or 'rank'

In some environments grade carries with it quite powerful connotations of status or rank. In itself this may not matter, but in extreme cases it may lead to distortions in evaluation and grading because of judgements being made about the characteristics of people in relation to the perceived requirements of a given 'rank' – quite at variance with real job content issues. Thus for example supervisory jobs may be undervalued because they are typically occupied by people promoted from the shop floor and not seen to equate to 'Grade X' type. Conversely other jobs may be overvalued because they are occupied by people judged to be 'of the right stuff'.

Obviously a grade structure does not create these circumstances, which are symptoms of deeper organisational attitudes to people, work and status which need to be addressed at source. However it may be easier to address them in the more neutral environment of an ungraded structure.

Natural groupings of jobs

Where jobs, and their evaluated sizes, fall into clear natural groupings, there are clear indications for a grade structure. Within each group, jobs would generally be perceived as 'similar' in level, and the differences between groups would be generally recognised.

Each group thus has a natural centre of gravity, different from the others, and only a minority of jobs fall at intermediate levels.

Conversely, if such natural groupings do not exist, then a grade structure is by no means precluded, but is more difficult to design, and to justify the sharp steps which it introduces.

History, culture and expectations

Most organisations have quite strong traditions about whether jobs are to be graded or not. Unless there is good reason to change this, then there is little to be gained from doing so. However, circumstances do exist where clear change in the 'tradition' is appropriate, in support of broader culture change objectives.

For example, an organisation replaced a graded structure for its middle management jobs, with an ungraded one, as part of a wider initiative aimed at sharpening managerial accountability and performance orientation, and breaking down a strong existing culture in which promotion through the grades was largely one of long service and good behaviour, rather than the job being done.

On the other hand, moving to a grade structure would be helpful in support of a requirement to increase flexibility and reduce detailed demarcation between individual jobs.

Grades for purposes other than basic pay structure

Even when grades are not used for the basic pay structure, boundaries based upon job evaluation results are frequently used to determine cut-off points for benefits (such as company cars) or to separate groups of jobs for which different terms and conditions of employment apply – for example notice period, nature of employment contract, etc.

In that the differences at such boundaries can be major (e.g. whether a car is provided or not is a significant step in the total remuneration package), such boundaries are often difficult to define, are in high focus and can cause concentrated pressure on the job evaluation system. Nevertheless, using job evaluation to determine any break-points which may be required is generally a more equitable, consistent and justifiable basis than alternatives such as reporting level, job title, or even less quantified means of expressing 'status'.

Grade design issues

If a grade structure is adopted, its design is critical: poor design can cause major boundary issues, can undo much good work which has gone into the job evaluation itself, and can generate a wide range of specific problems, including equal value problems. Some major issues which need to be addressed in developing a grade structure are listed below:

Common or different structures?

The first consideration is whether a single grade structure is to be developed to apply across all parts of the organisation, or whether separate structures are to be developed for different business units functions, departments or job categories. It is important to draw the distinction here between different *grade* structures and different *pay* structures. Even with a common *grade* structure, it is possible to attach different pay levels, ranges and progression arrangements to the same grade in different parts of the organisation, to reflect different market conditions and/or business economics. Thus for example an organisation may adopt a common grade structure but pay differently in its North of England operations from those based in the South East; or may pay business units differently based upon their profit performance. On an international scale, many multinational companies operate a common grade structure worldwide, but no-one would expect the pay for the same grade to be the same in the UK, Taiwan and the United States.

Our concern here is not whether different pay arrangements are developed, but whether fundamentally different *grade* structures should be used – i.e. different boundaries and/or grade widths in job size terms.

In the past, it was fairly common practice for different groups of jobs to have separate grade structures, usually based upon different evaluation/grading criteria. Thus in many manufacturing environments there were often separate grade structures for clerical staff, production operators, craft employees, supervisors, technicians, managers, etc. In many areas of the public sector there were similarly fragmented structures. Frequently, these separate structures were associated with different pay bargaining arrangements, with the result that there was little logic, equity or comparability between pay and grade in different groups. Not least, this has been a major cause of equal value problems when, as often happened, different groupings were associated with predominantly male or female employees.

Over recent years there have been two major trends in pay structure design, which at first sight appear to be contradictory, but on closer examination are seen to be mutually reinforcing.

Firstly, there has been a strong trend towards the integration of all aspects of employment conditions, including pay/grade structures, across different job groupings within organisations. Thus, multiple pay bargaining groups are being progressively replaced by single bargaining units, or at least greatly simplified arrangements. Previously fragmented grade structures based on separate employment categories are being replaced by integrated single grade structures, underpinned by a common job evaluation method. Such changes are driven by the more general move in most parts of the UK economy towards single status employment and a common basis for determining pay across the organisation, and reinforced by the recognition of equal value requirements.

In parallel with these integrative changes, there has been (and there is still continuing) a significant decentralisation of control of pay arrangements in most sectors. For example, in most parts of the private sector, there is major decentralisation to business units, divisions, subsidiary companies or sites. The privatisation of many utilities such as water, electricity supply and electricity generation has effectively separated and decentralised pay arrangements which were previously national and central; and in the public sector itself, there is widespread devolution of pay control to individual units – for example to the hospital trusts which have been generated within the NHS.

This decentralisation means that different grade structures may be developed by different units (even if underpinned by the same job evaluation method) to reflect their particular needs, organisation and job structures.

From this combination of events, what is emerging is a consolidation and integration of grade structures *within* units in an organisation, combined with a tendency to develop separate arrangements *between* units. Of course decentralisation of pay to units does not necessarily produce the need for different grade structures. Much depends on the degree to which decentralisation is really happening at a business level; the degree to which the organisation is trying to break the mould of centralised arrangements; and the degree to which there is a need to manage things like career development and staff moves between business units. One major multinational organisation for example has recently developed a common grade structure for worldwide application at all job levels, even though it is progressively decentralising business and pay control to its operating businesses, so as to maintain a strong corporate identity and grade 'language' throughout the organisation.

Determining grade boundaries

The objective of a grade structure is to group together those jobs which are of similar size, and separate those which are distinctly different. Thus the grade structure should, wherever possible, reflect the natural groupings of jobs which are seen to be present in the population. Because of this, grade structures and the positions of grade boundaries are best determined following evaluation – or at least following evaluation of a reasonable benchmark sample.

The implication of this is that there are no 'standard' positions for grade boundaries, even when a common evaluation method is used: boundaries need to be determined based upon inspection of actual evaluation results, the way they cluster, and the job groupings which they represent.

In some cases, the natural clustering of job evaluation results is strong, and the best positions for the grade boundaries are fairly clear. For example, Figure 11.1 shows a distribution of job sizes in which there are strong peaks (indicating job size clusters), and troughs at size ranges where few jobs have occurred. The troughs represent the best positions for the grade boundaries, since they separate the natural clusters and also give the least numbers of jobs in the contentious areas each side of the boundary. Conversely, drawing boundaries through the peaks would cut across natural clusters and would maximise boundary problems.

In principle, given such circumstances, there is no reason why boundaries should not be determined simply on this pragmatic basis. However, in most organisations there is a wish to build in some kind of logic or regularity to the grade widths and boundary positions, while still attempting to maintain the practical requirement to separate clusters. Such logic or regularity should mirror the underlying numbering basis of the job evaluation method used. Thus if arithmetic points scales are used, the grade boundaries should probably have an arithmetic relationship. If geometric scales are used, as for example in the Hay Guide Chart Profile method, then the grade boundaries should also demonstrate a geometric relationship.

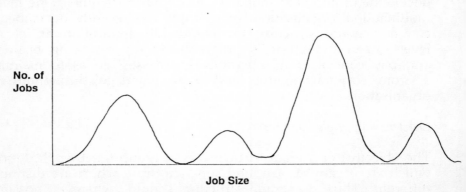

No. of Jobs

Job Size

Figure 11.1   Illustrative distribution of job size showing clear peaks and troughs.

Computer programs are now available which can search an evaluation listing for optimum grade structures, by identifying boundary positions which minimise the number of jobs close to the boundaries (i.e. find the troughs), consistent with a regular relationship between the boundary positions.

In other cases, the situation is more difficult, as natural peaks and troughs are not apparent. In such cases it is important to examine carefully the actual jobs in the population to identify which groups should be kept together and which should be separated – for example typically boss–subordinate relationships should be reflected in grade differences. Depending on the method of evaluation used, it may also be helpful to examine the detailed make-up of the evaluations factor by factor to see if this sheds any additional light on the natural groupings and divisions. Following this, alternative structures can be identified and examined, so as to select one which best reflects clusters of job type, and minimises contentious boundary separations.

Frequently, this type of uniform distribution without clear peaks or troughs is in fact a composite of a number of sub-distributions which separately do show peaks and troughs. This is illustrated in Figure 11.2, which shows an example where jobs in each function are clearly clustered, but the clusters occur at different job size levels. The aggregate distribution is thus much more uniform, without apparent peaks and troughs. In such circumstances, the 'ideal' grade structure say for the production function is different from the ideal structure to reflect the clusters in the research function. Assuming that a common grade structure is required, then a judgement needs to be taken as to what is the best compromise between the specific needs of each function. Analysing the aggregate population in this

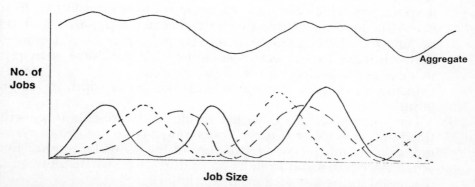

Figure 11.2   Illustrative distribution of job size for different functions.

way is helpful in arriving at this judgement logically and objectively, since it enables one to address questions like:

- Which cluster of production jobs most clearly belongs with which research cluster, which sales cluster, etc.?
- Which jobs must be kept together in the grade structure and which must be separated?
- Are there features in the detailed make-up of the evaluations in each sub-cluster which help determine which jobs naturally fall together?

A final, important, issue to bear in mind in determining grade boundaries, particularly where the natural positions are not self-evident, is the equal value requirement. Even if the evaluation method itself and the processes by which it is applied are entirely non-discriminatory, it is possible to arrive at a discriminatory result by inappropriate positioning of grade boundaries. For example, if a high proportion of jobs which turn out to be just below the chosen boundary are those typically occupied by women, then the structure could be seen to be biased. The fact that this may be entirely unintentional is no defence, if the bias is seen to be present in the actual structure. Hence grade structures should be carefully vetted from this perspective before finalisation and implementation.

Grade width and number of grades

In this context it is important to distinguish between grade width in job size terms – i.e. what range of job size is contained within a grade – from the size of any pay band which may be attached to the grade. The latter, the pay range associated with a grade, is to enable pay progression based upon criteria such as performance, length of service, skill acquisition or individual competence. It is *not* there to enable differences in job size to be reflected in pay within a grade. *The whole point about a grade structure is that for pay purposes, jobs within the grade are considered to be equal in size.* If this is not the desired aim, and fine difference in job size are required to be reflected, then a grade structure should not be used. Confusion between these two aspects is common, and the cause of frequent mis-use of grade structures and pay ranges.

In this discussion, our focus is on the grade width in job size terms.

For a given set of evaluation results, it is possible to generate finely tuned grade structures, containing a large number of narrow grades, or a much coarser structure of fewer, wider grades. Even when clear peaks and troughs occur in the job size distribution, as discussed in the last section, these options still exist.

For a fine structure, a grade may contain just one peak or cluster, with a boundary in every trough: coarser structures may contain two, three or more such clusters. As with virtually all aspects of pay structure design, there is no single 'right' answer: the choice depends both on the range of jobs involved and more particularly on what you want from the grade structure.

In the past, grade structures were typically characterised by a relatively large number of fairly narrow grades. In such structures the emphasis was on separating clusters of jobs from each other, rather than grouping clusters together. Since its use is widespread, and particularly because of the 'step-difference' concept on which it is built, the numbering pattern used in the Hay method will be used to describe such widths. Typically in the past grades have been constructed with widths of around one step – where one step represents a just perceptible difference, and two steps is a clear difference, often equating to a typical promotional interval in a traditional hierarchy.

Such structures satisfied well the needs of traditional hierarchical job structures: grade widths of less than a step would tend to cut through clusters of very similar jobs, whereas grades of two steps or more would tend to place many boss-subordinate relationships in the same grade – undesirable in classical pyramid job structures.

In the current environment, there is a growing tendency to develop coarser grade structures, comprising fewer, wider grades. Many organisations are currently reviewing their structures and seeking substantial simplification, often involving reducing the number of grades by up to a factor of two, in some cases even more. The reasons for this are the changes in organisational thinking described in earlier chapters, and further discussed here.

The first change of thinking is the de-layering of organisations to yield flatter structures. Care needs to be taken with this argument alone as the rationale for reducing the number of grades, since the number of grades does not necessarily equate to the number of levels in a reporting structure. A reporting structure of say five levels may be perfectly well represented (and may require) a grade structure of say 8 or 10 grades. In such a case, one department may have jobs at grades 1,3,5,7 and 9, while another may have jobs at grades 2,4,6,8 and 10. The confusion of grade with reporting position is widespread – in other words the assumption that a grade 1 has to report to a grade 2, which has to report to a grade 3, etc. In many organisations this has been the cause of artificially overlayered reporting structures, simply to use all the grades available.

A much more convincing argument for reducing the number of grades is the requirement in many organisations to increase job flexibility, promote teamwork and collaboration, reduce 'demarcation' and restrictive job design, and increase emphasis on skills, competencies and performance. In effect, a coarse structure of fewer, wider grades de-sensitises the pay structure to differences in job size. Moderate job size differences simply do not register, and only major and clear differences in size result in grade change. Thus, emphasis in the pay structure is shifted from job size consideration to managing pay progression within the pay range for the grade on whatever basis is seen to be appropriate – performance or skill/competency acquisition. The move to wider grades can provide positive support to the kind of changes in organisation, job design and culture which many businesses are undertaking. However, there are other implications, which need to be set against these organisational benefits:

Short-term cost

In moving from a structure of narrow grades to broader ones, there is likely to be a short-term implementation cost, due to the likelihood that some jobs gain an immediate pay increase on assimilation, while none are likely to receive a pay cut.

Cost potential

Wider grades are likely to be associated with bigger pay ranges to accommodate the desired pay progression based on performance/ skills/competence. Thus while short-term costs may be controlled by careful design of implementation arrangements, there is usually a longer term cost potential.

Ability to manage pay progression

The longer pay ranges which result put much more onus on the organisation's ability to manage pay progression, if cost drift and escalation is to be avoided. The evidence is that even with relatively narrow pay ranges, the ability of many organisations to manage such progression effectively is questionable, and the issue is more important the wider the ranges become. Organisations should only embark upon the introduction of wider grades with bigger pay ranges when they are confident that their performance management, skill assessment and/or competency assessment processes are sufficiently robust to take the extra strain. Without this confidence, cost escalation can result.

Therefore the judgement needs to be based upon an analysis of costs and benefits: the benefits in terms of greater productivity resulting from flexibility and skill/competency encouragement need to be seen to justify the actual and potential costs implied by a move to wider grades.

Change of grade relativities

In moving from narrow to wide grades, many jobs which were previously in different grades become graded together. Because of the status connotations of grade, this can cause significant employee reaction from individuals previously in the higher grade who feel 'downgraded' in relative terms now that they are put together with colleagues whom they previously thought of as lower grade. Such reaction needs to be anticipated and planned for if disruption and negative response is to be avoided. Of course it may be that an objective of the organisation, in going to wider grades, is in fact deliberately to break down such perceived status differences. As an example, a major company introduced a much coarser grade structure for its clerical staff quite explicitly for these reasons. Over time, in the old grade structure, a plethora of different jobs like 'senior clerk' had developed, often with ill defined relationships to the 'non-senior' clerks in the same area. The wider grade structure simplified the situation, so that only very clear job size differences were reflected in grade, and the features that justified 'seniority' – for example higher skill levels – were reflected directly in pay within the grade range.

In extreme cases, a structure of wider grades can produce a situation where boss–subordinate relationships come into the same grade. As organisations de-layer, the incidence of this will reduce, but some examples may still occur. If the reporting relationship between the two jobs is a real one, then placing them both in the same grade would generally be unacceptable. However, on examination, many such cases turn out to be less than full reporting relationships (like the clerk–senior clerk examples quoted above), in which case it may be appropriate to flush these out, and provide direct means of rewarding 'seniority' other than by largely unreal 'reporting'. What is required is careful examination of all specific cases which arise in any proposed structure, and appropriate design to minimise the number of real cases.

'Promotion'

For many years a widespread feature of UK practice has been 'reward by promotion'. This is not surprising, given that the facility to reward performance directly through pay has been very limited in many organisations in the past. Further, the culture in many UK organisations has in the past not been simply cash driven, but heavily influenced by considerations of status. (As an example, one company suffered extreme adverse reaction to a new job evaluation and grade structure, despite the fact that its employees were amongst the highest paid in the country, and the individual pay protection mechanisms that were agreed were comprehensive and long term: the issue was about disturbance to status and the disruption of understood 'promotion' routes.)

A structure of fewer, wider grades clearly reduces the number of grade promotions available, and the dwell time of an individual at any grade level is likely to be correspondingly higher. In parallel, the delayering of organisation structures similarly means that the number of hierarchical promotion steps available is less, and the dwell time at a given hierarchical level is extended. For individuals in a culture which expresses status in terms of hierarchical position and grade, this is a major culture shock, and while it may be a desirable and deliberate shock, it needs carefully managing through if disruption and demotivation are to be avoided.

Thus, in order to achieve the many positive benefits to be derived from broader grade structures in the right circumstances, clear processes for managing individual reward need to be put in place and communicated as the old props of grade status and hierarchical position are removed.

In summary, relatively narrow grades (corresponding for instance to 1–1.5 Hay steps) are probably most appropriate when jobs are largely structurally defined. Broader grades are indicated where the requirement is to support a move to greater job flexibility or the encouragement of skill/competency acquisition, and where jobs are defined in broader role terms. Where broader grades are used, particular attention needs to be given to the overall reward package, to ensure that emphasis is placed on appropriate aspects, and that cost drift is controlled.

12 Job Evaluation and Pay

Introduction

Throughout earlier chapters we have stressed that job evaluation does not in itself determine pay, and that a wide range of considerations beyond job size need to be taken into account in developing pay policies and practices. These are complex subjects in their own right and beyond the scope of this book.

Nevertheless, it is appropriate to provide some practical guidance on how job evaluation results can be used to help analyse pay practices and develop pay structures, recognising that other perspectives and issues need to be taken into account. This chapter provides such practical advice, together with a conceptual framework for pay policy which positions job evaluation in relation to these other perspectives, and the processes which are required to manage them.

Using job evaluation data to analyse pay practices

Having completed a job evaluation exercise, there is great temptation to rush straight into pay structure design, and produce the structure which is theoretically best, but careful thought should be given before such action is taken. Before, during and after conducting job evaluation in the organisation its employees are being paid, and an important consideration in pay determination for the future is understanding where you are starting from now. While this should not divert attention from deriving the ideal policies and structures, it profoundly affects the practicalities of getting there, and the time and costs likely to be involved.

Job evaluation results can be used to provide useful insights into current pay arrangements, and help build a clear picture of the starting point for future policy development.

Scattergrams

A widely used way of using job evaluation results for this purpose is to plot the current pay for each job against its evaluated job size – assuming that some form of points based job evaluation method has been used. Plots of this kind are usually referred to as scattergrams, and an example is illustrated in Figure 12.1.

Assuming that there is broad correlation between pay and job size – i.e. bigger jobs generally are paid more than smaller ones – then the scattergram will show the upward trend illustrated.

The detailed form of the scattergram depends both on the nature of the pay practice and the nature of the job size points scales used. Where there is a strong pay–job size relationship, the scatter typically has a linear form, when a geometric points scale is used, as for example in the Hay method. Arithmetic scales can produce curved relationships which are more difficult to analyse statistically,

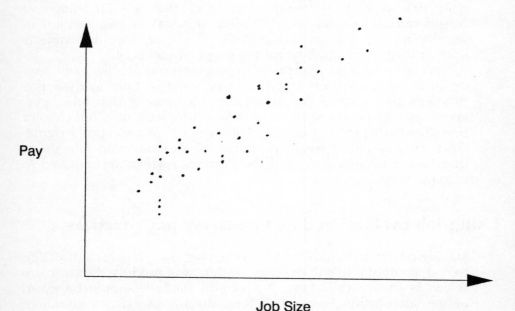

Figure 12.1   Scattergram of pay for individual jobs plotted against evaluated job size.

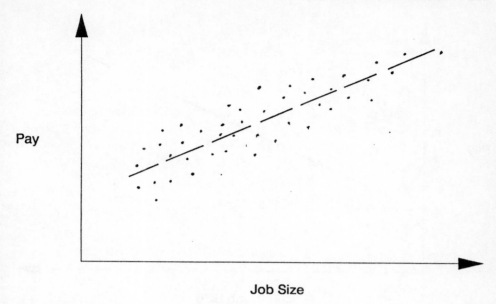

Pay

Job Size

Figure 12.2   Scattergram showing Line of Central Tendency (LCT).

so, for simplicity, the examples discussed below assume a geometric points scale of the Hay type.

With a scatter of broadly linear form, it is common practice to analyse the relationship statistically to calculate the line of central tendency, LCT (or line of best fit), using regression analysis, as illustrated in Figure 12.2. This line of central tendency is sometimes referred to as a 'practice line', though it must be noted that it only reflects the pay–job size relationship in the actual practice of the organisation.

Examination of the scattergram can give powerful insights into current practice, as illustrated in a few examples below.

Figure 12.3 (see p. 162)

In this case, there is almost a perfect correlation between pay and job size. This means that other factors like performance or market circumstances are having no effect at all. This would be symptomatic of pay arrangements wholly driven by job size, the defects of which were outlined in earlier chapters.

Figure 12.4 (see p. 162)

This represents a less extreme situation, where there is broad pay–job size correlation, but a fair amount of scatter. To understand

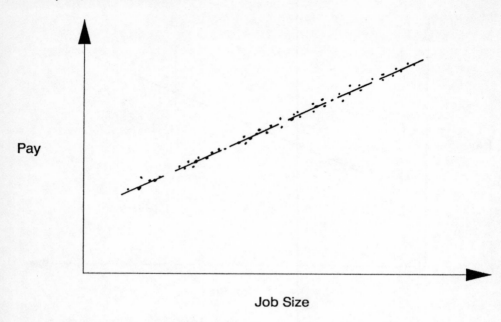

Figure 12.3   Scattergram showing very close correlation between pay and job size, with little apparent pay influence from other factors.

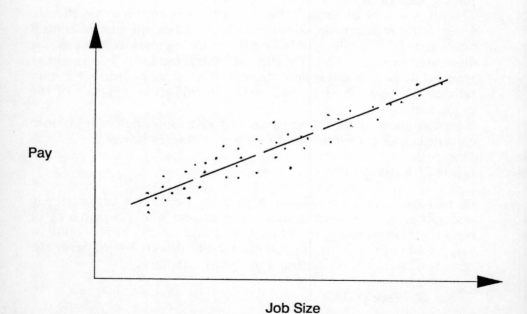

Figure 12.4   Scattergram with broad job size–pay relationship, but some scatter.

what such a relationship represents, it is important to analyse the scatter itself, to see if it is simply random, or whether it reflects other components of pay. For example, if pay is genuinely performance driven, one would expect the jobs above the LCT to be occupied predominantly by high performers: is this the case? Or are all the jobs above the LCT occupied by long serving employees, which would indicate pay for length of service?

Such further analysis might indicate, for example, that jobs in the sales function were paid typically above the LCT, while those in production were typically below. In this case, we would need to ask questions like:

- Is this intentional, and appropriate?
- Are the sales people typically higher performers than the production people?
- Or are they rated as higher performers because of inconsistent performance appraisal?
- Or are they just older?
- Or is it a response to a market situation, perhaps with a nationally dispersed sales force, but production located in a low market pay area?

We would need to understand issues like this, in order to consider the practical implications of whatever new pay arrangements were to be introduced.

In another case, it may be that jobs above the LCT are typically occupied by male employees while those below are typically female, in which case the analysis has revealed a clear equal value problem which needs to be addressed.

Figure 12.5

In this case, there is little apparent pay–job size relationship. A line of central tendency is not shown, since the statistical correlation is very low.

It is too easy to interpret such a situation over-simplistically, as a 'mess'. What it actually means is simply that whatever is driving current pay is not job size, as measured by the particular job evaluation method employed. It may be that the driving force is performance, age, perceived status, the result of 'buying' in individuals in a volatile market, etc. Whatever it is, it is profoundly important to understand it, before constructing a pay structure which gives a strong pay–job size relationship, since this would represent a major culture change requiring very careful implementation and management.

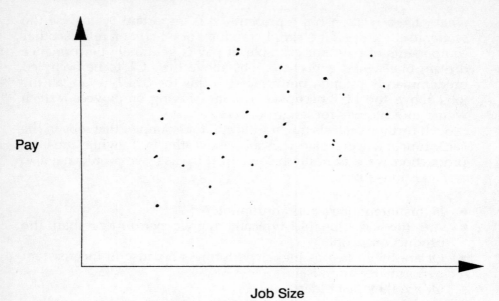

Figure 12.5   Scattergram showing little correlation between pay and job size.

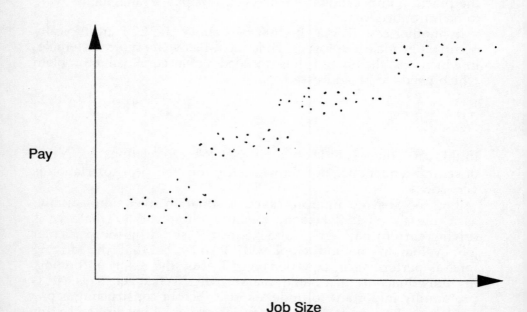

Figure 12.6   Scattergram showing evidence of an existing four grade structure.

Figure 12.6

This scattergram shows clear evidence of an existing grade structure in which there is good correlation between existing grade and job size. Such a grade structure may be explicit, or informal and implicit. Either way, it is important to know that current pay is clearly organised into four grades before designing a pay structure based on three, five or six grades.

Figure 12.7

This example also shows clear evidence of four existing grades (explicit or implicit), but in this case, the correlation between current grade and job size is much weaker, as shown by the horizontal overlap between the grade clusters. The shape of these clusters also shows evidence that many jobs are paid at one of four specific pay levels – probably grade maxima. Introduction of a grade structure (even one of four grades) based on job size will cause significant change in existing grade relativities, and will need careful management, particularly since many jobholders already appear to be paid at existing grade maximum.

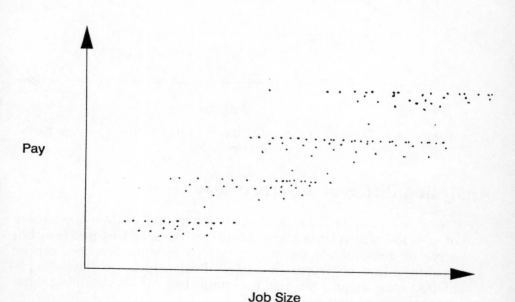

Figure 12.7   Scattergram showing evidence of four grade structure. Existing grades poorly correlated to job size, and pay concentrated at grade maxima.

Figure 12.8

In this example, the relationship clearly shows two parts. Up to a certain job size, the rate of progression of pay with increasing job size is fairly rapid – i.e. there is a clear positive slope to the graph. Beyond this point the relationship flattens, indicating that further increases in job size result in only small pay increases. Such relationships are not uncommon – for example in parts of the public sector – and indicate a situation where there is little financial incentive for employees to take on bigger responsibilities beyond a certain point.

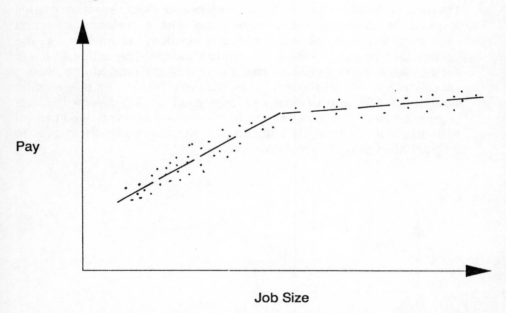

Figure 12.8   Scattergram showing different pay practices for two parts of the population.

Analysing different aspects of pay

The above examples are clearly only illustrative of the wide variety of pay–job size relationships which are observed in practice, but serve to demonstrate the way in which existing practices can be examined and analysed. In all the illustrations, we have simply plotted 'pay' against job size for simplicity, without defining what components of pay are included.

Further insights into pay practice can be obtained by analysing separately the various components of pay package, and their relationships to job size. Thus quite different relationships may be observed for base pay (i.e. basic wage or salary), and for total

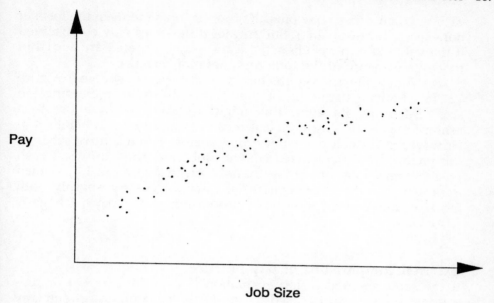

Figure 12.9(a)   Basic scattergram showing progressive flattening of the pay–job size relationship.

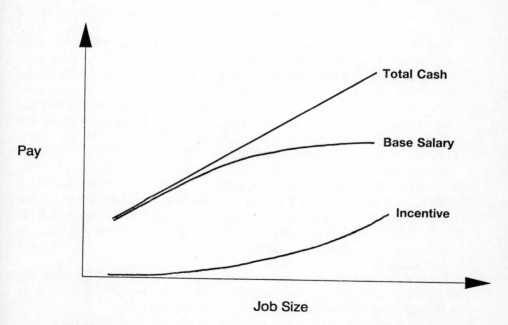

Figure 12.9(b)   Pay–job size relationship showing flattening of base salary line, counteracted by progressively increasing incentive. Total cash is sum of base salary plus incentive payment.

cash payments (base pay plus all other cash payments in the form of bonuses, incentives, etc.). Still further differences may be observed if the value of non-cash benefits (cars, pensions, etc.) are added in to give a measure of the total remuneration practice.

As a simple illustration, the base pay scattergram shown in Figure 12.9(a) shows a flattening of the relationship with increasing job size. Taken on its own, this might indicate (as in a previous example) a decreasing financial incentive to take on a bigger job. However, if the company concerned operated an incentive scheme, the payout of which increased with job size, then the total cash position may look more like that shown in Figure 12.9(b), which indicates that the overall financial reward goes up sharply with job size, but that an increasing proportion of the pay package is 'at risk'.

External comparisons of pay practice

If the same method of job evaluation is used in different organisations, then it can be used as the basis for comparing their pay practices on a like-for-like basis. This improves considerably the validity of external comparisons, which otherwise have to be based on methods like comparisons using job titles (which can mean very different things in different organisations) or direct job matching, which has some of the same problems and is limited to types of jobs which are common to different organisations.

The Hay job evaluation method is extensively used for this purpose both in the UK and internationally, and Hay maintain pay databases and conduct regular pay market surveys which use job size as the basis for comparisons. An example of a market pay chart from such a survey is shown in Figure 12.10, in which the base salary practices of a large group of organisations have been analysed at different job size levels, and expressed in terms of the observed median, upper and lower quartiles, and upper and lower deciles.

Using such data, the existing pay practice of an organisation can be compared directly with an appropriate 'cut' of the market data relating to a relevant segment of the market, to gain a view of the overall competitiveness. In the example illustrated in Figure 12.11, it is clear that the organisation has a highly competitive practice for smaller jobs, but appears to pay at a relatively low level in relation to the market for senior jobs.

Understanding both these external market relationships and the internal pay relationships described earlier are important first steps in developing future pay policies for an organisation.

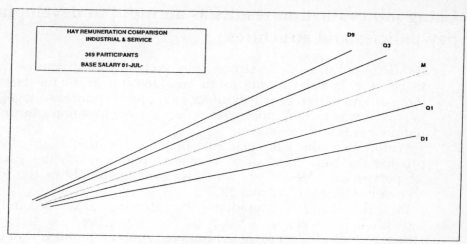

UNITS OF JOB CONTENT

Example of market pay chart
analysing the base salary
practices of a group of
companies, using job size
as the means of comparison.

Figure 12.10

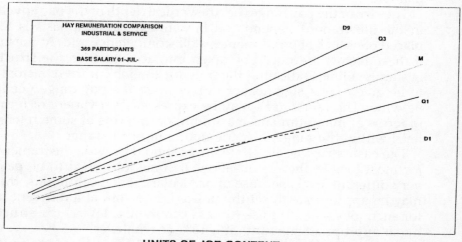

UNITS OF JOB CONTENT

Market chart with a company's
current practice superimposed
(dashed line).

Figure 12.11

Using job evaluation results as an input to developing pay policies and structures

As discussed in earlier chapters, pay policies and structures need to be built in such a way as to take account of all the factors, internal and external, which affect pay, and to put these together in such a way as to support and reflect the organisation's business requirements and emphases.

Within this, the particular role of job evaluation is usually to provide the basic framework to reflect internal relativities from a *job* perspective. Hence pay structures are frequently of the form shown in Figures 12.12 and 12.13.

In Figure 12.12 – ungraded – the structure takes account of individual job size, as evaluated. For any given job size, the structure indicates a pay range between minimum and maximum, within which actual pay is set and progressed based on whatever considerations of performance, skill, competency, etc. are deemed to be appropriate in the particular organisation's pay arrangements. The level at which the pay envelope is pitched takes account of the principal pay market in which the organisation operates, and the organisation's economics, performance, ability to pay, future requirements and current practices.

The slope of the pay envelope depends on the size of pay differentials which the organisation wishes to have between jobs of different sizes, taking into account both internal business-driven needs, and the kind of relationships typically found in the external market.

The size of the pay range (i.e. the vertical depth of the pay envelope in the illustration) depends on how much pay emphasis is to be placed on issues of performance, skill, competency, etc. At the limit, if these factors are not to be taken into account then the structure is simply a line, indicating the 'rate for the job'. If these factors are to be given great significance in pay, then the pay range needs to be wide. The range itself may be expressed in a variety of forms – in terms of minimum and maximum, or in terms of some reference level within the range, e.g. the midpoint of the range.

The basic structure illustrated here should provide the framework for most jobs in the organisation. If some jobs need to be paid at very different levels because of particular market conditions, then it may be appropriate to set the policy framework at a different level for such jobs – i.e. to raise (or less commonly, lower) the structure by an appropriate amount, 5%, 10% or whatever.

In the second case illustrated in Figure 12.13, a graded structure is used. The issues of establishing the grade structure itself in job size terms have already been discussed. The issues of setting the pay ranges associated with each grade are exactly the same as those

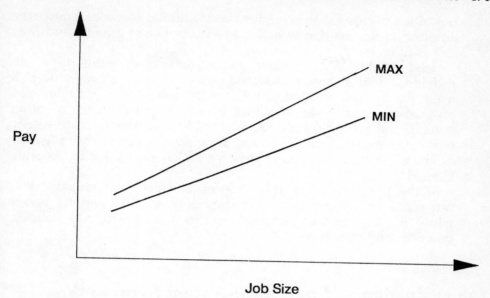

Figure 12.12   Typical ungraded salary structure showing maximum and minimum of pay range. Each job size has its own unique pay range, derived from this envelope.

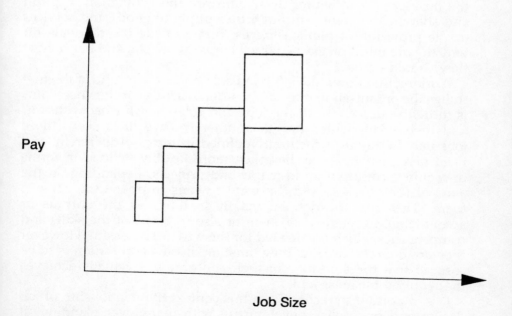

Figure 12.13   Typical graded salary structure. Each grade contains a range of job sizes. Each grade has its own minimum and maximum.

.

described in case (a) above, plus the additional consideration of the amount of pay overlap which is to exist between grades, and how this is to be used.

Used flexibly and sensibly, pay structures of either type can provide a logical and reasonable basis for pay determination. If used rigidly and mechanistically, with too little regard for pay progression within the structure based on performance or other criteria, and with too little regard for variations required to satisfy particular market needs, then the approach is open to the criticisms discussed in earlier chapters, and for which job evaluation is often blamed.

In the final section of this chapter, a conceptual framework is provided, showing the relationship between the various issues which need to be taken into account in determining pay policies, practices and structures.

Job evaluation and pay: a conceptual framework

This is summarised in Figure 12.14. In the explanation of this which follows, the numbers in parentheses refer to the numbered boxes on the chart.

Pay determination must begin from the aims and objectives of the business (1). Whether these aims are the generation of profit and shareholder wealth through the supply of goods and services or the provision of public services, they provide the rationale for why the organisation exists, why it employs people, and hence how they should be paid.

Working first down the left hand side of the chart, one of the first things the organisation must do in order to achieve its business aims is to define in some way the jobs and roles which exist within it, and their relationships one to another. As we have seen, these jobs may be highly structurally defined in terms of hierarchy and fixed tasks, or they may be much more flexibly defined in terms of required contribution to teams and projects, depending on the aims of the business and the way it needs to operate to achieve them. They may be defined mainly in terms of the outputs or accountabilities required of them or also in terms of the skills and competencies which are needed for them to be successful. However they are defined, defined they must be, if the organisation is to be assured that the sum total of their contributions actually achieves the required business aims.

It is important to recognise in this context the relationship of job design and pay policy development with manpower planning. If jobs are defined in such a way as to need more of them to achieve the same result, then for a given financial resource, the pay available

JOB EVALUATION AND PAY

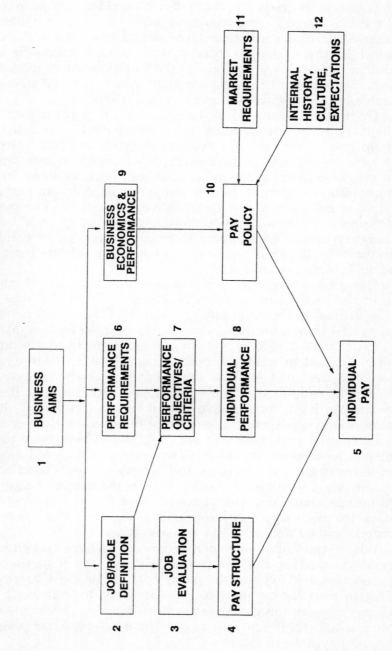

Figure 12.14   Job evaluation and pay.

per job is less. Hence in job definition, both the nature of the jobs and the number of jobs are both important, and inter-related.

Continuing down the left hand track, job definition (2) provides the raw material for job evaluation, which as we have seen considers the relative size or importance of each job, and provides a basic framework for pay structure (4) as described earlier in this chapter, which in turn feeds into individual pay determination (5). If that is all that happens, we are back to the situation where job size is the only determinant of pay, a situation which is unsatisfactory, and increasingly recognised as such by organisations.

The business aims (1) also determine the performance requirements of the business and its constituent parts (6). As with the aims themselves, they may take a variety of forms, and may be expressed in terms of financial performance, growth, market penetration, etc. or maybe in terms of service standards or similar criteria. Within an organisation, different units may have quite different performance requirements – not just quantitative differences, but qualitative differences as well, with 'performance' meaning totally different things. A critical requirement in building any kind of performance relationship to pay is first to clarify what is meant by 'performance' at the business or unit level.

The establishment of performance objectives or criteria at the individual level (7) needs to be based both on the way the job was defined in the first place (2), and the way overall performance is viewed from a business, unit, or function viewpoint (6).

Thus, as discussed previously, where performance is predominantly defined in terms of 'hard' output (profit, volume, etc.) *and* jobs are designed so that these criteria can be translated in a valid way to individual job level, then performance is likely to be defined in hard, quantitative output terms. Conversely, if overall performance is expressed more in terms of quality of service, or if the jobs in a particular area are designed to be service providers, then individual performance criteria are more likely to be expressed in terms of the competencies and behaviours associated with high quality service provision. Again, if the performance of a unit is seen to be principally dependent on whether the members of the unit have the necessary technical skills to operate, then performance criteria will be dominated by consideration of skills.

When (and only when) performance objectives and criteria have been clarified at the individual level (7), assessment of actual performance in relation to these criteria can be undertaken (8). This in turn can be used to provide input to individual pay (5), through one or more of the enormous range of mechanisms which are available for linking pay to performance – base pay progression, 'merit' pay, incentives, etc.

The third main strand derived from an understanding of the business and its aims (1) is the issue of hard economics – what it is possible and appropriate for the business to afford in terms of pay (9). In this context it should be remembered that in most organisations pay is one of the major cost items, and in some it is the dominant cost.

What the business can pay is partly a function of its performance, partly to do with its policies and practices on staffing levels (i.e. number of people), and partly a function of its basic economics. Different industries for example have quite different economic structures, and a useful way of illustrating this is to use the concept of the added value generated by an organisation, and which is used to pay its people, its investors, for reinvestment and to pay taxation. The added value generated per employee varies considerably between different industry types. For example, in light engineering manufacturing, the added value per employee is modest, and a high proportion of total added value is used on pay – i.e. it is labour intensive. In contrast, the oil industry generates higher added value per employee, but despite having typically higher pay levels, expends a lower proportion of its added value on pay – more being required for re-investment. Thus if a light engineering company attempted to pay oil-sector pay levels, the likelihood would be that the pay bill would exceed the total added value, and the company would very quickly end up in receivership.

The situation in non-profit making and public sector bodies is parallel, though different in detail. Whatever its purpose and ownership, any organisation has finite income, and only a proportion of this income which can be spent on pay. Pay levels which exceed the finance available are untenable. Hence, one of the major issues which feeds into pay policy determination (10) is the economics of the business (9).

But consideration of pay policy is not simply a matter of internal finance and economics. A second major input is the external pay market situation (11), which influences the pay levels which need to be paid to attract and retain the kind of people needed. As explained, the 'market' may be complex and heterogeneous, producing different considerations in different functions, business sectors and locations.

The third set of inputs to pay policy (10) are to do with the existing pay practices, history of pay, culture and attitudes to pay, and pay expectations which are present within the organisation. Pay policies either need to reflect these or, if the intention is to change them, support the change process in a measured and careful way. In practice, determining pay policy (10) requires the careful balancing of the economic requirements (9), market demands (11), and internal cultural requirements (12).

To summarise: Figure 12.14 illustrates a recurring theme of this book, that job evaluation is an important, but in itself incomplete,

input to pay determination. If it were missing from the considerations shown in Figure 12.14, then perspective of jobs and
their internal relative worth is lost. On the other hand, if it
dominates, then the significance of all the other vital issues involved
is diminished, and pay arrangements become mechanistic, and
unrelated to the real needs of the business.

13 Equal Pay and Job Evaluation

The impact of equal pay legislation

Paying women at the same rate as men for like work became a legal requirement in the UK under the Equal Pay Act 1970 which came into force in 1975. An issue avoided at that time was the enforcement of equal pay for work of equal value. This deficiency proved to be in contravention of the European Economic Community's Directive on Equal Pay, and was made good by the Government of the day with the equal value amendment to the Equal Pay Act which came into effect on 1 January 1984. Under this amendment women are entitled to equal pay with men (and vice versa) where the work is of equal value in terms of the demands of the job – 'for instance, effort, skill and decision'.

From that time employers have faced claims which cut across job families, occupational groups and bargaining units forcing comparison of intrinsic job content. Traditional – but under the terms of the amendment discriminatory – pay differentials have been questioned and upset. Neither the market value of jobs nor any internal disruption over differentials caused by a successful claim can come into the argument. There is no period of grace for employers facing increased employment costs, and inability to pay provides no defence.

Since 1984 there have been over 5000 claims to industrial tribunals claiming equal pay for work of equal value. In 1990 alone there were around 400 applications involving 32 employers (two-thirds of these applications were confined to two major clearing banks). The way the legislation is worded is complex and the processes put in place to hear equal value claims (see Figure 13.1 illustrating the tribunal stages; see p. 182) are complicated, time-consuming and costly. If this were not the case then there is no doubt that the number of claims would have been considerably greater.

At present, claims are mainly confined to those supported to establish precedents by major trade unions willing to bear the (considerable) cost of taking a case to tribunal – and beyond. As it is, many of the claims have been settled outside the formal process once the potential time and cost involved in pursuing a case has become clear.

Equal value is an area of major concern to many UK employers. Industries where claims have been upheld include:

- Retailing.
- Shipbuilding.
- Vehicle manufacture and distribution.
- Most types of manufacturing.
- Banking and insurance.
- Chemicals.
- Public services, e.g. local authorities, Post Office.
- Electricity supply.

Job comparisons that have led to successful claims have been mainly concentrated among more junior/support/technical roles. Typically they have compared traditionally 'female' jobs with traditionally 'male' ones – the expected areas of vulnerability where the market itself has been discriminatory, e.g.

- Divan cover machinists with quilting machine operator.
- Packer with labourer.
- Administration assistant in chief engineer's department with administration assistant in estate department.
- Clerical grades with kit marshaller, storeperson and tool storeperson.
- Print finishers with printers and guillotine operators.
- Computer operators/clerks with machine operators.
- Cook with painter, joiner and thermal insulation engineer.
- Accounts controller with applications engineer,
- Typists/secretaries with messengers.
- Cashiers with doorman.
- Laboratory assistant with laboratory technician.

Because of the time taken to take cases through tribunal – let alone appeals before the Employment Appeal Tribunal and the House of Lords – equal value is an area where case law has been slow to develop. Its development requires careful monitoring, and readers are strongly advised to keep up to date with rulings as they occur. (These are regularly and well reported in publications such as *IDS*

Brief and the *IRS Equal Opportunities Review* which does a full review of developments in the July/August issue each year). Our purpose here is to illustrate the issues as they affect job evaluation, not to provide a legal guide through a complicated and sensitive area of employment law.

Many would like to see change. It is not the place of this book to evaluate the criticisms emanating from various interest groups, but it can be said that the law as it stands reflects a rigid and somewhat idealistic view of job evaluation as it was practised in the 1970's. Inevitably this perception bears little relation to many of the processes and practices at the leading edge of job evaluation described in the rest of this book.

The implications for job evaluation

Job evaluation is central to the consideration of equal value claims because the jobs being compared must, by definition, be evaluated by some method to determine their relative value. Claims can be made whether a job evaluation scheme exists in the organisation concerned or not. An employer may defend a case on the basis that the job of the applicant has been evaluated as smaller than the job of the comparator. If a job evaluation method is used as a defence, the onus is on that employer to prove that the scheme meets the legal requirement to be an analytical approach which is free from sex bias in both design and implementation.

Equal value considerations have subjected many existing job evaluation systems to a level of scrutiny for which they were never intended. The legislation forces comparison of the content of jobs where neither employers nor union pressure might previously have demanded it. Many organisations with an old, decayed, unintentionally discriminatory system, or sometimes simply no current approach to job evaluation, are therefore at risk to an equal value claim. Many are also anxious to overhaul current approaches or implement a scheme which will help them put their house in order.

The hard message of experience to date is that a successful equal value claim against an employer means much more than meeting the costs of legal advice and paying compensation/back pay to the claimant(s). It is bad for any organisation's business reputation and its internal culture and climate, and is hardly an advertisement designed to attract, retain and motivate high quality employees.

Unless claims can be dismissed at or before the preliminary hearing or prehearing assessment, tribunals are required to commission a report by an 'independent expert' – drawn currently from a list of a dozen academics and consultants appointed by ACAS (the Advisory Conciliation and Arbitration Service). Independent experts then apply their own analytical approach to the assessment of equal value. These are often developed specifically for the requirements of the case, and on average independent experts take around a year to produce a report. They do not usually use numerical systems to assess job demands and avoid factor weighting. Independent experts typically use descriptive level definitions such as low, medium, high, against between five to seven factors. For example those used in *Bromley and others* v *H&J Quick* were:

- Knowledge
- Experience
- Judgement and decision-making
- Contacts
- Physical effort
- Consequence of errors

The tribunal stages of an equal value case are set out in Figure 13.1 (see p. 181).

Major case decisions as they affect job evaluation

Of the 80 or so cases referred to independent experts between 1984 and 1991, only a handful have produced decisions which affect job evaluation design and/or implementation. In outline, the cases and implications are as follows:

Hayward v *Cammell Laird (House Of Lords, 1988)*

The first successful case under the Equal Value Amendment was a cook Julie Hayward, who in 1984 claimed equal value with three male comparators – a painter, a joiner and a thermal insulation engineer. The independent expert appointed to examine the relative value of the work concluded that the cook's work was of equal value to the male comparators. The tribunal accepted this conclusion and ordered the employers to raise Hayward's pay in line with the pay of the comparators. The company refused to pay, arguing that a variety of benefits (sickness benefits, meals, meal breaks and extra holidays) to which she was entitled should be offset in the difference in base pay levels.

When the case reached the House of Lords it was held that a successful equal pay claimant is entitled to have each distinct term in his/her contract so that it is no less favourable than the corresponding term in his/her comparator's contract. Julie Hayward therefore gained equal basic pay and retained the additional benefits applicable to her job.

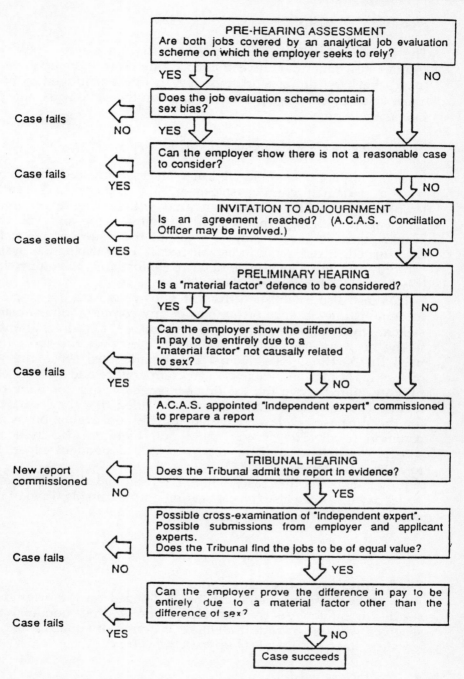

Figure 13.1   An equal value case: Tribunal stages.

Pickstone v Freemans (House Of Lords, 1988)

The significant ruling in this case was that employers could not counter a (woman operative's) equal value claim in comparison to (male checkers) doing work in a higher rate but judged to be of equal value by employing a 'token' man on the same work and pay rate as the woman.

Bromley and others v H&J Quick (Court Of Appeal, 1988)

In this complex case, nine clerical workers compared themselves with a partsman counter salesman and a parts clerk, and a telephonist/receptionist was compared with a van driver and a car cleaner. Although the detailed anatomy of the job evaluation system used by the employers was not the issue on which this case turned, it did serve to establish that a job evaluation system can only provide a legitimate defence against an equal value claim if it is analytical in nature.

This case also established that the onus rests with the employer to demonstrate absence of sex bias in any common job evaluation system which is to be relied on as a defence. It also drew attention to the need for exercising considerable care over the procedures used for 'slotting' jobs against benchmark jobs. Since the jobs of the applicants and their chosen comparators had neither been fully evaluated using the existing scheme's factors nor were they identical to the benchmark jobs, it was ruled that they were not, for the purposes of law, 'covered' by the job evaluation system common to all. The system could not, therefore, be used as a satisfactory defence and the report of an independent expert had to be commissioned.

Judgements in other cases where the claim failed and in straight equal pay cases can also have a bearing on the consideration of new equal value claims.

Discriminatory job evaluation
Any job evaluation scheme can be challenged on the grounds of sex discrimination. As we have already pointed out non-analytical schemes will not provide a defence in terms of equal value. The issues at stake for analytical approaches can be:

- The factors used.
- Any weightings attached to the factors chosen.
- Any element in the whole process of implementation and evaluation which is deemed to produce discrimination.

Example of discriminatory job factors

Factors	Maintenance Fitter	Company Nurse
(each factor is scored on a scale from 1 to 10) (for simplicity no weights have been applied)		
Skill		
Experience in job	10	1
Training	5	7
Responsibility		
For money	0	0
For equipment & machinery	8	3
For safety	3	6
For work done by others	3	0
Effort		
Lifting requirement	4	2
Strength required	7	2
Sustained physical effort	5	1
Conditions		
Physical environment	6	0
Working position	6	0
Hazards	7	0
Total	**64**	**22**

This set of factors is discriminatory because it contains many aspects of the male job and very few relating to the female job. There is also double counting, for example 'strength required' and 'lifting required' would frequently have similar scores, either high or low. See p. 184.

Figure 13.2   Example of discriminatory job factors.

The importance of factor choice

It is therefore essential to ensure that the choice of factors for any job evaluation scheme are representative of the whole range of work being evaluated, both men's jobs and women's jobs. To help employers and others concerned with job evaluation the Equal Opportunities Commission gives the example of discriminatory job factors shown in Figure 13.2.

This set of factors is discriminatory because it contains many aspects of the male job and very few relating to the female job. There is also double counting, for example 'strength required' and 'lifting required' would frequently have similar scores, either high or low. Figure 13.3 shows what in the EOC's opinion are less biased job evaluation factors.

Factor weighting

A scheme may also discriminate in the factor weightings used. Bias will creep in if the factors on which a male job scores highly are given higher weights than the factors on which a female job scores highest (or vice versa). Those accountable for designing schemes should review the factors with the highest and lowest weight to ensure that these can be justified and are not likely to favour jobs held by one sex.

The EOC example in Figure 13.4 shows how discriminatory factor weights produce a biased evaluation of the two jobs.

A single integrated scheme is advisable

The most effective method of ensuring a remuneration structure is unbiased is to evaluate all jobs using a common approach. This should provide vertical coverage from the largest to the smallest job and horizontal coverage across all occupational groups.

Indeed, the *relative* value of jobs throughout the organisation cannot be fully understood unless the measurement is by a single analytical method of job evaluation.

Where there are different methods of job evaluation covering different jobs, it is important that the 'read across' of the functions and jobs is understood. This can best be achieved by selecting a sample of jobs covered by different methods and evaluating them using a single analytical method which is appropriate to all jobs.

Example of non-discriminatory job factors

Factors	Maintenance Fitter	Company Nurse
(each factor is scored on a sale from 1 to 10) (for simplicity no weights have been applied)		
Basic knowledge	6	8
Complexity of task	6	7
Training	5	7
Responsibility for people	3	8
Responsibility for materials & equipment	8	6
Mental effort	5	6
Visual attention	6	6
Physical activity	8	5
Working conditions	6	1
Total	**53**	**54**

Figure 13.3   Example of non-discriminatory job factors.

Example of discriminatory factor weighting

Factors	Unweighted Scores Fitter	Unweighted Scores Nurse	Biased Weights	Weighted Scores Fitter	Weighted Scores Nurse	Un-Biased Weights	Weighted Scores Fitter	Weighted Scores Nurse
Basic knowledge	6	8	7%	0.42	0.56	5%	0.30	0.40
Complexity of task	6	7	8%	0.48	0.56	15%	0.90	1.05
Training	5	7	7%	0.35	0.48	15%	0.75	1.05
Responsibility for people	3	8	15%	0.45	1.20	15%	0.45	1.20
Responsibility for materials & equipment	8	6	15%	1.20	0.90	15%	1.20	0.90
Mental effort	5	6	8%	0.40	0.48	10%	0.50	0.60
Visual attention	6	6	10%	0.60	0.60	10%	0.60	0.60
Physical activity	8	5	15%	1.20	0.75	10%	0.80	0.50
Working conditions	6	1	15%	0.90	0.15	5%	0.30	0.05
Total	**53**	**54**		**6.00**	**5.66**		**5.80**	**6.35**

Figure 13.4   Example of discriminatory factor weighting.

Guidelines for implementation

Establishing and maintaining effective, non-discriminatory remuneration practices involves a number of key elements. A good example of the way in which the major aspects of the process surrounding implementation and the maintenance of these is contained in the Hay Management Consultants Code of Practice on Equal Pay for Work of Equal Value. The guidelines it gives are, in essence, those which would be regarded as appropriate to ensure fair treatment between individuals across any job or occupational groups, divisions or departments within an organisation. They reflect a fairly conventional job evaluation process but that may well be what is needed in areas where vulnerability to equal value claims is likely. In essence, the code says:

Involve women in the process

Women should be involved at all stages of the introduction and maintenance of job evaluation. The proportions of men and women involved should reflect the proportions employed across the organisation. If it is difficult to persuade women to become involved, and it often is, education and encouragement should be provided. This should emphasise the importance of active participation to minimise the risk of sex bias by ensuring all aspects of women's jobs are given full consideration.

Train all those concerned in equal value issues

All individuals involved should be thoroughly trained, not only in the techniques and approaches involved but also how to avoid sex bias at all stages of designing and implementing a job evaluation scheme. Job evaluation involves judgements and individuals will make judgements based on their own values – often discrimination is unconscious. Those involved must therefore be made aware of how sex bias can creep in however unintentionally.

Ensure balanced steering and review arrangements

The steering panel, responsible for planning and coordinating the introduction and maintenance of job evaluation, should have representation from all 'interested' parties. Both men and women should be involved and representatives of all parties should be open minded.

Prevent bias in job analysis and in job description

Because the prime source of information for job evaluation is typically job descriptions, it is as important that the compilation and presentation of job descriptions be free of sex bias. A uniform format should be used for all jobs. Job titles should not give any indication of the sex of the job holder; operative, clerk, supervisor and manager are all acceptable as descriptive of either sex. Foreman, manageress, chambermaid, are not. Words such as he, she, his, her, should be avoided and substituted with terms such as jobholder. Names of jobholders should not be included on copies of job descriptions given to evaluation panels. It is the job that is being evaluated not the jobholder, and inclusion of information indicating the gender of the jobholder increases the likelihood of bias in the evaluation process.

Job descriptions should of course be agreed as representative by the jobholder(s), line management and (where applicable or if part of a union agreement covering job evaluation) union/staff representative.

Where job analysts are used to produce job descriptions the group should include both men and women. Each analyst should be trained in the approach to collecting and presenting information to be used. They should be concerned that sex bias can creep in the way jobholders are questioned, in discussions about the job and in the choice of words used to describe the job and shown how to prevent this.

Ensure an unbiased selection of benchmark jobs

Most schemes involve the selection of benchmark jobs to provide a framework for evaluations, or to provide the basis for factor selection. These jobs are normally selected because they are representative of grades, levels and/or functions within the organisation. Discrimination can be introduced in the selection of these jobs by the selection of too many jobs held predominantly by men. To avoid this, the selection of benchmark jobs should include a representative sample of those jobs predominantly held by women e.g. secretaries, catering supervisors and sales staff.

Prevent bias appearing in the job evaluation process

However inherently free of sex bias the method of job evaluation is, bias can be introduced in the evaluation process. As the EOC states 'A commitment to fair job evaluation may require that some traditional assumptions are changed regarding the value attributed to work predominantly carried out by women'. Job evaluation is judgemental and bias can be introduced to the most carefully selected scheme by discriminatory judgements by the panel. Often these judgements are unwitting and can only be prevented by careful explanation.

The composition of the panel should follow the principles already described, that is reflecting the distribution of men and women throughout the organisation/jobs involved, individuals trained to avoid bias and with the qualities of open mindedness and fair judgement. Panel members must have an understanding of the jobs they are evaluating, and the panel should ideally be composed of representatives of the jobs which are to be evaluated.

The decisions emerging from operation of the panel should be monitored by the chairperson and active involvement of all the members encouraged to prevent 'railroading'. The resulting evaluations should be consensus decisions, based on the job, not jobholders, and without reference to historical position in the pecking order (which might well, however unintentionally, have been discriminatory).

Records should be kept of the reasons behind the evaluation decisions to enable appeals to be considered, and, if necessary, for evidence if a claim for equal pay is made. Experience confirms that the basis for decisions will not be remembered some months or years later without documentation. These 'rationales' will also help in reviewing the whole exercise to ensure that the evaluation judgements have been consistent throughout.

Watch decisions on grade boundaries

If the salary structure involves the use of grades, there are several pitfalls to be avoided in order to ensure the structure is free of sex bias. The positioning of grade boundaries can introduce bias in the allocation of basic pay and benefits.

The approach used for the allocation of points levels to grades should be consistent across the hierarchy of jobs. Grade boundaries should not be placed between jobs evaluated as virtually indistinguishable. Inevitably, the most potentially biased position for a grade boundary is between jobs which are traditionally male and those which are traditionally female.

Alternative grade structures should be closely examined for discriminatory sensitivities by reviewing the positioning of male and female dominated jobs before a structure is finally agreed. The potential for a claim challenging the structure is likely to be least where grade covers only a narrow range of job 'sizes' and particularly where there is also some pay overlap.

Scrutinise the whole reward structure

The legislation is concerned with 'work' whilst job evaluation is concerned with 'job'. There are many other influences on pay aside from evaluation and these must be given as much attention as the evaluation process to ensure a remuneration structure free of bias.

The entitlement to each element of remuneration should be determined free of sex bias. This includes the provision of benefits, e.g. car, the cut off points for additions to pay, e.g. overtime, and the procedures for dealing with promotion, demotion and transfer of employees.

Performance-related pay, bonus and incentive schemes can have a considerable impact on total pay. The criteria upon which assessment of performance is made, the extent of employee coverage, or simply the way it is operated by line management could create sex bias in remuneration and this alone could result in discriminatory treatment. In 1992, such a claim was made by the First Division Association – the trade union for senior civil servants.

Watch external market comparisons – the market can be discriminatory

Pay and benefits surveys are typically used as a means for discovering the 'going' rate for jobs. Surveys are concerned with reporting information on current practice amongst the contributors. If the market at large has for some time been biased against women/female dominated jobs, (i.e. paid them less) surveys will do no more than reflect precisely the situation which the law demands be avoided.

Market information is very valuable but must be interpreted with great sensitivity when taking the data into consideration in setting remuneration levels. Where it is clearly discriminatory, i.e. for traditionally segregated jobs in such areas as the retail and clothing manufacturing sectors difficult and sometimes expensive decisions are having to be made to reduce the 'pay gap' between traditionally male and female jobs.

The tricky issue of material factors

The legislation provides a 'material factor' defence. This states that an equality clause which entitles a woman to no less favourable terms of employment than her comparator shall not operate if the employer proves that the variation in their pay is genuinely due to a material factor which is not the difference of sex.

The material factor defence, in effect, operates as an explanation of a pay difference which would otherwise be presumed to be discriminatory. The crux of the defence lies simply in the proof that a pay differential is due to an objectively justifiable reason. This may be a difference in the 'personal equation' (e.g. their performance) of the female applicant and male comparator, or, in equal value cases, on much broader grounds.

There is much debate on the extent to which material factors will eventually prove a defence to equal value claims. To date, there is only limited guidance from case law. In the area of market forces, since the market rate for 'women's' jobs is traditionally less than the market rate for 'mens' jobs, reliance on the prevailing market rate is not likely to provide a sufficient defence for employers. Functional market premia for groups of workers (e.g. data processing/systems or accounting jobs) may well be material factor differences but will have to be defended on hard evidence of labour shortages or other reasons which do not have their basis in sex differences.

The importance of a positive approach

Experts in human resources management generally agree that the solution to the fundamental problems giving rise to equal value claims is through the promotion of equality of opportunity for women in recruitment, training and career development. The way forward in terms of the Equal Pay legislation as it affects job evaluation is through joint management and union involvement where unions are part of the picture, involving women as well as men at all stages and approaching the subject in an unbiased, open minded way. The principles and practices that lie behind scheme design and operation must be appropriate to ensure fair treatment, irrespective of gender, and that can be a very important retention factor for any employer. Employers who gain the reputation for fostering equal opportunities in their working practices are likely to fare better in times of skills shortage because they can better attract and keep the people they need. When employees are facing the prospect of being in a 'sellers' market', the evidence is that they select employers on the basis of the quality of working life on offer. Equal treatment is a pretty important ingredient.

Areas equal value legislation does not yet address

Throughout this book we have sought to show how new processes and approaches to job evaluation are replacing the 'set piece' implementation methodologies that were received wisdom in the 1970's. However, we are faced with equal value legislation which enshrines the perception of job evaluation and how it worked a decade and more ago. Among the untested but increasingly used approaches in this context are:

- Job family models.
- Non-employee panel based approaches to evaluation (e.g. management/specialist only panels).
- Computer assisted job evaluation (the existence of discriminatory algorithms?).
- Broader ranges of job 'scores' linked to fewer, broader salary ranges.

Skill and competency based pay approaches were certainly not considered and indeed hardly existed when equal value legislation went on the statute book. No one appears to have explored whether such approaches when used separately from job evaluation contain the potential to deliver unequal pay for work of equivalent value. The issues perhaps lie more in terms of equal opportunities than equal pay – but the former has an unfortunate habit of influencing the latter.

One thing is certain, literacy in the equal value implications of these new approaches will have to be developed and measures taken to prevent sex discrimination in these as in the more conventional world they are starting to replace.

14 Job Evaluation and Organisation Analysis

Introduction

On a number of occasions in earlier chapters, we have referred to the value of job evaluation as a tool of organisational analysis and understanding. In this chapter, the ways in which it can provide this are briefly reviewed.

It is important to note that job evaluation does not provide a comprehensive approach to organisation analysis: for full understanding of how an organisation works and how it could be improved, a variety of approaches must be brought into play. Nevertheless, job evaluation can provide an important and useful perspective on organisation, which can represent significant additional added value from the evaluation process.

The second important point is that organisation is more than just structure. As illustrated in Figure 14.1, an organisation needs to be considered in terms not only of structure, but also in terms of:

- The major management processes, formal and informal by which the organisation actually works.
- The way in which it is resourced.

In addition, understanding of the culture and history of the organisation is needed – especially if changes are to be made, as is the way top direction is exercised and transmitted.

Many observers would argue that it is more important to have good processes than good structure. Inadequacies of structure can often be overcome by effective processes of planning, communi-

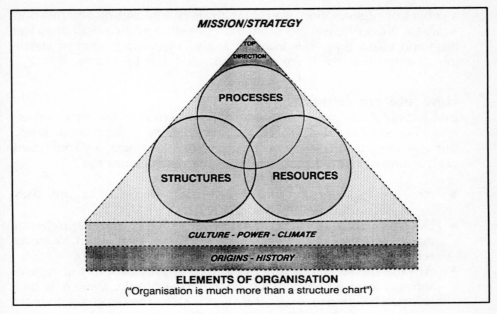

Figure 14.1   Mission/Strategy.

cation and control, but there is no way that even the most elegant of structures can compensate for poor processes. Most organisat'ons can quote examples of planned organisational change, in which the structure was changed, new organograms drawn and new job descriptions issued – but nothing actually happened, because the processes were not considered. The way that organisations are now developing, with greater emphasis on flexibility and teamwork, puts even more emphasis than before on process issues.

Properly used, job evaluation can give important perspectives on both structural and process aspects of organisation.

Finally, it needs to be recognised that organisational perspectives gained through job evaluation are essentially diagnostic and not prescriptive. It provides a spotlight on issues in the current organisation, and can be used to test alternative arrangements, but it cannot, by itself, indicate the 'best' organisation in any particular case.

The following sections outline some of the ways the job evaluation process can be used to provide such perspectives.

Job analysis

A primary source of organisational analysis and understanding is through the job analysis process. This is not surprising: jobs are a subset of organisation, so job analysis is a subset of organisation analysis. Nevertheless it is often overlooked, and the result of all the time and effort that goes into job analysis is simply a set of sterile job descriptions which are evaluated, filed and forgotten.

How jobs are defined
In Chapter 8 we raised the questions of what is meant by a job and how should jobs be defined. At its most fundamental level, the answers to these sorts of questions provide an important organisational perspective, since they address issues like:

- Are jobs specifically and individually defined, or are they expressed more flexibly and generically?
- Does the organisation rely heavily on structure and hierarchy, or does it work more through team work and 'horizontal' working relationships?
- Are the management processes used appropriate to the organisational form which actually exists? For example, there may be a mismatch between an organisation which relies strongly on team work and collaboration, and a set of processes which emphasise control, approval and restrictions on individual freedom.

Job relationships
In addition to these broad organisational perspectives, job analysis can provide important insights at the level of individual jobs and job relationships. For this to be effective, the quality of job analysis needs to be satisfactory, or false conclusions can be reached. If, for example, the organisation appears to contain ambiguities or lack of clarity, it is first necessary to ensure that these observations are not just the result of sloppy job analysis, and are indeed a true reflection of how the organisation actually operates.

Job analysis format
The format in which job information is expressed can also have a bearing on the effectiveness with which job analysis can be used to reach organisational conclusions.

Job description formats which emphasise detailed individual tasks are not very satisfactory in this respect, since they tend to be inward looking and focus on the internal detail of the job, rather than its outputs and hence interactions with other jobs. Job descriptions containing sections on the purpose of the job, and its principal accountabilities, as outlined in Chapter 8, are much more powerful from this point of view, since they stress the outputs and achievements required from jobs – why does the job exist, and what is it meant to achieve?

In general, job descriptions of the conventional type are more useful in providing organisational analysis than multiple choice questionnaire of the 'universal' type. However, job family questionnaires provide powerful, though different, perspectives on organisation. Since they focus on the features which differentiate between levels of work within a family, their construction depends upon a deep analysis and exploration of how work is organised and managed within that family. Hence consideration of the organisational issues involved is concentrated at the stage of developing the questionnaire and its content, rather than being done on a job-by-job basis as is the case for more conventional job descriptions.

The types of organisational observation which can be made through job analysis, and through the debate on jobs which occurs in panel based job evaluation processes are outlined in the sections which follow.

Organisational clarity

Clarity is not synonymous with rigidity. However flexible an organisation is, there needs to be clarity about the nature of that flexibility and how it works. If it is defined ambiguously, or interpreted differently by different job holders, then the result is not flexibility but chaos.

Hence whatever the nature of the organisation job analysis can be used to reach conclusions on issues such as:

- Is there clarity in the way the organisation operates – in terms both of structure and of processes?
- Are there areas of ambiguity in the organisation, open to different and potentially conflicting interpretations?
- Are there examples of directly contradictory interpretations about the organisation – for example different jobs claiming accountability for the same thing (or denying accountability for it), or describing quite different versions of how job inter-relationships operate?

Vertical overlap

Vertical overlap occurs when responsibilities are replicated at different organisational levels. It may occur at an overall functional level, or at the level of individual job relationships.

Vertical overlap in functions occurs typically in such relationships as

- Between head office and regions.
- Between regions and areas.
- Between parent company and subsidiaries, etc.

Sometimes this kind of overlap results in simple duplication of activity – for example, two lots of people consolidating financial data, or developing new accounting procedures. In other cases, it may result in conflicting activities – for example if head office and an operating unit were to develop mutually incompatible HR policies – or it may simply result in confusion. If a business unit believes it has responsibility to set pay levels, it may do so, only to be told by headquarters that its decisions may have knock-on effects in sister businesses and must therefore be reconsidered. Symptoms of this sort of situation are evidence of lots of meetings and 'to-ing and fro-ing' between head office and units whenever important decisions have to be made.

At the level of individual jobs, overlap may occur in boss–subordinate relationships. If the relationship is sensibly constructed, the purpose and accountabilities of the subordinate job should be consistent with and supportive of those of the superior job. A common problem is when the purpose and accountabilities of the two jobs are virtually indistinguishable. In such circumstances it is necessary to question who really is accountable, and whether both levels are actually required. A good approach to this is to question what unique added value each job provides to the work process. In some cases this will demonstrate simply that one or other of the levels is unnecessary. In other cases, it may show that the nature of the two levels needs clarifying and refining. Two common examples of this may serve to illustrate.

In an engineering department, the formal organisation structure may be expressed as shown in Figure 14.2, with groups of engineers reporting to senior engineers who report to principal engineers and so on. The job descriptions may reveal that the purpose and accountabilities of several of the layers in the structure are remarkably similar. This is often a case of a 'technical hierarchy' being confused with – and expressed as – a reporting hierarchy. In such cases, engineers do not really 'report to' senior engineers, though they may receive technical guidance and supervision from them. Most of the 'management' activities are actually undertaken by the department head, who will relate directly to the individual engineers at all levels. Thus the 'real' organisation may be better expressed as shown in Figure 14.3, with engineers at different levels reporting directly to the head.

The problem with expressing it in the hierarchical form is that it causes confusion about the nature of the 'middle' level roles. Senior and principal engineers may be conscious that they apparently have supervisory accountabilities, but are not sure what they are, and may feel ill-equipped to do anything about them. Much better to reflect the reality that their seniority is technical, not managerial and let them get on with what they are good at – being an engineer. Such situations are common in a wide range

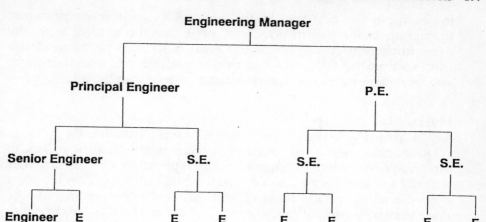

Figure 14.2   Reporting structure as expressed in organisation chart.

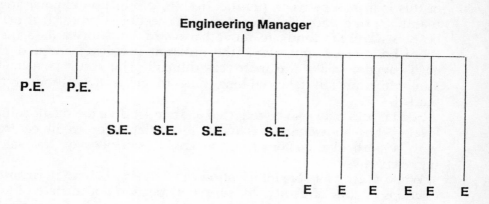

Figure 14.3   Management reporting relationships in a technical hierarchy.

of technical/professional functions, as well as in other 'knowledge worker' areas such as clerical/administrative groups.

A different situation is that of, say, a sales force comprising a national sales manager, regional managers, area managers and representatives. The purpose and accountabilities of regional and area managers may be very similar, with both levels claiming accountability for managing the sales force, setting prices, developing sales forecasts and targets, etc. This may of course indicate that one or other level is unnecessary, or it may be that the distinction between the respective roles needs clarifying. Thus for example the real role of the area manager may be primarily to provide a flow of information, or it may be to deal with the more important customers in the area. If so, it is better to clarify this, so that the nature of the role is understood, and that more appropriate selection and performance criteria can be set.

Horizontal overlap

Again, this may occur at a functional or individual job level.

Horizontal overlap of functions occurs when there is a lack of integration between functions and a replication of like activities within functions. For example if individual functions develop their own planning, policy making and administrative arrangements, there may be incompatibility or duplication of activity. This may not matter if the functions can act with reasonable independence from each other, but if coordinated corporate approaches are needed, there will be problems. These problems usually surface in complex planning procedures with lots of paper, lots of meetings and lots of people attending – and slow decision taking. A common example of this is liaison between product design, production engineering, manufacturing and sales. For a complex technical product, it may be necessary constantly to move backwards and forwards across these boundaries, but often, the different processes adopted by each function make the interfaces difficult. The result is usually straightforward: it takes a long time to get a new product to market.

Such issues may also be reflected at an individual job relationship level. Who, for example, is really accountable for credit control with a particular customer – the credit controller or the sales representative?

While much valuable information can be gained about horizontal overlaps or lack of clarity, by simple inspection and debate of job descriptions, this can usefully be supplemented by a technique called inter-accountability analysis. In this, a matrix is constructed, showing a series of major accountability or key result areas on one axis, and the jobs involved on the other. In each box is entered the nature of the impact which each job has on that particular result area – prime controlling impact, shared, contributory (advisory) or remote (information provision). An extract from such a matrix is illustrated in Figure 14.4.

This approach can show very clearly features such as:

- Those result areas where no-one seems to have direct account-ability, and everyone is contributory (indecision?)
- Those where several jobs think they are prime (conflict?)
- Those where hardly anyone seems to have an impact (neglect?)
- Those where everyone seems to have an impact (cooks and broth?)

KEY RESULT AREAS	1 Service commitments met / Usage parameters achieved	2 Services properly managed & operated to regulations	3 Supporting equipment & stock kept at optimum levels & reliability	4 Lines, structures, stations, works, depots, etc. safe & adequate for operating needs	5 Prices, information & other services run adequately & efficiently	6 Collection of revenue	7 Department run within agreed annual finance & manpower limits
DIRECTOR	P (Controls Ops)	P (Controls)	P (Maintenance)	C (Oprtng exp)	P (Controls)	P (Control)	P (On ops)
CONTROLLER PLANNING AND DEVELOPMENT	-	-	S-	-	-	-	S- (Staff budget)
CONTROLLER INSTALLATIONS	-	-	-	-	S+ (Sales & prms)	-	S- (Staff budget)
CONTROLLER SERVICES	-	-	S+ (Standards)	P (Controls)	-	-	S- (Staff budget)
CONTROLLER FINANCE	-	-	C (Stock control)	-	C (Fincl apprsl)	C (Bling System)	S (Mntr Staff)
ADMINISTRATOR ENGINEERING SERVICES	-	-	-	-	-	-	-

Figure 14.4 Extract from Inter-Accountability Matrix.

Job evaluation results

While much useful organisational information can be gained directly from job analysis and the debate about jobs which occurs during the evaluation process, the results of job evaluation can also be used in this mode, particularly if factor based evaluation methods are used.

The details of how this can be done depend to a large degree on the specific method used, the factors, numbering pattern, etc. Hence to illustrate the types of analysis possible, we will refer to a particular method, the Hay Guide Chart Profile Method. This is widely used for this purpose, not least because a number of features in the method make it particularly amenable for use in this way, especially:

- The 'step difference' concept which underpins all the factor scales used (one 'step' being the smallest perceptible difference between two jobs in any factor). This provides a consistent way of expressing intervals between jobs in terms of steps.
- The profile concept, in which the 'input' factors of Know-How and Problem Solving are related to the 'output' factor of Accountability.
- Several of the evaluation elements themselves (e.g. Breadth of Management Know-How, and Impact on end results) provide specific focus on organisation issues.

Before using any job evaluation results to reach organisational conclusions, it is first essential to have confidence in the quality and consistency of the results themselves. Otherwise, erroneous conclusions can be reached, if apparent organisational issues are just a function of inconsistent evaluation, not of the organisation itself.

Specific types of technique which can be used include:

Points inventory

The total of the job size points for all jobs in a particular business, unit or department provides a useful measure of the total weight of effort being applied to running that particular unit. Simply using personnel numbers may conceal the fact that some units have fewer, larger jobs while others may have more smaller ones. Using total payroll costs may make inter-unit comparisons difficult, if different pay practices apply to the various units.

While the total job size points cannot be used in any absolute sense they can be used in a relative way to compare organisational arrangements.

As an example, consider an organisation containing several regional operations, essentially similar in nature, but differing in scale. An issue may well be to compare the amount of management effort used to run each region.

The total of the job size points for the management jobs in each region provides this, and can be used to calculate relevant ratios, such as:

- Ratio of management points to total number of staff: this provides a measure of the efficiency of the management operation in terms of the people-management task to be undertaken.
- Ratio of management points to revenue or income: this provides a measure of the efficiency of management effort in terms of the financial scale of the business.

Such ratios can be used both to test relative management efficiencies, but also to provide insights on, for example, the optimum unit size to make best use of management resource.

For a single unit operation, such comparisons are not feasible, but tracking points totals or similar ratios over time can provide a means of assessing changes in operational efficiency and productivity.

Interval or gap analysis

In this approach, intervals or gaps between the sizes of jobs are examined – usually between boss and subordinate jobs. The results can be used to indicate unusual features or potential anomalies in the structure.

Normally, when using the Hay method, the intervals between jobs are expressed in terms of number of 'steps' between jobs in the three evaluation factors of Know-How, Problem Solving and Accountability.

Thus for example, a typical boss–subordinate interval in a conventional hierarchical structure is

2 steps different in Know-How.
1 step different in Problem Solving.
3 steps different in Accountability.
(in shorthand – 2:1:3)

This generates an interval in total job size of around 2½ steps.

As organisations de-layer, this 'classical' gap changes, with intervals such as 3:1:4 or 3:2:5 becoming more common, and more variety in the gaps between a manager and different subordinates.

Closer intervals indicate heavy layering. For example intervals such as 1:1:2 are often found for one-on-one reporting relationships, 'deputy' jobs, or where the need for one of the layers is questionable.

Similarly, gaps of 1:1:2 or even 1:0:1 are typical in the kinds of technical hierarchies referred to earlier, where the 'reporting' relationship is technical rather than managerial, or simply an artifice of the organisation chart. Other types of reporting relationships and spans of control are typically reflected in other characteristic intervals and different types of organisation may exhibit different typical relationships. For example in smaller companies the intervals are often wider than in larger ones.

Testing specific intervals against these sorts of criteria, and against intervals commonly found in the organisation can help identify structural features which may need attention – e.g. apparently surplus layers in the structure.

Such analyses can also be used to highlight management development and succession issues. A typical promotion interval is often of the 2:1:3 type. Single-step promotions across gaps much bigger than this are often difficult, overstretching and risky. If the organisation typically has gaps above this size (as is increasingly common in delayered structures) or if there are specific areas where this is the case, then management development/succession planning processes will need to provide the means for diagonal, 'sideways' and multi-step moves, to replace the traditional stepwise ascension of the hierarchical ladder.

Profile analysis

In the Hay method, the profile is an expression of the relationship between the three factor scores, and indicates the 'shape' of the job.

A simple way of expressing the profile is in terms of the number of steps between the points for Accountability and Problem Solving (which is itself a function of Know-How). For example if the Accountability is three or four steps above the Problem Solving, the job is sharply orientated to Accountability and output. Such profiles would be characteristic of jobs such as sales representatives, sales managers, production supervisors, chief executives, etc.

Conversely, profiles in which Problem Solving is two or three steps above Accountability would be more characteristic of basic research jobs. In many staff or functional areas (personnel, finance, etc.) Accountability is often one or two steps above Problem Solving.

Once there is understanding of the characteristic profiles of different types of jobs, this can be used to examine both individual job relationships and the range of profiles in different units to reach conclusions on relative results orientation.

Impact analysis

One element of Accountability in the Hay method is Impact on end results, which is expressed at four levels: Prime, Shared, Contributory and Remote. Rather like the inter-accountability approach referred to earlier, analysis of Impact evaluations across different parts of an organisation can provide valuable insights into how Accountability is distributed. Figure 14.5 shows an example of the results of Impact Analysis across the five business units and headquarters of a company.

IMPACT ANALYSIS

BUSINESS UNITS	Prime	Prime-Shared	Shared	Shared-Contributory	Contributory	Contributory Remote	Remote	Total
A	12	8	26	3	14	1	0	64
B	13	9	26	3	16	1	1	70
C	4	6	17	4	10	1	1	42
D	9	3	20	4	10	1	0	47
E	5	7	17	5	13	1	0	48
TOTAL UNITS	43	32	108	19	62	5	2	271
HQ	49	5	69	23	130	16	28	310
TOTAL	92	37	167	42	192	21	30	581

Figure 14.5   Impact analysis.

15 Job Evaluation in the Future

Predicting the future for job evaluation may be providing hostages to fortune, especially given the current challenges to the process and the variety of ways in which practice is responding and developing to meet these challenges.

Nevertheless, clear trends are discernible which enable future patterns of application to be predicted with a reasonable degree of confidence.

First, the concept of 'role' will persist in most organisations. This may be somewhat differently defined from traditional views of a job, but will remain an essential organisational concept. Only through clarifying and understanding roles can the organisation ensure that its business requirements will be met, and manage the balance of capability required to deliver them.

The current questioning of the validity of defining jobs, and the suggestion that this should be totally replaced by focus on people and their skills and competencies, is a swing of the pendulum. This swing is an understandable reaction to the over-emphasis of the past on rigidly defined jobs and the lack of consideration of the impact of people. There are already signs that pendulum is moving towards a sensible equilibrium position in which the importance of role from an organisational perspective is balanced with recognition of the way, in practice, people influence the role they are fulfilling, and the performance they achieve within it.

The issue of internal relativities between roles in an organisation will continue to be an essential component in considering pay, as will the concept that one ingredient of internally equitable pay arrangements is the relative size or importance of role.

The clear implication of this is that some means of assessing the relative size of roles within an organisation will remain as one of the cornerstones of pay management. In other words, 'job evaluation' in some shape or form will continue to be required.

There will be continuing change in the way jobs and roles are defined. Undoubtedly in some circumstances 'jobs' will continue to be defined in largely traditional terms of structure and account-abilities: in a growing number of cases, however, roles will be much more flexibly defined, with less emphasis on structure and hierarchical position, and more consideration of the skills and competencies associated with them. Nevertheless, organisations will still demand clear definition of the outputs and achievements required from roles, and the ways in which these relate to the skills and competencies needed to support them. Integrated role definition models of the type outlined in Chapter 3 will increasingly provide the framework for this: traditional job definition is simply a special case of this broader framework.

Such integrated role analysis models will be used as the basis for job evaluation (or 'role sizing' if that title is preferred) as well as career development, performance management, selection and training.

There are major implications in this for the way the human resources function is organised and managed in most businesses. To date, it has been common to split responsibility for such aspects as job evaluation, pay, career development, training and selection between separate individuals or departments. This is particularly true of large organisations. The integration of these processes will increasingly demand different organisational arrangements to avoid continued fragmentation and pigeon-holing of these issues.

The basic methods used for job evaluation (as distinct from the processes for their application) will come under continued scrutiny to ensure that they can deal with the changing definition of jobs and roles. Methods in which factors relate specifically to structural or hierarchical features will require modification or replacement. Methods in which the factors do not assume any particular organisational model will increasingly be preferred as the rate of organisational change continues. Similarly methods in which the relationship between input and output factors is explicitly considered will increasingly be used to support and reflect the sort of integrated role definitions noted above.

The processes for applying job evaluation will continue to develop and evolve. Traditional 'panel-type' processes will continue to be used where added value is gained from the panel debate, or where the size of the population does not warrant developing more structured approaches or models. However such processes will become steadily 'slicker' and more efficient, and will increasingly rely on computer based administrative support.

Computer assisted processes of the 'universal' questionnaire type will become widely applied for large job populations, where there is significant variety of job type, and where jobs continue to be defined individually. Increasingly, integrated questionnaire approaches will be used, combining 'job size' issues with competency analysis considerations.

Job family models will increasingly be applied to 'knowledge worker' categories of jobs, and will be closely linked to skill and competency analysis, career development and performance management. Where high degrees of flexibility are required, or where there are large populations of relatively similar roles, there will be greater use of frameworks of flexible generically defined roles, by family or sub-family. In this context, job evaluation may simply be used to assess the size of the roles and levels represented in the framework, and provide the means of reading across between levels in different families. Where jobs continue to be considered individually, questionnaire methods will be used to help allocate particular jobs to the right position in the framework of roles.

The way job evaluation results are used as an input to pay decisions will continue to develop, to achieve a better balance between the various factors and issues involved. In most organisations, the over-concentration of the past on job size will reduce as considerations of performance and external market gain greater significance and acceptance. Job evaluation in the future will no longer be seen as a centralised pay control mechanism, but as a tool to help manage pay more effectively, alongside a range of other tools.

In summary, this represents a very different picture from how job evaluation was practised and used in the past. Unfortunately, the image and reputation of job evaluation with many line managers and employees – and indeed with many HR professionals – is the image of the past. As demonstrated in this book, current practice is quite different from that of say, the 1970's, and all the indications are that this rate of change will continue. In this context, perhaps the most important challenge for job evaluation is to shed the image of the past, and for its practitioners to demonstrate through the way they operate, that the old image is no longer justified.

Appendix 1

Approaches available from management consultants

This appendix summarises the main features of the following most commonly used management consultants' job evaluation schemes: The summaries are in large part drawn from descriptions given in Armstrong M & Murlis H., Reward Management, Kogan Page, 1991.

- Hay Guide Chart – Profile Method
- PE International – Pay Points and Direct Consensus Method
- PA Consulting Group
- Price Waterhouse – The Profile Method
- Saville-Holdsworth – the SHL Method
- The Wyatt Company – The EPFC method
- Ernst and Young International (Employment Relations Associates) – The Decision Band Method
- Institute of Administrative Management – Office Job Evaluation
- Towers Perrin – WJQ
- KPMG Management Consulting – EQUATE

The Hay Guide Chart – Profile method of job evaluation

History and development
The Hay Guide Chart Profile Method of Job Evaluation is the most

widely used single job evaluation method in the world, being used by over 7000 profit and non-profit organizations in some 40 countries. While it is perhaps best known for its application to management, professional and technical jobs, it is also extensively used for clerical and manual jobs, and when a single top-to-bottom evaluation method is required as the basis for integrated pay and grading structures.

It was initially conceived in the early 1950s, having its roots in factor comparison methods in which Edward N. Hay was a pioneer, and has evolved by practical application into its present form.

Its widespread use, and the consistency of the job size numbering scale used, enables it to provide the basis for valid pay comparisons between organisations, nationally and internationally. Comprehensive pay and benefits surveys, using job-size based comparisons are conducted by the Hay Group in over 35 countries.

The method can be applied by a wide variety of processes, both manual and computer assisted, tailored to the particular requirements of the user organisation.

Basis of the method

The method is based upon the following principles and observations.

- While there are many factors which could be considered in developing a job evaluation scheme, these can be grouped into three broad factors: the knowledge and skills required to do the job; the kind of thinking needed to solve the problems commonly faced; and the responsibilities assigned to the job.
- This provides the basis of the three main factors of the Guide Chart Profile Method – Know-How, Problem Solving, and Accountability – which are common to all jobs, and which are subdivided into several elements.
- For any given job, there will be a relationship between the three factors. Thus the output or end results expected from the job (the Accountability), will demand a certain level of input (Know-How), and processing of this Know-How (Problem Solving) to enable delivery of the output.

This can be represented by the simple model:

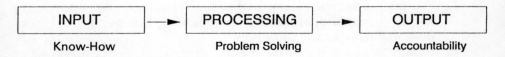

INPUT	PROCESSING	OUTPUT
Know-How	Problem Solving	Accountability

- Thus jobs can be characterised not only by the size or level of each factor, but also by the balance between the factors – the

Profile – which reflects the 'shape' of the job. Thus for example a research job is likely to be heavily loaded towards Know-How and Problem Solving, whereas for a sales representative or production manager, the balance will be shifted towards Accountability. In addition to evaluating each factor, evaluators also assess the profile of the job, which provides an important check on consistency of treatment.

- The ability of evaluators to discern a difference between two jobs depends not only on the absolute difference, but on how big this difference is in relation to the size of the jobs themselves. Thus the numbering patterns used in the Guide Charts are based upon a geometric scale, each number being a constant percentage greater than the previous one. This percentage has been empirically determined at 15 per cent, as best representing the ability of experienced evaluators to discern a difference in any factor between two jobs. This 'step difference' concept provides the basic building block for the scales and for the comparisons between jobs, with one step representing a 'just discernible difference'.
- Jobs should not be evaluated in isolation, but viewed in their organisational context, so that working relationships both vertically and horizontally throughout the organisation are taken into account.
- In order that the focus is on jobs, not the performance of jobholders, 'standard acceptable performance' is assumed. Similarly, jobs are evaluated independent of any market-driven pay conditions which may pertain, recognising that these require addressing explicitly as pay issues, not job-size considerations.

Components of the method
The method has three main factors and eight dimensions as follows:

Know-How

The sum of every kind of knowledge, skill and experience, however acquired, needed for acceptable job performance. Its three dimensions are requirements for:

1. Practical procedures, specialised techniques and knowledge within occupational fields, commercial functions, and professional or scientific disciplines.
2. Integrating and harmonising the diverse elements involved in managerial situations. This involves, in some combination, skills in planning, organising, executing, controlling and evaluating and may be exercised consultatively as well as executively.

3.   Active, practising person-to-person skills in work with other people, within or outside the organisation.

Problem Solving

The original, self-starting use of Know-How required by the job to identify, define, and resolve problems. 'You think with what you know'. This is true of even the most creative work. The raw material of any thinking is knowledge of facts, principles, and means. For that reason, Problem Solving is treated as a percentage of Know-How.

Problem solving has two dimensions:

*   the environment in which thinking takes place
*   the challenge presented by the thinking to be done.

Accountability

The answerability for action and for the consequences of that action. It is the measured effect of the job on end results of the organisation. It has three dimensions in the following order of importance:

1.   Freedom to act: the extent of personal, procedural, or systematic guidance or control of actions in relation to the primary emphasis of the job.
2.   Job impact on end results: the extent to which the job can directly affect actions necessary to produce results within its primary emphasis.
3.   Magnitude: the portion of the total organisation encompassed by the primary emphasis of the job. Where possible, magnitude is expressed in annual financial figures representing the area of primary emphasis of the job.

Beyond these three factors of job content, additional scales can be used to assess factors relating to the context in which the job operates; for example unpleasant working environment, hazards, physical demands, sensory attention, etc. When such factors are important for the jobs under consideration, scales are generated to enable their assessment within the context of the organisation.

The Guide Charts

A Guide Chart for each factor (see Figures 1, 2 and 3) contains semantic scales which reflect levels of each dimension. Each chart, except for Problem Solving, is expandable to reflect the size and complexity of the organisation to which it is applied. The language of the scales, carefully evolved over many years and applied to

DEFINITION:
Know-How is the sum of every kind of knowledge, skill and experience required for standard acceptable job performance. It is the fund of knowledge (however acquired) which is made use of, rather than the value of many.

* The requirement for Know-How in practical procedures, specialised techniques and professional disciplines.

** The requirement for Know-How in integrating and harmonising the diverse elements involved in managerial situations. This Know-How may be exercised in an advisory capacity as well as executively. It involves combining to some degree the skills in planning, organising, controlling, coordinating and innovating and takes account of size, functional or organisational diversity, and time scale.

*** The requirement for Know-How in working with and through people (within or outside the organisation).

MEASURING KNOW-HOW:
Know-How has both breadth and depth. Thus, a job may require some knowledge about a lot of things, or a lot of knowledge about a few things. The total Know-How is the sum of breadth and depth. This concept creates a practical way of comparing and weighing the total Know-How content of different jobs in terms of: 'HOW MUCH KNOWLEDGE ABOUT HOW MANY THINGS'.

HayGroup

HAY GUIDE CHART FOR EVALUATING KNOW-HOW

*** **HUMAN RELATIONS SKILLS**

1. **BASIC:** Ordinary courtesy and effectiveness in dealing with others is required.
2. **IMPORTANT:** Understanding, influencing, and communicating with people are important but not overriding considerations.
3. **CRITICAL:** Skills in influencing, developing and/or motivating people are critical to the achievement of job objectives.

* **DEPTH AND RANGE OF TECHNICAL KNOW-HOW**

(left side vertical bands: PRACTICAL PROCEDURES / SPECIALISED TECHNIQUES / PROFESSIONAL DISCIPLINES)

A **PRIMARY:** Jobs requiring Secondary education only, plus some work indoctrination.

B **ELEMENTARY VOCATIONAL:** Jobs requiring familiarisation in unmolved/standardised work routines and/or use of simple equipment and machines.

C **VOCATIONAL:** Jobs requiring procedural or systemic proficiency, which may involve facility in the use of specialised equipment.

D **ADVANCED VOCATIONAL:** Jobs requiring some specialised (generally non-theoretical) skills gained by on the job experience or through part professional qualification.

E **BASIC PROFESSIONAL:** Jobs requiring sufficiency in a technical, scientific or specialised field based on an understanding of concepts and principles normally associated with a professional or academic qualification or gained through a detailed grasp of involved practices and procedures.

F **SEASONED PROFESSIONAL:** Jobs requiring proficiency in a technical, scientific or specialised field gained through broad and deep experience built on concepts and principles, or through wide exposure to complex practices and precedents.

G **PROFESSIONAL MASTERY:** Jobs requiring determinative mastery of concepts, principles and practices gained through wide experience and development in a highly specialised field or through comprehensive business experience.

H **UNIQUE AUTHORITY:** Jobs requiring ... and command of a ...

** **PLANNING, ORGANISING, CONTROLLING – BREADTH OF MANAGEMENT KNOW-HOW**

	0. TASK Performance of a task (or tasks) highly specific as to objective and content and not involving the supervision of others			I. ACTIVITY Performance or supervision of work which is specific as to objective and content with appropriate awareness of related activities.			II. HOMOGENEOUS Internal integration of operations which are relatively homogeneous in nature and objective and which involve associated functions			III. HETEROGENEOUS Operational or conceptual integration of functions which are diverse in nature and in objective in an important management area, or central co-ordination of a strategic function			IV. (TOTAL)		
	1.	2.	3.	1.	2.	3.	1.	2.	3.	1.	2.	3.	1.	2.	3.
A	38	43	50	50	57	66	66	76	87	87	100	115	115	132	15
	43	50	57	57	66	76	76	87	100	100	115	132	132	152	1
	50	57	66	66	76	87	87	100	115	115	132	152	152	175	2
B	50	57	66	66	76	87	87	100	115	115	132	152	152	175	
	57	66	76	76	87	100	100	115	132	132	152	175	175	200	2
	66	76	87	87	100	115	115	132	152	152	175	200	200	230	2
C	66	76	87	87	100	115	115	132	152	152	175	200	200	230	2
	76	87	100	100	115	132	132	152	175	175	200	230	230	264	3
	87	100	115	115	132	152	152	175	200	200	230	264	264	304	
D	87	100	115	115	132	152	152	175	200	200	230	264	264	304	
	100	115	132	132	152	175	175	200	230	230	264	304	304	350	
	115	132	152	152	175	200	200	230	264	264	304	350	350	400	
E	115	132	152	152	175	200	200	230	264	264	304	350	350	400	
	132	152	175	175	200	230	230	264	304	304	350	400	400	460	
	152	175	200	200	230	264	264	304	350	350	400	460	460	528	t
F	152	175	200	200	230	264	264	304	350	350	400	460	460	528	6
	175	200	230	230	264	304	304	350	400	400	460	528	528	608	7
	200	230	264	264	304	350	350	400	460	460	528	608	608	700	
G	200	230	264	264	304	350	350	400	460	460	528	608	608	700	
	230	264	304	304	350	400	400	460	528	528	608	700	700	800	
	264	304	350	350	400	460	460	528	608	608	700	800	800	920	
H	264	304		350	400	460	460	528	608	608	700		800	920	
	304	350		400			528	608	700	700	800		920	1056	

Figure 1   Part of the Hay Know-How Guide Chart.

HayGroup

DEFINITION: Problem Solving is the "self starting" thinking required by the job for analysing, evaluating, creating, reasoning, arriving at and drawing conclusions. To the extent that thinking is circumscribed by standards or covered by precedents, or referred to others, Problem Solving is diminished.

Problem Solving has two dimensions.
● The environment in which the thinking takes place.
●● The challenge presented by the thinking to be done.

MEASURING PROBLEM SOLVING: Problem Solving measures the intensity of the mental process which employs Know-How to (1) identify, (2) define, and (3) solve a problem. "You think with what you know." This is true of even the most creative work. The raw material of any thinking is knowledge of facts, principles and means, ideas are put together from something already there. Therefore, Problem Solving is treated as a percentage utilisation of Know-How. (The Problem Solving score can be readily derived from the conversion table printed on the back of the Know-How Guide Chart.)

HAY GUIDE CHART FOR EVALUATING
PROBLEM SOLVING

●● THINKING CHALLENGE

● THINKING ENVIRONMENT – FREEDOM TO THINK	1. REPETITIVE Identical situations requiring solution by simple choice of things learned		2. PATTERNED Similar situations requiring solution by discriminating choice of things learned		3. VARIABLE Differing situations requiring the identification and selection of solutions through the application of acquired knowledge		4. ADAPTIVE Situations requiring analytical, interpretative, and/or constructive thinking and a significant degree of evaluative judgement		5. UNCHARTED Pathfinding situations during creative and the developing of new concepts and approaches contributing significantly to the advancement of knowledge thought	
A STRICT ROUTINE: Thinking within detailed rules, instructions and/or rigid supervision	10%	12%	14%	16%	19%	22%	25%	29%	33%	3€
B ROUTINE: Thinking within standard instructions and/or continuous close supervision	12%	14%	16%	19%	22%	25%	29%	33%	38%	4.
C SEMI-ROUTINE: Thinking within well defined procedures and precedents, somewhat diversified and/or supervised	14%	16%	19%	22%	25%	29%	33%	38%	43%	5(
D STANDARDISED: Thinking within substantially diversified, established company procedures and standards, and general supervision	16%	19%	22%	25%	29%	33%	38%	43°	50%	5
E CLEARLY DEFINED: Thinking within clearly defined company policies, principles and specific objectives, under readily available direction	19%	22%	25%	29%	33%	38%	43%	50%	57%	66
F BROADLY DEFINED: Thinking within broad policies and objectives, under general direction	22%	25%	29%	33%	38%	43%	50%	57%	66%	76
G GENERALLY DEFINED: Thinking within general policies, principles and goals under guidance	25%	29%	33%	38%	43%	50%	57%	66%	76%	87?
H ABSTRACTLY DEFINED: Thinking within business human...	29%		34%		50%		66%		87%	

© 1990 These charts are for use in the United Kingdom by the client named above and may not be reproduced without the permission of Hay Management Consultants Limited.

Figure 2   Part of the Hay Problem Solving Guide Chart.

HayGroup

DEFINITION: Accountability is the answerability for action and for the consequences of that action. It is the measured effect of the job on end results. It has three dimensions in the following order of importance:

■ **Freedom to Act** – measured by the existence or absence of personal or procedural control and guidance as defined in the left-hand column below.

●●● **Job Impact on End Results** – as defined at upper right.

●●● **Magnitude (Area of Impact)** – indicated by the general size of the area(s) most clearly affected by the job (measured on an annual money basis.)

IMPACT OF JOB ON END RESULTS

INDIRECT
- **REMOTE:** Informational, recording, or incidental services for use by others in relation to some important end result.
- **CONTRIBUTORY:** Interpretative, advisory or facilitating services for use by others in taking action.

DIRECT
- **SHARED:** Jointly accountable with another—others (except own subordinates and superiors) within or outside the organisational unit, in taking action and exercising a controlling impact on end results.
- **PRIME:** Controlling impact on end results, where shared accountability of others is subordinate.

HAY GUIDE CHART FOR EVALUATING

ACCOUNTABILITY

			●●● MAGNITUDE Figures for use in 1991/92 Adjusted figures for 19 (Magnitude figures for use in the following year are published each September)	(0) MINIMAL Under £33,000				(1) VERY SMALL £33,000 – £330,000				(2) SMALL £330,000 – £3.3M				(3) MEDIUM £3.3M – £33M				(4) LARGE £33M – £330M			
		●● IMPACT		R.	C.	S.	P.	R.	C.	S.	P.	R.	C.	S.	P.	R.	C.	S.	P.	R.	C.	S.	P.
A	**PRESCRIBED:** These jobs are subject to — Direct and detailed instructions — Close supervision			8 9 10	10 12 14	14 16 19	19 22 25	10 12 14	14 16 19	19 22 25	25 29 33	14 16 19	19 22 25	25 29 33	33 38 43	19 22 25	25 29 33	33 38 43	43 50 57	25 29 33	33 38 43	43 50 57	43 50 57
B	**CONTROLLED:** These jobs are subject to — Instructions and established work routines — Close supervision			12 14 16	16 19 22	22 25 29	29 33 38	16 19 22	22 25 29	29 33 38	38 43 50	22 25 29	29 33 38	38 43 50	50 57 66	29 33 38	38 43 50	50 57 66	66 76 87	38 43 50	50 57 66	66 76 87	66 76 87
C	**STANDARDISED** These jobs are subject, wholly or in part to — Standardised practices and procedures — General work instructions — Supervision of progress and results			19 22 25	25 29 33	33 38 43	43 50 57	25 29 33	33 38 43	43 50 57	57 66 76	33 38 43	43 50 57	57 66 76	76 87 100	43 50 57	57 66 76	76 87 100	100 115 132	57 66 76	76 87 100	100 115 132	100 115 132
D	**REGULATED** These jobs are subject, wholly or in part to — Practices and procedures which have, clear precedents or are covered by closely defined policies — Managerial control — Review of results			29 33 38	38 43 50	50 57 66	66 76 87	38 43 50	50 57 66	66 76 87	87 100 115	50 57 66	66 76 87	87 100 115	115 132 152	66 76 87	87 100 115	115 132 152	152 175 200	87 100 115	115 132 152	152 175 200	152 175 200
E	**DIRECTED:** These jobs are subject to — Broad practice and procedures covered by functional precedents and policies — Achievement of a circumscribed operational activity — Managerial direction			43 50 57	57 66 76	76 87 100	100 115 132	57 66 76	76 87 100	100 115 132	132 152 175	76 87 100	100 115 132	132 152 175	175 200 230	100 115 132	132 152 175	175 200 230	230 264 304	132 152 175	175 200 230	230 264 304	230 264 304
F	**GENERALLY DIRECTED:** These jobs by their nature or size are subject to — Functional policy objectives — General direction			66 76 87	87 100 115	115 132 152	152 175 200	87 100 115	115 132 152	152 175 200	200 230 264	115 132 152	152 175 200	200 230 264	264 304 350	152 175 200	200 230 264	264 304 350	350 400 46	200 230 264	264 304 350	350 400 46	350 40X 4€
G	**GUIDED:** These jobs are subject only to guidance and broad direction on orientation of policy			100 115 132	132 152 175	175 200 230	230 264 304	132 152 175	175 200 230	230 264 304	304 350 400	175 200 230	230 264 304	304 350 400	400 460 528	230 264 304	304 350 400	400 460 528	528 608 700	304 350 400	400 460 528	528 608 700	528 608 700
H				152 175 200	200 230 264	264 304 350	350 400 460	200 230 304				264 304	350 400 460	460 528 608	608 700 800	350 400 460	460 528 700	608 700	800 920 1056	400 460 528	528 700	608 700 920	800 920 1056

● **FREEDOM TO ACT**

AREA AND TYPE OF IMPACT

© 1991 These charts are for use in the United Kingdom by the client named above and may not be reproduced without the permission of Hay Management Consultants Limited.

Figure 3   Part of the Hay Accountability Guide Chart.

literally millions of jobs of every kind, has remained fairly constant in recent years but is modified, as appropriate, to reflect the unique nature, character, and structure of any given organisation. The numbering pattern in each chart is based upon the 15% difference concept noted above.

To illustrate the use of the charts, consider the Know-How chart (1). If for example a job is considered to fall squarely into E Technical Know-How II Breadth of Management and 3 Human Relations Skills, then the chart indicates a Know-How value of 304 units. The 264 and 350 values are to allow for fine tuning or shading when one of the elements is considered light or heavy compared with the basic definition or with comparator jobs.

The same total Know-How score of 304 units can of course be arrived at in a variety of ways. For example F+12 304 indicates a job which is significantly more technical, but less demanding in terms of management and human relations skills – but on balance requiring the same total volume of knowledge and skills. In addition to their primary purpose of arriving at a job size, this illustrates the way that the Guide Charts are frequently used to provide a language in which jobs can be described and characterised in a consistent way.

Use of the other two Guide Charts is similar, though in the case of Problem Solving, the chart yields a percentage value which is applied to the Know-How score to give Problem Solving units. Total job size is the sum of the three factor scores.

Consistency checks
- Profile: this is used as a powerful check for internal consistency within an evaluation. If for example the evaluation shows an Accountability score three 15 per cent steps higher than the Problem Solving score, it would be recorded as A3 (sometimes 'plus 3' or 'up 3').
- Evaluators make a separate judgement on the profile expected for the job. Thus, typically, jobs in line functions would be expected to have strongly Accountability orientated profiles, jobs in basic research would have strong Problem Solving orientation (P), while jobs in many staff functions like personnel, finance, etc. are likely to have the two more in balance. If the profile which emerges from the evaluation does not agree with the evaluators' view of the appropriate profile, it indicates an inconsistency of treatment between the factors, and causes the evaluators to reconsider the evaluation.
- Rank Order: Testing of rank order to identify anomalies is an important part of the process. It can be done at the level of total job size; by factor (e.g. total Know-How); or by individual dimension (e.g. freedom to act).

Application of the Guide Chart Profile method

The basic measuring instrument of the Guide Charts can be applied through a wide variety of processes, both manual and computer assisted. The choice of a particular application process depends principally on the purpose for which the job evaluation is being undertaken, the size and diversity of the job population under consideration, and the time and resource constraints which exist. Thus traditional processes, based upon multi-functional evaluation committees, can provide great sensitivity to a wide diversity of jobs, and can generate valuable output in terms of organisational analysis and clarification, though they are demanding in terms of time and resources. Computer assisted processes reduce the time and resource demands, particularly for large populations, but may reduce the opportunity for organisational debate and analysis. Hay consultants advise client organisations on the most appropriate process to meet particular needs and circumstances. The range of processes is illustrated in the following examples.

Committee based process

In this, the most commonly applied traditional process, evaluation judgements are made by a committee (or committees), trained in the use of the Guide Charts, and using job information in the form of job descriptions.

The process usually starts with the selection of a benchmark of jobs, to reflect the range of job types and levels in the population, and to enable basic evaluation standards and interpretations to be set.

Job descriptions for the benchmark jobs may be prepared by trained analysts, by jobholders or their managers – depending on circumstances. In most cases, approval of the final document by both jobholder and manager is adopted, whoever has prepared the description. A variety of job description formats may be used, but an important feature of Hay job descriptions is an emphasis on the results expected from a job – the principal accountabilities – which assists clarity and conciseness, and can provide links into related processes such as organisational analysis and performance management.

The benchmark committee is selected, usually including members from a range of functions, not purely HR specialists, so as to provide a range of inputs and perspectives, and foster ownership of the results. Depending on the organisation's needs, the committee may be a management group, or may include peer group members and/or trade union representatives.

The committee is trained and guided by a Hay consultant, and evaluates the benchmark sample to provide clear reference points, and standards and principles to assist evaluation of non-benchmark jobs.

An important component of this process is the establishment of evaluation interpretations which reflect the organisation's values and emphases, within the Guide Chart framework.

For a small population or in a highly centralised organisation, the same committee may proceed to evaluate the remaining jobs. Otherwise, additional committees are selected and trained (for example divisional committees in a diversified business), and processes established to ensure application of common standards.

Computer based administrative support is available to assist this process, in the form of the QED Chart component of the HayXpert® suite of software. This enables recording and storage of job evaluation data, evaluation rationales and, if required, job descriptions, for rapid sorting and access when comparisons or rank order checks are being made.

Comparison and classification methods

The Guide Chart Profile method can also be used to underpin a variety of comparison or classification approaches, particularly for large and relatively homogeneous populations.

These processes normally start with committee evaluation of a benchmark sample, using the Guide Charts in the conventional way.

Based on the results of this sampling and standard setting, a classification or 'slotting' framework can be established, to facilitate evaluation of remaining jobs by direct comparison. This can be presented in written 'workbook' form, or as a computer based framework in HayXpert® software.

Such methods can achieve very rapid evaluation of large populations and provide for significant devolution of responsibility for evaluation, with relatively low training requirements.

Computer assisted evaluation processes

In these processes, the use of job descriptions and committees for the bulk of the job population is replaced by structured questionnaires, processed by computer to generate evaluations directly, using an algorithm which has been established from full evaluation of a benchmark sample.

Where a single approach is required to cover all (or most) of the jobs in an organisation, a single, comprehensive questionnaire is constructed. A benchmark sample of jobs is evaluated conventionally, using the Guide Charts, to provide the basic standards to underpin the process. The same jobs are also rated on the questionnaire and an algorithm built to replicate Hay job unit results from the questionnaire responses and programmed into HayXpert® software. For non-benchmark jobs, questionnaires are completed and processed through the computer (batch or interactive) to yield comparative evaluations. Quality checks are built in, both to the software and processes to ensure consistency.

An alternative approach, for a more tightly defined job group is the job family questionnaire. This provides a shorter, more focused questionnaire which is typically developed in conjunction with members of the family in question to reflect quite explicitly the key differentiating factors which affect job size in that family, expressed in their language. It is often used when relationships between job evaluation, career development and competency analysis are important. The process for its implementation is similar to that described for the 'universal' questionnaire.

Mixed processes

Since all these application processes are underpinned by the same Guide Chart principles and numbering scales, they yield comparable results and so different processes can be applied to different job groups without loss of compatibility.

PE International Pay Points

History and development
PE International Pay Points was developed in 1979 based upon the experience and developmental work undertaken by Inbucon Management Consultants over some 30 years. It can be applied to determine market-related salaries for senior executives and middle management jobs and as an analytical method of job evaluation extending down to clerical level. The system has the advantage of an automatic link to PE International's salary database derived from their regular surveys of executive salaries and fringe benefits.

The evaluation process
Concise job descriptions are prepared and points are awarded against levels under five factors in the traditional analytical points rating manner. The factors cover:

- knowledge and experience
- complexity and creativity
- judgements and decisions
- influence on results
- contacts.

Depending on the number of jobs to be considered the system may be applied to a sample of jobs first which can then be used as benchmarks or reference jobs for evaluating others. Jobs can be left individually scored or put into a grading structure with each grade having a specific range of points. Job scores are converted into market-related salaries by the application of two multipliers derived from PE International's own extensive database. The first multiplier called 'company factor' takes account of the size and characteristics of the particular company or operating unit in which the job is situated. The second multiplier called 'salary factor' simply converts points scored into an assessed market salary for the job which then becomes the mid-point of a salary range. There is provision in the system for taking account of industry and regional salary differentials and of specific job premiums where a market scarcity applies. Salary ranges can also be pitched at market median, upper quartile or other intermediate values depending on a particular company's salary policy. The system has been extensively applied in both public and private sectors in the UK and Europe.

PE International Direct Consensus Method (DCM)

History and development
DCM was first developed by PE International some 25 years ago, and uses job ranking by paired comparisons. Jobs are compared within a number of different factors to develop a factor plan. The system is highly flexible and is suitable for both large and small organisations. It can cover senior management, as well as clerical and manual jobs. DCM can be applied with full employee participation, or purely as a management exercise.

The evaluation process
For job populations above 70–80, a series of jobs, typically 40–60, would be selected for ranking as benchmarks. In the case of a participative exercise, employees whose jobs will be covered by the evaluation are first of all briefed on the project, and a judging panel of 6–16 panelists is chosen to represent a cross section of the organisation by level, function and sex. The panel then decides the factors which will be used in the evaluation.

There is complete flexibility as to the factors chosen. The main criteria are that they need to suit the jobs which are being evaluated. Thus, it may be expedient to use different factors for managerial, clerical and manual jobs, although otherwise the approach is the same. Care must be taken to ensure that the selected factors are free from sex bias. If job descriptions do not already exist, these must be prepared with due prominence being given to each of the selected factors. Jobs are then arranged in pairs on a ranking form with each job paired with every other job against each of the chosen factors.

Although job descriptions are available the judges are required to familiarise themselves with the jobs to be ranked. They then record their decisions on the ranking forms provided, by marking the job with the greatest demands in each pair of jobs against each factor. After individual factor assessments have been completed, each pair of jobs is separately compared on a 'total factor' basis.

Analysing the results and providing weightings

The judging panel's decisions are processed by computer, which prints out the rank orders of jobs as decided by the panel, both for each factor and also on a 'total factor' basis. The program also produces decision matrices, which highlight judgements contrary to the general consensus so that these can be examined and resolved. The implied factor weights are then calculated by computer, based on the judges' decisions in ranking jobs against individual factors and on a total factor basis. In this way, a factor plan is prepared which is unique to the organisation and the evaluated jobs. The ranking is divided into a number of grades and the remaining jobs, i.e. those not ranked, are then fitted into grades by the application of the factor plan.

Using the concepts of DCM outlined above, tailor-made analytical factor points systems are also developed and applied.

PA Consulting Group

History and development

The factor based approach to job evaluation developed by the PA Consulting Group gives greater prominence to internal relativities than external comparisons. PA emphasise that their experience has shown people at work place a relatively higher importance on pay comparisons with colleagues than with those doing similar work in other organisations. Each scheme is therefore developed to meet the client's own needs, particularly in the selection of factors. The approach utilises the advantages of the traditional paired comparison method in developing the system parameters by using cross ranking, allowing a line of best fit between results obtained from the paired comparison and the factor plan. All jobs are finally ranked by their weighted factor scores alone.

Particular care is taken throughout the process, both at the stage of factor choice and definition and during evaluation meetings, to avoid any bias and this applies particularly to sex bias, in line with the spirit of the Equal Pay (Amendment) Regulations.

Recent developments include:

- the availability of a 'standard PA system' which encapsulates PA's job evaluation experience in six pre-defined factors, each with two dimensions.
- the 'PA/Monitor' expert system, which enables consistent and reliable evaluation of jobs through direct entry by jobholder and manager to a PC based questionnaire, eliminating all paperwork and panel meetings.

Scheme development

There are three broad stages involved in developing a client-tailored scheme:

- factor selection and definition
- evaluation of benchmark jobs
- analysis and review of results and development and testing of the final structure.

  Plus, increasingly

- tailoring the PA/Monitor system to replicate the benchmark panel's decision processes.

The end of the development phase results in a unique, validated scheme for each client.

Basis of the scheme

For those clients looking for a tailored scheme factors are selected and defined uniquely for each client and, typically, between six and ten factors are chosen. These will normally be developed from the six standard PA factors including for example 'judgement'; job impact; communication and theoretical knowledge and application. But it is up to the client organisation to select which factors it considers important. Each factor will normally be divided into two logically linked dimensions, both having levels or degrees, with narrative descriptions using client terminology.

The evaluation process

The client is encouraged to set up a steering group to oversee the process. That group will select 30 to 40 benchmark jobs which are representative of both senior and junior levels in the organisation and of all functions. The steering group will appoint a panel including a wide cross section of people in the company, to evaluate the jobs.

Company job descriptions are completed, either by the job holder or by an analyst, depending on time and cost constraints. As well as a traditional job description, a factor based questionnaire is also completed. These are reviewed for consistency prior to the panel meeting.

At the evaluation meeting, each job is considered in turn, separately from the other jobs. The chairman of the panel introduces the job and ensures there is sufficient discussion to enable each panel member to examine the scope and responsibilities of the job. Factors are considered one at a time and the appropriate degree finally selected by a majority vote. At least a two-thirds majority is required and discussion continues until there is this level of consensus.

Each panel member then separately completes the paired comparison exercise. This involves comparing each job with each other job on paired comparison sheets. This process of course involves subjective judgement, but panel members will have gained an up-to-date knowledge of the scope of these jobs during their discussion in the factor analysis process. Again stress is placed on the need to avoid sex discrimination, and to think to the future rather than to justify the status quo.

Analysis, development and validation of the scheme

All results are processed by computer, using PA's own software. First, the paired comparison results are checked for consistency between judges and the average rank order then compared with the factor analysis scores. Weightings are produced which give the closest fit between the paired comparison results and the factor analysis.

These results are then carefully reviewed with the client to ensure that the scheme which has been developed is the optimum scheme for that client. Thus the parameters of the system are tested and refined before proceeding to the application stage.

Application and use of the scheme – manual system

The remaining jobs are evaluated using the factors; weightings are developed in the previous phase. (The benchmark jobs, having been evaluated during the development phase, do not need re-evaluation.)

Participation and disclosure: There is potential for this system to be highly participative at every stage. A manual is produced for use by the job evaluation panel at its meetings, containing all the information necessary to conduct future evaluations and to deal with new jobs as they are created. The information disclosed to employees will typically include a summary of the purpose, processes and results of the scheme but will usually exclude factor weightings.

When the results are announced, employees are normally allowed to appeal against the grading, following a procedure recommended by the consultant. Once these appeals have been considered and settled, the scheme is in full operation. New and changed jobs are evaluated as necessary.

Maintenance: To ensure the scheme keeps up to date and is responsive to changes in the clients' situation, various levels of maintenance are recommended, and detailed in the manual. In the short term, annual job content reviews are recommended, in the longer term (three to five years), factor and weighting audits.

Application and use of the scheme – computerised system

Following the validation of the tailored system by the evaluation panel, the PA/Monitor system will itself be tailored to reflect the client's new system. This involves modifying and adding to the question library (the standard system has over 200 questions) the answer options and the 'evaluation rules' which the system will use to replicate the decision processes of the benchmark panel re-evaluating the jobs on the system.

The remaining jobs are then evaluated by the jobholder and manager following the questioning sequence presented to them on the PC. (The system runs in 'Windows' and 'help' screens are available throughout so that the ability to operate a 'mouse' is all that is required.) The evaluation of any one job will typically trigger a route through about 50 relevant questions (selected by the system on the basis of previous responses). Automatic validation is built in and after the final question has been answered a 'job overview' is produced which describes the job in terms directly related to the evaluation factors and provides a detailed rationale for the evaluations produced.

PA claims that the system is truly 'paperless' and user-friendly, being open for any jobholder to 'appeal' by re-evaluating their own job. The evaluation process is devolved to line management with Personnel Department retaining only the overall audit, validation and control functions.

Price Waterhouse: The Profile Method

The Profile Method is based on an approach developed by Urwick Orr and Partners, who merged with Price Waterhouse in 1985. The method is designed to help organisations develop tailored schemes to meet their own needs quickly and easily. In recent years it has been developed to cover all jobs ranging from board level to the shop floor, across a wide range of industries and sectors. Profile Method schemes are robust in equal value terms, and can also be developed as 'expert system' applications.

Main components of the system

The Profile Method builds schemes around a tailored set of factors, termed 'characteristics', which are selected to meet an individual client's needs. Similarly, weightings developed for the characteristics are specific to each client company. Price Waterhouse stress the difficulty in consistently evaluating jobs when the rating scale comprises too many levels. Typically, their Profile Method uses only between four and eight levels within each characteristic.

As experience is gained during the design and operation of the scheme, guidelines are drawn up for ensuring consistency. Typical characteristics cover the areas of responsibility, knowledge, social skills and mental skills.

Benchmark jobs are selected by a steering committee, and job descriptions completed. Where possible, in-house analysts are trained to minimise dependency on external consultants.

The benchmark jobs are looked at in two ways. First, they are compared analytically, characteristic by characteristic, to produce 'profiles' of the jobs. Second, they are compared on a whole-job basis, to place them in a simple felt-fair rank order. These two sets of data are compared statistically to produce a set of weightings that enable the 'profiles' to be converted into an evaluation score. The weighting computation is carried out using a specially developed computer program designed to place greatest weighting on those characteristics that are most highly correlated with the felt-fair rank order.

The remaining jobs are then also profiled and scored using the weighted characteristics, to provide detailed evaluations of all jobs. Alternatively, a grading structure can be developed around the benchmark job results, with the remaining jobs slotted into grades by comparing them with the grades of benchmarks.

Throughout each assignment, consultants encourage full participation and discussion. Evaluation teams may be wholly management led, or include employees from a range of levels. The atmosphere in which the evaluations are conducted is important, and in-house involvement in the development of the scheme ensures greater acceptability. It also prolongs the life of the scheme by achieving high consistency in assessment.

Saville and Holdsworth – The SHL approach to job evaluation

History and development

An integral feature of the SHL approach to job evaluation is the linkage with the Work Profiling System of job analysis, which provides a comprehensive range of human resource management applications.

The WPS is standardised job analysis questionnaire which is normally completed by the jobholder and is then read by an optical scanner. The computer produces both a detailed technical report and a short summary report on the job. It is possible for a number of jobholders in the same job to complete the questionnaire and produce a combined report showing the mean and standard deviation for up to 99 jobholders.

The WPS has been developed over four years and was sponsored by 21 major UK organisations.

More than 1000 jobs were submitted to quantitative scaled questionnaires (critical component questionnaires) as well as qualitative research via repertory grid, critical incidents and paired comparisons techniques. This led to three structured trial questionnaires with over 800 questions between them and the generation of a human attribute model covering over 200 attributes.

Main components of the scheme
The use of the WPS allows information to be collected about a job in a structured way using either paper and pencil or computer administration. The expert aspect of the WPS computer system is in the:

- 800 plus equations used to predict human attributes from job task and context information
- linking assessment methods to the human attribute model
- matching procedure for individuals to jobs
- standardised guidance in setting interview questions and personality link caveats.

For job evaluation purposes organisations have the choice of selecting relevant factors from the 28 sections in Part II of the WPS questionnaire or if necessary the 32 sections in Part I of the WPS. Thus each organisation may develop a unique job evaluation system from the same menu of variables.

The scheme is introduced by means of the following eight steps:

Step one: steering committee appointed
The steering committee, comprising management and staff representatives, has three main tasks:

- agreeing the principles of the job evaluation scheme
- helping in the smooth introduction of the scheme
- monitoring the long-term performance.

Ideally, the steering committee should collectively have knowledge of all the jobs covered by the scheme. This helps in the various decisions that need to be made and provides confidence to staff that the scheme will be administered fairly.

It is important that all members of the steering committee have a basic understanding of the job evaluation process and the Work Profiling System. The first meeting will be largely devoted to these two objectives.

It is desirable for the appeals procedure to be defined at an early stage. This is likely to take the form of a sub-committee of the steering committee. Time periods should be set for the receipt of appeals following the announcement of the results of job evaluation.

A sample of benchmark jobs need to be selected which reflect a clearly perceived hierarchy within the current pay structure. Benchmark jobs are chosen to represent the full range of job values and are jobs about which there is substantial agreement on current relative value. Being selected as a benchmark does not mean that a job will necessarily remain on the same grade once the exercise has been completed. Those jobs selected as benchmarks would then be analysed using the Work Profiling System.

Step two: job analyst training
Validating the Work Profiling System questionnaires will be a key element in the job evaluation process. Job analysts will require comprehensive knowledge of the WPS and specific training in the validation interview. This will help to develop the skill and expertise of the organisation's own job analyst team.

Step three: selection of evaluation dimensions
From approximately 30 main sections in Part I of the WPS and the 21 sectors in Part II the steering committee selects those dimensions which reflect the needs of the organisation. At this stage it is possible to attach additional items that may not appear in the WPS, and yet be of importance to the organisation and relevant to the jobs under review. Having identified the key dimensions for the scheme it is then required to allocate weightings to them for inclusion in the WPS analysis. SHL provides guidance on the various ways of doing this.

Step four: evaluation of benchmark jobs by steering committee
Using job objectives and key job tasks produced via the WPS, the steering committee evaluates the benchmark jobs on a 'felt-fair' basis, and creates a metric derived from the rank order of

jobs. Paired comparison technique can be used for this procedure, although other methods are available.

Step five: evaluation of benchmark jobs by WPS
The benchmark jobs are put through the WPS and evaluation scores generated as weighted aggregates. These are then validated by correlating against the felt-fair metric. If the degree of correlation is inadequate, a review of differences is undertaken. This could result in a revision of weights and re-validation.

Step six: preparation of explanatory documentation
To keep staff informed of the scheme, a general explanatory document and technical manual will need to be prepared. These documents may well be supported by other activities – for example, staff meetings to introduce the evaluation method.

Critical monitoring of the job analysis process will be required on an ongoing basis, including the validation interviews.

Step seven: data preparation
Once all the jobs have been analysed using the WPS it will be necessary to collate the scattergram of scores and present this to the steering committee to aid their decision on relating points to salary grades.

Step eight: review of appeals
Due to the thoroughness of the WPS as a means of analysing jobs it is unlikely that many appeals will arise on the grounds of an inadequate job description. However, some appeals may occur where jobholders feel there is inequity in the grading of their own job compared with that of another staff member perceived to be performing similar duties.

Wyatt – The Employee Points Factor Comparison Method (EPFC)

History and development
This variation on points rating was developed in 1978–79 by the Wyatt Company UK Ltd. It is the product of a search for a method which is quantifiable and avoids the problem encountered in some factor schemes of scoring jobs twice on the same factor, and yet which arrives at an integrated evaluation of jobs at all levels. Since such a scheme would provide an acceptable framework for the collection of comparative pay information, Wyatt devised the

EPFC as a necessary preliminary to the establishment of their Remuneration Data Service (RDS). At that stage the scheme was not primarily intended for use by companies as a method of in-house job evaluation. Company in-house adoption of the scheme came at the request of individual participants and is not a condition of membership of the RDS.

Current components of the scheme
The EPFC approach is essentially a factor based points rating scheme. It is based on the premise that since jobs cannot be carried out without people, why not measure them by reference to the demands the job makes on the people doing them? Employees have two attributes to offer in fulfilling the requirements of any job: knowledge and personal skills. Wyatt therefore base their scheme on a detailed analysis of these two dimensions as follows.

Knowledge
Knowledge is measured by the combination of formal learning (education) and practical application (experience). The education breakdown measures the jobholders' required store of knowledge that can only be gained by formal education or training. The experience analysis measures the knowledge and skills which cannot be gained by formal education or training but which are essential for satisfactory job performance. A section illustrating the knowledge chart is shown below. The full chart contains eight degrees of education and seven degrees of experience.

Skills
The axes for the chart measuring skills are mental aptitude, human relations skills and physical skills. The mental 'aptitude' elements define the range of mental skills required and start from simple observance of limited rules governing basic tasks through various levels of analysis, decision-making and original thought. The human relations breakdowns define the levels of influence required for effective job performance. Physical skills are scored against three levels from no special skills to highly developed skills. A section of the skills chart is illustrated below. The full chart contains six degrees for human relations and seven degrees for mental aptitude. This chart appears to be more complex than the knowledge chart, because it has to represent three factors rather than just two.

For the purposes of comparison with the RDS the scheme divides into level or grades from 1, e.g. cleaner/janitor, to 24, e.g. international chief executive. Company structures vary from this pattern but are carefully cross checked by Wyatt for the purpose of salary comparisons on the data bank.

EDUCATION	I. Experience is limited to basic exposure to the routines of life. Little or no previous business or commercial experience required.			II. Jobs requiring work related experience to gain limited but specialised knowledge of machinery, processes, procedures and work routines.			III. Jobs requiring experience of a range of business procedures, specialised experience of complex industrial machinery or processes, or technical sufficiency in a specialised subject.		
A. Jobs requiring minimum formal education or general work training.	23	27	32	32	38	44	44	52	61
	27	32	38	38	44	52	52	61	72
	32	38	44	44	52	61	61	72	85
B. Jobs requiring either general schooling in a range of subjects, probably to 'O' level GCE standard, or specific training in one specialist subject or skill.	32	38	44	44	52	61	61	72	85
	38	44	52	52	61	72	72	85	100
	44	52	61	61	72	85	85	100	115
C. Jobs requiring a craft apprenticeship, City and Guilds, qualification or ONC.	44	52	61	61	72	85	85	100	115
	52	61	72	72	85	100	100	115	132
	61	72	85	85	100	115	115	132	152
D. Jobs which require either: general schooling in a wide range of subjects, probably to 'A' level GCE standard, or specialist training eg City and Guilds technical qualifications or HNC.	61	72	85	85	100	115	115	132	152
	72	85	100	100	115	132	132	152	175
	85	100	115	115	132	152	152	175	201

Figure 4: Section of a knowledge chart – Wyatt EPFC Method.

The evaluation process

Wyatt recommends that evaluations are based wherever possible on up-to-date job descriptions, although it is recognised that the design of these will in each case need to be consistent with the needs, goals and culture of the organisation. Jobs should be evaluated where practicable by panels of four to six members (although larger groups may be necessary where wider representation is required) including representatives of different areas of the organisation. All evaluation decisions should be recorded formally with a written justification of the score allotted to each job. Within this framework it is understood and accepted that no two organisations will want their job evaluation system to be implemented in the same way, and Wyatt's approach is appropriately flexible. Wyatt prefer to use the method most suitable to an organisation's culture. However, they insist that good records are the key to a fully supported job evaluation programme and full notes of both job details and the evaluations are kept as part of the programme.

The scheme has been used in a variety of environments, including both staff and union representatives.

MENTAL APTITUDE	PHYSI-CAL SKILLS	I. No more than ordinary courtesy required.			II. Jobs requiring the serving of others, perhaps in answering queries from the public, explaining instructions, supervising a team on routine work or in circumstances requiring tact and diplomacy.			III. Understanding and serving people is important for supervising a small team on technical work or a larger team on routine work, explaining complex technical material or organising others outside the establishment.		
A. Simple repetitive duties requiring no special mental skills. Job limits are defined by regulations and procedures and continuously available direction.	1 2 3	61 85 115	72 100 132	85 115 152	85 115 152	100 132 175	115 152 201	115 152 201	132 175 231	152 201 266
B. Routine duties requiring mental or visual concentration, attention to detail or simple analysis. Judgements are uninvolved and based upon standard instructions and procedures with readily available direction.	1 2 3	85 115 152	100 132 175	115 152 201	115 152 201	132 175 231	152 201 266	152 291 266	175 231 306	201 266 352
C. Jobs requiring mental alertness and concentration for controlling machinery or making judgements within well defined procedures and precedents, and with readily available advice.	1 2 3	115 152 201	132 175 231	152 201 266	152 201 266	175 231 306	201 266 352	201 266 352	231 306 405	266 352 465

Figure 5: Section of a human relations skills chart –
Wyatt EPFC Method.

Ernst and Young – Employment Relations: the decision band method (DBM)

History and development
DBM was devised by Dr T T Paterson who applied it in Africa and Europe. It has been applied extensively in the USA and Canada by Arthur Young Management Consultants. In 1981, Arthur Young acquired the world rights to implement DBM, DBM is available in the UK through Employment Relations Associates Ltd – part of Arthur (now Ernst and Young) Young (UK). DBM is a registered trademark.

DBM is derived from Dr Paterson's work on organisational theory and practice. As such it is an aid to organisational analysis as well as a job evaluation and pay determination method.

In common with many other job evaluation methods, DBM requires three stages: analysis of jobs, grading of jobs and pricing of jobs. DBM is a relatively simple method to implement.

Components of the scheme

A common characteristic of all jobs is that they are required to make and/or advise those making decisions. As such decision-making/advising can be used as a means of comparing jobs in an organisation. The nature of the decision ranges from the most far-reaching decisions on policies to simpler decisions such as how fast to clean an area or key in data. Dr Paterson observed that there are six levels (termed bands) of decision-making/advice present within organisations. The bands form an end-means continuum, i.e. the higher band, sets the end for the next band, etc. These six bands form the basic framework of the grading approach and incorporate various aspects of decision-making which are treated as separate factors in some other methods. Other factors such as skill are also considered as explained below.

The six bands are summarised below.

Band F – corporate policy-making decisions

Decisions that determine the scope, the direction, the overall goals of the total enterprise, subject to few constraints other than those imposed by law and/or economic conditions. These decisions take into consideration the functions of the enterprise. Such decisions also set the goals of the major functions and set the limits of the funds available to each and to the extent of their intended programmes. Band F decisions are of the kind made at Board or chief executive level.

Band E – programming decisions

Decisions on the means of achieving the goals (ends) established by Band F decisions – specifying goals for the constituent functions of these major functions, and allocating resources (facilities, people, money, materials) among these constituent functions in order to achieve the goals.

Band D – interpretive decisions

Decisions on the means of achieving the goals (ends) established by Band E decisions specifying what is to be done in lower bands, and deploying the allocated resources. If circumstances change, involving uncertainty of information or outcome, a Band D decision

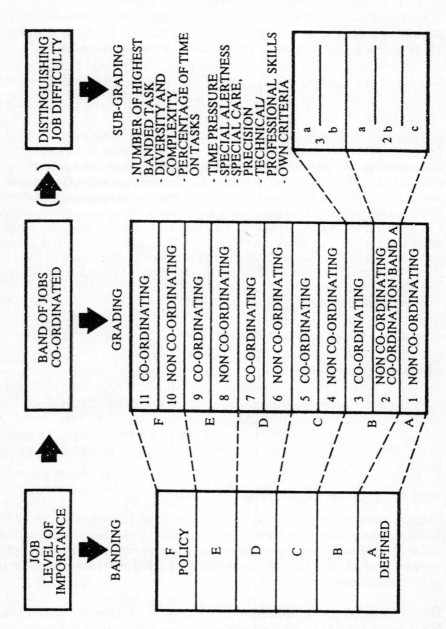

Figure 6: Decision banding method.

is required to establish what is to be done in similar circumstances in the future.

Band C – process decisions

Decisions on the means (selection of a process) of achieving the goals (ends) established by Band D decisions, subject to the limits imposed by the available technology and resources, and the constraints set at Band D. The selection of the process is a decision that must precede the carrying out of the operations that constitute the process. That is, the process decision specifies what is to be done at Band B.

Band B – operational decisions

Decisions on the carrying out of the operations of a process specified by a Band C decision. There is, within the limits set by the specific process, a choice as to how the operations are carried out, but not as to what operations constitute the process.

Band A – defined decisions

Decisions on the manner and speed of performing the elements of an operation. There is, within the limits set by the prescribed operation, a choice as to how the elements are performed, but not as to what elements constitute the operation.

The grading method

When each job has been analysed, the jobs are then banded, graded and sub-graded, if appropriate. The need and the extent of sub-grading depends upon the nature and requirements of the organisation. The three steps are:

1. *Banding*: Each job is placed in an appropriate band.
2. *Grading*: Each band has an upper and lower division (termed grades). If a job has a coordinating responsibility for other jobs in the same band as itself, it is placed in the upper division, if not it is placed in the lower division.
3. *Sub-grading*: Degrees of job difficulty can be distinguished within the grades by comparing jobs on aspects such as diversity and complexity of tasks, need for special alertness, precision, technical or professional skills.

The grading steps are illustrated in Figure 6. It does not mean that posts must appear in all the bands and grades. This will depend on the organisation, e.g. Band E tasks are often undertaken by Band F postholders in small/medium-size organisations. In practice, it is often found that a maximum of three sub-grades are required for the lower grades of each band and two sub-grades for the higher grade.

The grading of jobs is usually undertaken by a group of managers and employees.

The Institute of Administrative Management – Office Job Evaluation

The Institute of Administrative Management's (IAM) approach to job grading was born in 1942 but has evolved considerably since those early days. It is essentially a job classification scheme developed to cover all aspects of office work. The classification currently divides into nine grades (Grades A–F and M1–M3). These Grade Definitions are given in Figure 7.

For each of the following office activities typical tasks are described and defined in some detail:

- Audit.
- Computers.
  - Computer analysis;
  - Computer operators;
  - Personal Computers;
  - Computer Programming;
  - Systems Control and Management;
  - Visual Display Unit (VDU) operating.
- Depot Operation.
- Document Reproduction.
- Filing.
- Financial Accountancy.
- Foreign Exchange.
- Insurance.
- Libraries.
- Management Accounting.
- Marketing and Advertising.
- Organisation and Methods.
- Personnel.
- Post.
- Production Control.
- Facilities Management.
- Purchasing Administration.
- Sales Administration.
- Statistics.
- Telecommunications.
- Travel.
- Typing and Secretarial Duties.

Grade Definitions

A
Jobs or duties that require no previous work experience and are
1. simple enough to require very limited training;
2. closely controlled by supervision or self checking procedures.

B
Jobs or duties which remain simple but require a short period of training. Duties consist of standard routines following well defined rules less closely controlled.

C
Jobs or duties which require some experience or special aptitude. The duties are generally standardised with regular control but there is little scope for initiative to be developed.

D
Jobs or duties requiring considerable experience and a limited degree of initiative but remaining mostly within predetermined procedures. Routines may vary and be without close supervisory control.

E
Jobs or duties which require either or both of the following:
1. a technical or specialist knowledge at a basic level applied where the occasional use of discretion and initiative is necessary;
2. work supervision normally of up to five lower grade staff.

F
Jobs or duties which require the application of both knowledge and experience in one or more of the following:
1. technical or professional operations at intermediate qualification level of an appropriate professional institute;
2. performance or control of complex work whether secretarial, technical or administrative where judgement and initiative is called for;
3. supervision requiring leadership, guidance on work procedures, training of others and motivation covering a team where control of work alone is delegated to a lower level grade.

M1
Jobs or duties require one or more of the following:
1. professional or specialised knowledge beyond the intermediate level examination of an appropriate professional institute but not necessarily to a final qualification of such institutes;
2. performance or control of work of wide complexity including non-routine decisions and regular use of judgement and initiative within determined policy;
3. management of sufficient numbers of staff to require grade F level activities to be carried out by more than one subordinate.

M2
Jobs requiring one or more of the following:
1. the final qualification of an appropriate professional institute or a University degree with some experience;
2. performance or control of work of significant complexity and importance requiring regular non-routine decisions, using initiative and judgement, and assistance in the development of policy changes;
3. management of specialist functions where more than one level of supervision is necessary to control the range of activities involved (e.g. with responsibility for one or more M1 level staff).

M3
Jobs requiring one or more of the following:
1. in addition to a final qualification and/or equivalent University degree (first or higher), a period of typically several years experience consistent with the level of authority;
2. performance or control of work over several functions demanding general as well as specialist expertise and involvement in policy making at the highest level;
3. management of a series of specialist functions where management level jobs report in for guidance, control and monitoring.

Figure 7 Institute of Administrative Management – Office Job Evaluation.

These tasks have each been allocated a grade level. Job grading is achieved by matching actual tasks against graded definitions and deciding the dominant grade level for each job under consideration. The IAM manual gives detailed guidance on this, together with advice on the implementation and maintenance of the scheme and broader pay related issues.

This approach forms the basis of job matching for IAM's regular Office Salaries Analysis. It is supported and developed through the Office Job Evaluation User Group and through training courses and certification of practitioners.

Towers Perrin – WJQ (Weighted Job Questionnaire)

This computer assisted approach to analytical factor/points based job evaluation can either be based on five 'core' job factors or applied in the 'WJQ Custom' form which allows for tailor-made factors or skills/competencies. Both are described below and are subject to continuing support and development.

Core WJQ

At the heart of this approach is a questionnaire designed to gather accurate and specific job data. The questionnaire contains 13 measurement sections representing the different dimensions of the five core job factors contained in the WJQ. These are:

1. *Skill and knowledge*
   - level of formal/academic training
   - technical complexity
   - craft, athletic or artistic talent
   - level of proficiency
2. *Problem solving*
   - fact-finding and analysis
   - originality and creativity
3. *Contacts*
   - internal/external contacts
4. *Scope of responsibility*
   - organisational authority level
   - scope of people management responsibility
   - impact of errors
   - scope and degree of monetary responsibility
5. *Working conditions*
   - physical activity
   - work environment.

Each section of the questionnaire contains one or more 'items' requiring a response and in total there are 65 items requiring responses. These may be either numeric responses such as number of subordinates or responses selected from multiple choice 'response tables'.

'Core' WJQ allows for customisation to client needs both through tailoring of the factors, responses and questions to reflect an organisation's culture, values and language and through customised factor weighting and scoring routines.

WJQ – Custom

Released in the UK some two years ago, this is a highly flexible approach accommodating job evaluation or skills based pay. Essentially the factors and questionnaire are created specifically for the client, whilst all the benefits of established WJQ software routines can be used, e.g.

Challenger –	checking the consistency of a given job's responses
Up/down comparator –	comparing a job profile with those of the positions above and below it
Inter-rater –	comparing multiple responses for the same job and reporting on any deviates
Factor comparisons –	providing a hierarchy of predicted factor levels
Levels summary –	lines of predicted factor levels by all factors used
Points summary –	displaying the points hierarchy for each factor as well as total points and grade assignments for selected jobs.

WJQ is well established around the world and is now quite widely used in the UK in both the public and private sectors. The software, which can operate in a 'Windows' environment, also contains modules for additional salary management applications. These include job description production, salary survey analysis and remuneration planning.

KPMG Management Consulting – EQUATE

A relative newcomer to the UK computer assisted job evaluation scene, EQUATE was initially developed by Link Consultants with whom KPMG entered into a joint agreement a few years ago. Essentially it is an expert system shell-software environment which has been designed to accept and help manage and audit any analytical factor based points rating job evaluation system. It can, therefore, be used as a means of managing existing 'manual' schemes, as a basis for auditing and restructuring schemes subject to decay and drift as well as the implementation of newly designed schemes.

Its main features are as follows:

- flexibility over factor selection and definition.
- a customised questionnaire design and validation process for job data collection.
- an algorithm building process to programme in the evaluation rules into the system shell
- a weighting process designed to reflect the needs and values of the organisation.
- a series of software routines for checking the validity of job data, comparing and validating factor scores.
- salary management software.

EQUATE links into an integrated job information system (currently under development) so that the job database derived from questionnaires can be used to build:

- a salary management process.
- a job evaluation module.
- a selection module aimed at giving recruitment specifications and selection test criteria.
- a competency specification module aimed at delivering job performance criteria.
- a training module which links in training needs analysis.

A version of EQUATE-MEDEQUATE has been developed to service clients in the Health Services sector.

Other job evaluation approaches are available from:

Mercer Fraser – Compmaster

Hewitts

Many smaller H.R./personnel consultancies are able to develop 'tailor-made' approaches.

Appendix 2a

Example of a job description in narrative format

JOB DESCRIPTION

Job Title: Marketing Director

Reports To: Managing Director

Date:

PURPOSE

To develop and, after agreement, direct the implementation of short- and long-term sales and marketing plans which will provide for the achievement of the Company's objectives of growth and profitability.

DIMENSIONS

Annual Turnover:	£78 million
Staff:	46
Overseas Sales Companies	9

PRINCIPAL ACCOUNTABILITIES

1. Develop short- and long-term sales and marketing plans which

will provide for the realisation of the Company's strategic objectives.

2. Direct and control the Company's sales and marketing operations to ensure the achievement of agreed profit and turnover objectives.

3. Review, develop and maintain an organisation which will maximise the effectiveness of the Company's sales and marketing operations.

4. Recruit, motivate and develop senior sales and marketing managers to ensure commitment and consistently high performance.

5. Develop and guide overseas sales companies to ensure profitable operation and growth in line with established corporate objectives.

6. Effectively represent the interests of the Company to major customers and lead negotiations for major contracts.

7. Identify new markets and liaise with Production Director to ensure product development which will increase the Company's market penetration and growth.

8. Contribute, as an executive director, to the identification and formulation of strategic objectives for the Company.

NATURE AND SCOPE OF POSITION

The Marketing Director reports directly to the Managing Director of the company along with the Finance Director and the Operations Director. Under the leadership of the M.D., these four posts make up the executive board which is the main policy making body within the Company. Together they provide the direction necessary to the achievement of agreed strategic objectives and coordination between them is achieved primarily through a weekly meeting, chaired by the M.D. In addition to discussing plans and monitoring their implementation, this meeting provides a regular forum in which sales achievement can be translated into production activity.

The jobholder is responsible for the development and, after agreement, implementation of sales and marketing plans. Whilst the largest single market remains the UK only 25% of the Company's production is sold in the home market. 25% is sold direct into overseas market with territory sales managers selling primarily to approved agents and distributors. The remaining 50% is sold into overseas market through nine overseas subsidiaries, established to market and sell the Company's products. Two of these subsidiary companies have been established in the USA whilst the remaining seven are concentrated on particular European countries or countries which form part of the old Commonwealth. The Managing Director of each of the nine companies reports direct to the Marketing Director along with:

- Sales Manager – There are four territory sales managers covering in broad terms all those countries where there is no overseas subsidiary. The four territories are the UK, Europe, Australia and Asia and the Middle East and Africa. Their activities are coordinated by the sales manager who is also responsible for market research, sales publicity and promotion and after sales service.

- Commercial Manager – Advice and support on the form of contract is provided by this manager who is also responsible for a team of contract managers who are the main point of customer contact and liaison during the production process. In addition the Commercial Manager is also responsible for the distribution and storage of the company's products and the sale of spares.

The Marketing Director sees the development of strategy as very much a personal responsibility and works closely with the M.D. in the formulation of sales plans and the assessment of market priorities. There is little scope for fundamental innovation in the form of product the company is offering and little can be achieved by any significant diversification. The development of the company and continued growth of turnover therefore very much depends upon which markets are developed, the optimal timing for their development and the way in which the market is entered.

Information and intelligence to enable the development of the marketing strategy are gathered through the territory Sales Managers and the Sales Manager with specialist support from the Market Research Manager and the Technical Services Manager. The Technical Service Manager's contribution in this area is largely related to monitoring developments with regard to prime movers (the diesel engines which drive the generators). The Marketing Director also liaises closely with the Finance Director in considering the most appropriate forms of market entry.

Plans are produced on a one plus five year basis and once approved are translated into targets for the territory Sales Managers. This translation process is largely carried out by the Sales Manager subject to the approval of the Marketing Director. The Marketing Director works directly with the Managers of the overseas companies setting targets in terms of volume, turnover, profit and sales costs.

The market for the company's product is fairly well established and most potential customers are readily identifiable.

Field sales effort is therefore largely one of establishing and maintaining contact with likely users. Once real sales potential has been identified initial contact and negotiation is carried out by Territory Sales Managers operating within price and contract norms, determined by the Marketing Director. Price norms are reviewed regularly in the light of the company's business circumstances and the jobholder will expect to discuss changes to these with other Executive Directors. Most of the contracts carried out by the Company are of sufficient business significance to warrant senior management involvement and many of the major contracts would be handled personally either by the Marketing Director or indeed on occasions by the M.D.

The Marketing Director has a brief weekly meeting with the Sales Manager and the Commercial Manager which is essentially a pre-briefing prior to meeting with the M.D. and other Executive Directors. The jobholder expects however, to be kept closely in touch with the sales situation. The jobholder endeavours to see the overseas subsidiary managers between two and four times per annum depending upon the confidence placed in the individuals, and monitors the activities of these subsidiary companies largely through the receipt of monthly reports.

Appendix 2b

Example of a short-form job description

JOB DESCRIPTION

Job Title: Management Accountant

Reports To: Financial Controller

Business: Food and Speciality Chemicals

Location:

Jobholder: A.N. Other

Date:

Job Ref: 17

PURPOSE

Maintain and develop the company's management information and product costing systems to aid the decision making process.

DIMENSIONS

Turnover	£50 million
Payroll Costs	£7.0 million
Manufacturing Costs	£10 million
Staff	3

ORGANISATION CHART

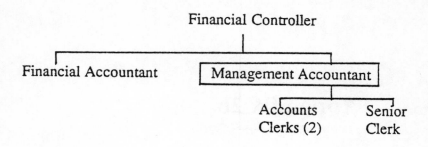

PRINCIPAL ACCOUNTABILITIES

1. Collate and prepare the information required for the Company budget which meets the corporate objectives and which provides the basis for management decision-making.

2. Provide accurate and up-to-date product cost information so that product prices can be maintained at levels which will ensure that Company profit targets are achieved.

3. Prepare accurate, timely and cost effective management accounts and highlight variances so that management can take effective action to improve operating performance.

4. Evaluate stock holdings and determine valuations which reflect current costs and conform to accounting standards.

5. Plan and control the day-to-day activities of the department to ensure that the information provided is accurate and punctual.

6. Liaise with Directors and Senior Managers regarding the establishment of effective information systems, recommending changes and developments to the Financial Controller and I.T. Manager.

SPECIAL FEATURES

The jobholder is responsible for keeping track of product costs accurately and regularly updates the records to keep pace with cost increases. The jobholder is also responsible for the evaluation of all stocks, the organisation of physical counts and the evaluation of their accuracy. Being able to monitor profit margins and derive the best possible pricing structure is an important component in improving the business performance.

The jobholder works with the Financial Accountant in the preparation of company statutory accounts, and liaises with the external auditors when required. All budget preparation and planning is managed by the jobholder, working with various Department Heads to produce balanced and accurate figures.

The I.T. systems are now rather old and inappropriate for the current business complexity and the jobholder is working with the systems people to develop new ways of dealing with the financial information for costing and forecasting purposes.

Appendix 2c

Example of a job description in structured format

JOB DESCRIPTION

Job Title:	Sales Promotion Manager	**Agreed:**
Location:		**Date:**
Jobholder:	A.N. Other	**Jobholder:**
Report to:	Marketing Support Manager	**Superior:**

---

1. PURPOSE OF THE JOB

Coordinate and implement all sales promotion activities for the company, managing them within agreed budgets and in accordance with Company policies so as to contribute to achievement of sales targets.

2. ORGANISATION CHART

Marketing Support Manager

Contracts Manager   SALES PROMOTION MANAGER   Sales Administrator

Sales Promotion Assistant

3. JOB FACTS AND FIGURES

Sales Promotion Expenses	£545,000
Department Expenses	£15,000
Employees	1

4. PRINCIPAL ACCOUNTABILITIES

1. Formulate in conjunction with appropriate Product Managers a sales promotion plan to contribute to the achievement of agreed sales objectives.

2. Ensure sales promotion expenditure is maintained within agreed budget.

3. Manage the implementation of assigned promotional events to give best possible exposure within agreed budgets.

4. Plan and control press activities to establish Company image and product awareness in line with corporate objectives and new product launches.

5. Personally organise VIP tours, visits and meetings on behalf of other Managers to build Company image.

5. JOB CONTEXT AND CONTENT

The Sales Promotion Manager is responsible for the whole of the company's promotional activities and therefore contributes significantly to the achievement of total order plan. The jobholder is assisted by the Sales Promotion Assistant.

The market for the Company's products is highly competitive and promotional activity is key to the success of the business.

The jobholder must ensure the development of good relations within the organisation and with external advisers.

6. PROBLEMS FACED

The increasing complexity of the business has demonstrated the need for a more flexible approach to enable the Company to respond to rapidly changing demands of customers.

Among the more significant of the problems with which the jobholder is faced is the need to satisfy potentially conflicting demands of different Product Group Managers. Further problems arise through the need to ensure that a range of deadlines are met for the implementation of the programmes and production of material.

7.   PLANNING AND ORGANISING

The Sales Promotion Manager is required to develop short to medium term strategies (one to two years) for achieving proposed sales promotion programmes. These programmes are produced on a quarterly basis and discussed with and updated by Product Group Managers and the Marketing Support Manager. Measures to achieve greater efficiency are kept under review by the jobholder.

The day-to-day organisation of the workflow and utilisation of the Sales Promotion Assistant are handled by the jobholder.

8.   DIRECTION RECEIVED

The job holder reports formally to the Marketing Support Manager on a monthly basis and is in weekly contact to discuss matters of priority. The Company has a range of standard products and therefore of promotional programmes but new developments are frequently required for new products.

Within standard guidelines the jobholder has considerable freedom to operate, including handling of relations with external agencies.

9.   WORKING CONTACTS

The jobholder has weekly contacts with the Product Group Managers, the Sales Managers and a range of other managers as required. Externally, relations are with consultants, agencies and on occasion customers. The jobholder is required to deal with top level sales contacts and customer problems on a monthly basis.

10.   KNOWLEDGE AND EXPERIENCE

A thorough knowledge and experience of sales promotion, sales activity and of the electronics industry are essential and in addition the job holder should have a wide range of contacts among sales promotion and advertising agencies. The position demands substantial organisational and human relation skills.

11.   ADDITIONAL INFORMATION

BOOKS AND PAMPHLETS

Advisory Conciliation and Arbitration Service. Job evaluation: an introduction. London, Advisory Conciliation and Arbitration Service, 1990.

Armstrong M.; Murlis H. Reward Management: a handbook of remuneration strategy and practice, 1991. 591pp.

Elizur, D. Systematic job evaluation and comparable worth. Aldershot, Gower, 1987. xxiv, 290pp.

Hastings, Sue. Developing a less discriminatory job evaluation scheme. Oxford, Trade Union Research Unit in conjunction with the TUC Working Group on Equal Value, 1991. 20pp. (Technical notes, 109).

Hewitt Associates. Total compensation management: reward management strategies for the 1990s, 1991. vii, 319pp.

Incomes Data Services Limited. Blue collar job evaluation. London, IDS, 1985. 44pp. Class No: FFH 143 pa.

Incomes Data Services Limited. Job evaluation review. London, IDS, 1986. 74pp.

Johnson C.; Dewsbury, C. Equal pay for work of equal value: a guide to the non-discriminatory use of job evaluation.

Knell A. Remuneration and benefits handbook, 1991. Various paging.

Labour Research Department. Winning equal pay: the LRD guide to job evaluation and equal value. London, Labour Research Department, 1989. 24pp.

Rock, M. L; Beruer, L. A. The compensation handbook: a state-of-the-art guide to compensation strategy and design, 1991.

Scott, K. Office job evaluation. Rev. ed. Orpington, Kent, Institute of Administrative Management, 1989. Various paging.

Thomason, G. Job evaluation: objectives and methods. London, Institute of Personnel Management, 1980. 218pp.

Working Time Analysts. A guide to the Hay job evaluation package. Oxford, Working Time Analysts, 1986.

JOURNAL ARTICLES

'The computerised way to evaluate jobs'. H. Murlis and D. Pritchard. **Personnel Management.** Vol 23, No 4, April 1991. pp48-50,53.

'Delayering at Rolls Royce'. **IDS Top Pay Unit Review.** No 123, May 1991. pp5-6.

'EC 92: are your compensation programs ready?'. B. Brooks, M. C. Haller and J. R. Viguie. **Benefits & Compensation International.** Vol 19, No 7, January 1990. pp11-14.

'Equal value through job evaluation: perspectives on recent British experience'. S. Richebll. **Equal Opportunities International.** Vol 7, No 2, 1988. pp21-29.

'Evaluating jobs for pay'. D. Pritchard. **Payroll Manager's Review.** Vol 3, No 5, March 1989. pp33-34.

'Factors contributing to the implementation of unbiased job evaluation schemes'. A. Ghobadian. **Personnel Review.** Vol 16, No 5, 1987. pp21-25.

'Flexible pay arrangements – the need for a systematic approach'. M. Palmer and G. Martin. **Health Services Management.** Vol 86, No 1, February 1990. pp12-15.

'Integrated job evaluation'. M. Saxby. **Management Services.** Vol 31, No 12, December 1987. pp20-22.

'Job evaluation and equal value: recent development'. **Industrial Relations Review and Report.** No 455, 10 January 1990. pp11-14.

'Job evaluation and gender'. **Industrial Relations Review and Report.** No 489, 7 June 1991. pp4-11.

'Job evaluation in changing world'. H. Murlis and D. Fitt. **Personnel Management.** Vol 23, No 5, May 1991. pp39-43.

'Job evaluation: a barrier to excellence?'. S.M.Emerson. **Compensation and Benefits Review.** Vol 23, No 1, January-February 1991. pp39-51. Std No: 133122

'Job evaluation: equal work – equal pay?'. J. McNally and S. Shimmin. **Management Decision.** Vol 26, No 5, 1988, pp22-27.

'Job evaluation: the next generation'. M. F. Emig. **Personnel Journal.** Vol 65, No 11, November 1986. pp52-55.

'Job evaluation: the road to equality?'. **Industrial Relations Review and Report.** No 448, 26 September 1989. pp5-10.

'Job evaluation: trade union and staff association representatives perspectives'. A. Ghobadian. **Employee Relations.** Vol 12, No 4, 1990. pp3-9.

'Job evaluation under review'. **Industrial Relations Review and Report.** No 423, 30 August 1988. pp2-7.

'Job evaluation: still at the frontier. **Compensation and Benefits Review.** Vol. 23 No. 4 July August 1991. pp53-67.

'A job evaluation case history. E. Wilde. **Work Study.** Vol 41, No 2 Mar/Apr 1992. pp6-11.

'New factors in job evaluation'. S. Fouracre and A. Wright. **Personnel Management.** Vol 18, No 5, May 1986. pp40-43.

'Personnel policies, structural characteristics, and equity in job-evaluated payment systems'. A. Ghobadian and M. White. **Personnel Review.** Vol 17, No 5, 1988. pp29-32.

'Policy and analysis skill competency and reward'. **IDS Top Pay Unit Review.** No 128 Oct 1991. pp18-23.

'Staff job evaluation – 1: review of schemes'. **Industrial Relations Review and Report.** No 310, 20 December 1983. pp2-8.

'Staff job evaluation – 2: making the evaluations'. **Industrial Relations Review and Report.** No 311, 10 January 1984. pp2-7.

'Staff job evaluation – 3: establishing pay rates'. **Industrial Relations Review and Report.** No 314, 21 February 1984. pp2-5.

'Worth wiles'. H. Falconer. **Personnel Today.** 16 April 1991. pp31,33

HISTORICAL REFERENCES

The following references of American origin provide a perspective on the early development of modern evaluation methods.

Eugene J. Benge, Samuel L. H. Burk, and Edward N. Hay, **Job Evaluation Manual** (Harper and Brothers, New York, 1941)

William D. Turner, 'The Per Cent Method of Job Evaluation', **Personnel** 24:6 (May, 1948)

Edward N. Hay, 'Four Methods of Establishing Factor Scales in Factor Comparison Job Evaluation', **Personnel** 23:6 (1946)

Edward N. Hay, 'Creating Factor Comparison Key Scales by the Per Cent Method', **Journal of Applied Psychology** 32:5 (October 1948)

Edward N. Hay and Dale Purves, 'The Profile Method of High Level Job Evaluation', **Personnel** 28:2 (September 1951)

Edward N. Hay and Dale Purves, 'A New Method of Job Evaluation – The Guide Chart-Profile Method', **Personnel** 31:1 (July 1954)

Edward N. Hay, 'Setting Salary Standards for Executive Jobs', **Personnel** 34:4 (January-February 1958)

Index